A WAY OF
BEING

A WAY OF BEING

Carl R. Rogers

Introduction by
Irvin D. Yalom

Houghton Mifflin Company
Boston   New York

For information about permission to reproduce selections from
this book, write to Permissions, Houghton Mifflin Company,
215 Park Avenue South, New York, New York 10003.

Library of Congress Cataloging-in-Publication Data

Rogers, Carl Ransom, date.
A way of being.
Includes bibliographies and index.
1. Humanistic psychology. I. Title.
BF204.R64 150'.19 80-20275
ISBN 0-395-75530-1

Printed in the United States of America

QUF 10 9 8 7 6 5

Acknowledgments begin on page 377.
Part opening abstract art by Tonia Noell-Roberts

For information about this and other Houghton Mifflin
trade and reference books and multimedia products, visit
The Bookstore at Houghton Mifflin on the World Wide Web at
http://www.hmco.com/trade/.

Contents

Introduction

In his first teaching position, Carl Rogers huddled together with a group of psychology students. He was in his late thirties. It was shortly after electromagnetic tapes had been introduced, and the group listened excitedly to a recording of a psychotherapy interview. Again and again Rogers stopped and replayed sections of the session in order to pinpoint where the interview went wrong or to delineate those moments when the client made a significant step forward.

That is one image of Carl Rogers to be found in *A Way of Being*. There are many others. Imagine another scene, one that occurred when he was twenty years older.

At an academic symposium on Ellen West, a heavily studied patient who committed suicide several decades before, Rogers startled the audience by the depth and intensity of his reaction. He spoke about Ellen West as though he knew her well, as though it were only yesterday that she had poisoned herself. Not only did Rogers express his sorrow about her tragically wasted life, but also his anger at her physicians and psychiatrists who, through their impersonality and preoccupation with precise diagnosis, had transformed her into an object. How could they have? Rogers asked. If only they had known that treating a person as an object always stands in the way of successful therapy. If only they had related to her as a person, risked themselves, experienced her reality and her world, they might have dissolved her lethal loneliness.

And still another image, fifteen years later. Carl Rogers was seventy and had been invited to deliver an honorary lecture at the annual convention of the American Psychological Association. The audience sat back, relaxed in their chairs, awaiting the expected mellow retrospective of a revered septuagenarian. Instead, Rogers rocked them with a series of challenges. He urged school psychologists not to content themselves merely with treating students damaged by an obsolete and irrelevant educational system but to change the system, to participate in designing an educational experience that would liberate the students' curiosity and enhance the joy of learning. Later he railed against the constrictions of professionalism and suggested that the efforts of certification and licensure had not been worth the cost: there were as many credentialed charlatans as uncredentialed ones, too many gifted therapists had been denied access to the profession, and the rigid bureaucracy of the American Psychological Association had frozen the field in the past and stifled creativity. No one slept during that talk.

In these scenes, and in so many others evoked in *A Way of Being,* Carl Rogers's commitment to the growth of others is evident. "Person-centered"—that was Rogers's preferred term for his approach. Concern and respect for the client's experiential world have been paramount in Rogers's work ever since the beginning of his career when, for twelve years, he worked with delinquent and underprivileged children in Rochester. He began to formulate ideas about therapy that revolved around his belief that one must rely upon the client to delineate the direction of the therapeutic work—that the client knows what hurts, what experiences need to be uncovered, and what problems are crucial. A textbook he wrote in his mid-thirties on the treatment of the problem child attracted wide academic attention and led to a professorship at Ohio State University.

There he offered a pioneering course on counseling. (Remember that in the late 1930s the field of clinical psychology, as we know it today, did not exist.) Soon, as his ideas about therapy crystallized, he wrote a textbook, *Counseling and Psychotherapy,* which his publishers were reluctant to publish; they would prefer, they told him, a text for a course and a field that existed! Ultimately, *Counseling and Psychotherapy* was destined, along with Rollo May's book *The Art of Counseling,* to play a significant role in the birth of clinical psychology and to shape the future of a humanistically oriented therapeutic approach.

Carl Rogers was a hardy warrior who fought many battles—territorial battles with the field of medicine and psychiatry, which tried to prevent psychologists from treating patients; ideological battles with reductionists, such as B. F. Skinner, who denied the centrality of choice, will, and purpose; and procedural battles with psychoanalysts who considered his client-centered approach simplistic and anti-intellectual.

Today, a half century later, Rogers's therapeutic approach seems so right, so self-evident, and so buttressed by decades of psychotherapy research that it is difficult to appreciate the intensity of these battles or even to comprehend what they were all about. Experienced therapists today agree that the crucial aspect of therapy, as Rogers grasped early in his career, is the therapeutic relationship. *Of course,* it is imperative that the therapist relate genuinely to the patient—the more the therapist becomes a real person and avoids self-protective or professional masks or roles, the more the patient will reciprocate and change in a constructive direction. *Of course*, the therapist should accept the patient nonjudgmentally and unconditionally. And, *of course*, the therapist must enter empathically into the private world of the client.

Yet these were once such novel ideas that Rogers had to bludgeon the profession into taking note of them. His primary weapon was objective evidence, and he was the creative force behind the use of empirical research to elucidate the process and outcome of psychotherapy. His studies of the critical aspects of the therapist-client relationship—empathic understanding, genuineness, and unconditional positive regard—continue to be considered by social scientists as a model of research elegance and relevance.

Rogers was joined in his lifelong efforts to create and nurture a humanistic approach to psychotherapy by the powerful voice of Rollo May. Though the two men fundamentally agreed about the goals and approach to therapy (and though both were educated at the Union Theological Seminary), they drew their convictions from very different sources: Carl Rogers from empirical research and Rollo May from the study of literature, philosophy, and myth.

Union

During his career Rogers was attacked for the supposed simplicity of his therapeutic approach, and many practitioners caricatured client-centered therapy as the method in which the therapist merely repeats the last words of the client's remarks. Yet those who knew Rogers, who watched him interview, or who read his work with care knew that his approach was neither simplistic nor restrictive. It is true that Rogers always proceeded from the bottom up rather than from the top down—that is, he first grounded himself in his immediate observations of therapeutic work, his own and others', and generated low-level but testable hypotheses. (That was always a major difference between a Rogerian approach and a psychoanalytic one, which drew high-level inferences to construct an untestable theory, which subsequently informed and regulated therapeutic procedure.) But it is also true that early in his career Rogers arrived at several fundamental assumptions upon which his subsequent work rests.

He was persuaded of the reality and significance of human choice; he believed that experiential learning was a far more powerful approach to personal understanding and change than an endeavor resting upon intellectual understanding; he believed that individuals have within themselves an actualizing tendency, an inbuilt proclivity toward growth and fulfillment. Rogers often spoke of his belief in the existence of a formative impulse (counterbalancing an entropic force) in all of organic life. In his belief in an actualizing tendency he joined the ranks of a skein of humanistic thinkers like Nietzsche, Kierkegaard, Adler, Goldstein, Maslow, and Horney, who believed in the existence within each individual of a vast potential for self-understanding and personal change. Thus Nietzsche's first "granite sentence" of human perfectibility was "Become who you are," and Karen Horney, a maverick psychoanalyst, believed that "just as the acorn will develop into an oak, the child will mature into an adult." The therapeutic task emanating from this position, then, is not one of construction or reconstruction or manipulation or shaping. Instead, it is one of facilitation, of removing obstacles to growth and helping to release that which has always been there.

The person-centered approach generated so much power for personal change, Rogers believed, that there was no reason to confine it to the psychologically troubled. Consequently he sought to harness its power for use in many nonclinical arenas. For decades he was actively involved in educational programs urging that education en-

acorn

compass affective as well as cognitive learning, that teachers focus on the whole person, that a learning environment of acceptance, genuineness, and empathic understanding be created, that teachers and institutional
personnel be trained in a person-oriented approach, that
efforts be made to build self-esteem in the student and to
unlock natural curiosity.

Encounter groups were sometimes characterized as
"group therapy for normals." They straddled the fine line
between education and therapy or, as it has been put less
reverently, between "head shrinking and mind expansion." In the 1960s Rogers understood that the intensive
group experience contained enormous potential for
change. He plunged into the encounter group movement
and made significant contributions to the technology of
group leadership. Taking a stand against coercive and manipulative leadership styles, he urged that the same person-oriented approach so essential to individual counseling was equally essential in the group experience. Leaders
had to be participants as well as leaders; they could best
shape a facilitating environment by their own example.
Rogers followed his own prescriptions, and protocols of
his groups reveal his breathtaking honesty: as in his individual work, he revealed not only his own personally troubling issues but also his fantasies of other members—insofar as he deemed they might lead others toward
constructive introspection.

What was true for the small group was true for the large
group as well. At the age of seventy-five Rogers led groups
of several hundred people in community-building endeavors. He believed that person-oriented groups offered a
powerful tool to resolve human conflict, both national and
international. Determined to have an impact on cross-cul-
tural and ethnic tensions, Rogers traveled widely in the
last ten years of his life. He conducted communication

groups of blacks and whites in South Africa, spoke to
large audiences in Brazil (then a dictatorship) about individual freedom and self-actualization, facilitated a four-
day conflict-resolution workshop for high officials of
seventeen Central American nations, and demonstrated
client-centered counseling in crowded workshops in the
then Soviet Union. His international efforts were so exten-
sive that he was nominated for the Nobel Peace Prize.

A Way of Being begins with Rogers's views on communication. Few things mattered more to him than the accurate and honest communication of his feelings and
thoughts. He eschewed any impulses to awe, to persuade,
or to manipulate. In a sense, this makes the task of an in-
troducer superfluous. Though few deserve an introduction
more, no one needs it less. As the reader shall see, Rogers
speaks for himself—and speaks with extraordinary clarity
and grace.

Irvin D. Yalom

Preface

Sometimes I am astonished at the changes that have occurred in my life and work. This book encompasses the changes that have taken place during the past decade—roughly, the seventies. It brings together diverse material which I have written in recent years. Some of these thoughts have been published in a variety of journals, some have never been published. Before I endeavor to introduce you to the contents, I would like to look back at a few landmarks of my own change.

In 1941, I wrote a book on counseling and psychotherapy, published the next year. It was spawned by my awareness that I was thinking and working with individuals in ways which were quite different from other counselors. The book was completely focused on verbal interchange between a helper and a person in need of help; it contained no suggestion of broader implications.

A decade later, in 1951, this point of view was presented more fully and more confidently in a volume on client-centered therapy. In this book there was a recognition that the principles of therapy had application in other fields. In chapters written by others, or drawn largely from the experience of others, there was discussion of group therapy, group leadership and administration, and student-centered teaching. The field of application was widening.

I cannot believe how slow I was in facing the ramifications of the work that I and my colleagues were doing. In 1961, I wrote a book to which I gave the title, "A Therapist's View of Psychotherapy," indicating that the focus of all the papers was individual work, though actually various chapters dealt with the ever broadening fields of application. Fortunately, the publisher was not impressed by the title and, modifying one of the chapter titles, suggested that I call it *On Becoming a Person.* I accepted the suggestion. I had thought I was writing for psychotherapists, but to my astonishment discovered I was writing for *people*—nurses, housewives, people in the business world, priests, ministers, teachers, youth—all manner of people. The book, in English and in its many translations, has now been read by millions of people all over the globe. Its impact forced me out of my parochial view that what I might say would be of interest only to therapists. The response broadened my life as well as my thinking. I believe that all of my writing since contains the realization that what is true in a relationship between therapist and client may well be true for a marriage, a family, a school, an administration, a relationship between cultures or countries.

So now I wish to return to this book and what it holds. I have grouped together at the outset five papers which are very personal—revealing my experiences in relationships, my feelings as I grow older, the origins of my philosophy, my perspective on my career, a personal view of "reality." Essentially these were written not only by me, but for me. Whether they will touch you and your experience, I cannot predict.

In this section, and throughout the book, the writings can be partially dated by my handling of the "he-she," "him-her" problem. Thanks to my daughter and to other friends with feminist leanings, I have become more and more sensitive to the linguistic inequality between the sexes. I have, I believe, *treated* women as equals, but only in more recent years have I been clearly aware of the put-down involved in the use of only masculine pronouns in statements with generic meaning. I have preferred to let the papers stand as written, rather than endeavoring to bring the language up to my present-day standards, which would seem somehow dishonest. I said what I said. Some of the papers are also dated by the references to our (in my opinion) incredibly stupid, impersonal, and destructive war in Vietnam, as tragic for Americans as for the Vietnamese.

The second part of the book centers on my professional thoughts and activities. The breadth of their application is indicated by the change in the terminology categorizing my views; the old concept of "client-centered therapy" has been transformed into the "person-centered approach." In other words, I am no longer talking simply about psychotherapy, but about a point of view, a philosophy, an approach to life, a way of being, which fits any situation in which *growth*—of a person, a group, or a community—is part of the goal. Two of these papers were written during the past year, while others were produced somewhat earlier, but taken together they present the major facets of my work and thought as of today. Personally I am fond of the chapter containing six vignettes—snapshots of experiences from which I have learned deeply.

The third section deals with education, a field of application in which I feel some competence; I offer some challenges to educational institutions and some thoughts about what we may be facing in the years ahead. I am afraid that my views are quite unorthodox and that they may not be popular in a temporarily conservative mood in education, in an era of shrinking budgets and short-range views. These are thoughts about the far future of learning.

In the final section I give my view of the drastic transformation which faces our culture due to little known advances in scientific thinking and new developments in many other fields, and I speculate about the manner in which the shape of our world will change. I also give my views as to the nature of the person who can live in that transformed world.

Several chapters have been published previously in different form. Chapter 4, "Growing Old: Or Older and Growing? " Chapter 9, "Building Person-Centered Communities: The Implications for the Future," and Chapter 15, "The World of Tomorrow, and the Person of Tomorrow," are published here for the first time.

The theme holding the book together is that every chapter expresses, in one form or another, a way of being toward which I strive—a way of being which persons in many countries, in many occupations and professions, in all walks of life, find appealing and enriching. Whether this will be true for you, only you can determine, but I bid you welcome, as you journey through this "way."

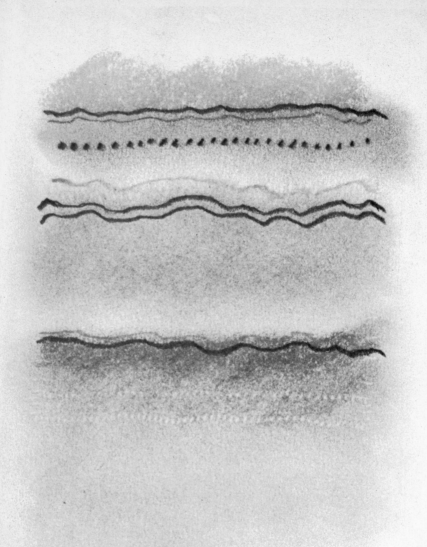

Part I

PERSONAL
EXPERIENCES
AND PERSPECTIVES

Experiences in Communication

In the autumn of 1964, I was invited to be a speaker in a lecture series at the California Institute of Technology in Pasadena, one of the leading scientific institutions in the world. Most of the speakers were from the physical sciences. The audience attracted by the series was known to be a highly educated and sophisticated group. The speakers were encouraged to put on demonstrations, if possible, of their subjects, whether astronomy, microbiology, or theoretical physics. I was asked to speak on the subject of communication.

As I started collecting references and jotting down ideas for the talk, I became very dissatisfied with what I was doing. The thought of a demonstration kept running through my mind, and then being dismissed.

The speech that follows shows how I resolved the problem of endeavoring to *communicate*, rather than just to speak *about* the subject of communication.

I have some knowledge about communication and could assemble more. When I first agreed to give this talk, I planned to gather such knowledge and organize it into a lecture. The more I thought over this plan, the less satisfied I was with it. Knowledge *about* is not the most important thing in the behavioral sciences today. There is a decided surge of experiential knowing, or knowing at a gut level, which has to do with the human being. At this level of knowing, we are in a realm where we are not simply talking of cognitive and intellectual learnings, which can nearly always be rather readily communicated in verbal terms. Instead we are speaking of something more experiential, something having to do with the whole person, visceral reactions and feelings as well as thoughts and words. Consequently, I decided I would like, rather than talking *about* communication, to *communicate* with you at a feeling level. This is not easy. I think it is usually possible only in small groups where one feels genuinely accepted. I have been frightened at the thought of attempting it with a large group. Indeed when I learned how large the group was to be, I gave up the whole idea. Since then, with encouragement from my wife, I have returned to it and decided to make such an attempt.

One of the things which strengthened me in my decision is the knowledge that these Caltech lectures have a long tradition of being given as demonstrations. In any of the usual senses what follows is not a demonstration. Yet I hope that in some sense this may be a demonstration of communication which is given, and also received, primarily at a feeling and experiential level.

What I would like to do is very simple indeed. I would like to share with you some of the things I have learned for myself in regard to communication. These are personal learnings growing out of my own experience. I am not attempting at all to say that you should learn or do these same things but I feel that if I can report my own experience honestly enough, perhaps you can check what I say against your own experience and decide as to its truth or falsity for you. In my own two-way communication with others there have been experiences that have made me feel pleased and warm and good and satisfied. There have been other experiences that to some extent at the time, and even more so afterward, have made me feel dissatisfied and displeased and more distant and less contented with myself. I would like to convey some of these things. Another way of putting this is that some of my experiences in communicating with others have made me feel expanded, larger, enriched, and have accelerated my own growth. Very often in these experiences I feel that the other person has had similar reactions and that he too has been enriched, that his development and his functioning have moved forward. Then there have been other occasions in which the growth or development of each of us has been diminished or stopped or even reversed. I am sure it will be clear in what I have to say that I would prefer my experiences in communication to have a growth-promoting effect, both on me and on the other, and that I should like to avoid those communication experiences in which both I and the other person feel diminished.

The first simple feeling I want to share with you is my enjoyment when I can really *hear* someone. I think perhaps this has been a long-standing characteristic of mine. I can remember this in my early grammar school days. A child would ask the teacher a question and the teacher would give a perfectly good answer to a completely different question. A feeling of pain and distress would always strike me. My reaction was, "But you didn't hear him!" I felt a sort of childish despair at the lack of communication which was (and is) so common.

I believe I know why it is satisfying to me to hear someone. When I can really hear someone, it puts me in touch with him; it enriches my life. It is through hearing people that I have learned all that I know about individuals, about personality, about interpersonal relationships. There is another peculiar satisfaction in really hearing someone: It is like listening to the music of the spheres, because beyond the immediate message of the person, no matter what that might be, there is the universal. Hidden in all of the personal communications which I really hear there seem to be orderly psychological laws, aspects of the same order we find in the universe as a whole. So there is both the satisfaction of hearing this person and also the satisfaction of feeling one's self in touch with what is universally true.

When I say that I enjoy hearing someone, I mean, of course, hearing deeply. I mean that I hear the words, the thoughts, the feeling tones, the personal meaning, even the meaning that is below the conscious intent of the speaker. Sometimes too, in a message which superficially is not very important, I hear a deep human cry that lies buried and unknown far below the surface of the person.

So I have learned to ask myself, can I hear the sounds and sense the shape of this other person's inner world? Can I resonate to what he is saying so deeply that I sense the meanings he is afraid of yet would like to communicate, as well as those he knows?

I think, for example, of an interview I had with an adolescent boy. Like many an adolescent today he was saying at the outset of the interview that he had no goals. When I questioned him on this, he insisted even more strongly that he had no goals whatsoever, not even one. I said, "There isn't anything you want to do?" "*Nothing*. . . . Well, yeah, I want to keep on living." I remember distinctly my feeling at that moment. I resonated very deeply to this phrase. He might simply be telling me that, like everyone else, he wanted to live. On the other hand, he might be telling me—and this seemed to be a definite possibility—that at some point the question of whether or not to live had been a real issue with him. So I tried to resonate to him at all levels. I didn't know for certain what the message was. I simply wanted to be open to any of the meanings that this statement might have, including the possibility that he might at one time have considered suicide. My being willing and able to listen to him at all levels is perhaps one of the things that made it possible for him to tell me, before the end of the interview, that not long before he had been on the point of blowing his brains out. This little episode is an example of what I mean by wanting to really hear someone at all the levels at which he is endeavoring to communicate.

Let me give another brief example. Not long ago a friend called me long distance about a certain matter. We concluded the conversation and I hung up the phone. Then, and only then, did his tone of voice really hit me. I said to myself that behind the subject matter we were discussing there seemed to be a note of distress, discouragement, even despair, which had nothing to do with the matter at hand. I felt this so sharply that I wrote him a letter saying something to this effect: "I may be all wrong in what I am going to say and if so, you can toss this in the wastebasket, but I realized after I hung up the phone that you sounded as though you were in real distress and pain, perhaps in real despair." Then I attempted to share with him some of my own feelings about him and his situation in ways that I hoped might be helpful. I sent off the letter with some qualms, thinking that I might have been ridiculously mistaken. I very quickly received a reply. He was extremely grateful that someone had *heard* him. I had been quite correct in hearing his tone of voice and I felt very pleased that I had been able to hear him and hence make possible a real communication. So often, as in this instance, the words convey one message and the tone of voice a sharply different one.

I find, both in therapeutic interviews and in the intensive group experiences which have meant a great deal to me, that hearing has consequences. When I truly hear a person and the meanings that are important to him at that moment, hearing not simply his words, but him, and when I let him know that I have heard his own private personal meanings, many things happen. There is first of all a grateful look. He feels released. He wants to tell me more about his world. He surges forth in a new sense of freedom. He becomes more open to the process of change.

Sr Maureen

I have often noticed that the more deeply I hear the meanings of this person, the more there is that happens. Almost always, when a person realizes he has been deeply heard, his eyes moisten. I think in some real sense he is weeping for joy. It is as though he were saying, "Thank God, somebody heard me. Someone knows what it's like to be me." In such moments I have had the fantasy of a prisoner in a dungeon, tapping out day after day a Morse code message, "Does anybody hear me? Is anybody there?" And finally one day he hears some faint tappings which spell out "Yes." By that one simple response he is released from his loneliness; he has become a human being again. There are many, many people living in private dungeons today, people who give no evidence of it whatsoever on the outside, where you have to listen very sharply to hear the faint messages from the dungeon.

If this seems to you a little too sentimental or over-drawn, I would like to share with you an experience I had recently in a basic encounter group with fifteen persons in important executive posts. Early in the very intensive sessions of the week they were asked to write a statement of some feeling or feelings which they were not willing to share with the group. These were anony-mous statements. One man wrote, "I don't relate easily to people. I have an almost impenetrable facade. Noth-ing gets in to hurt me but nothing gets out. I have repressed so many emotions that I am close to emo-tional sterility. This situation doesn't make me happy, but I don't know what to do about it. Perhaps insight into how others react to me and why will help." This was clearly a message from a dungeon. Later in the week a member of the group identified himself as the man who had written that anonymous message, filling out in much greater detail his feelings of isolation, of complete coldness. He felt that life had been so brutal to him that he had been forced to live a life without feeling, not only at work but also in social groups and, saddest of all, with his family. His gradual achievement of greater expressiveness in the group, of less fear of being hurt, of more willingness to share himself with others, was a very rewarding experience for all of us who participated.

I was both amused and pleased when, in a letter a few weeks later asking me about another matter, he also included this paragraph: "When I returned from [our group] I felt somewhat like a young girl who had been seduced but still wound up with the feeling that it was exactly what she had been waiting for and needed! I am still not quite sure who was responsible for the seduction—you or the group, or whether it was a joint venture. I suspect it was the latter. At any rate, I want to thank you for what was a meaningful and intensely interesting experience." I think it is not too much to say that because several of us in the group were able genuinely to hear him, he was released from his dungeon and came out, at least to some degree, into the sunnier world of warm interpersonal relationships.

Let me move on to a second learning that I would like to share with you. I like to *be heard.* A number of times in my life I have felt myself bursting with insoluble problems, or going round and round in tormented circles or, during one period, overcome by feelings of worthlessness and despair. I think I have been more fortunate than most in finding at these times individuals who have been able to hear me and thus to rescue me from the chaos of my feelings, individuals who have been able to hear my meanings a little more deeply than I have known them. These persons have heard me without judging me, diagnosing me, appraising me, evaluating me. They have just listened and clarified and responded to me at all the levels at which I was communicating. I can testify that when you are in psychological distress and someone really hears you without passing judgment on you, without trying to take responsibility for you, without trying to mold you, it feels damn good! At these times it has relaxed the tension in me. It has permitted me to bring out the frightening feelings, the guilts, the despair, the confusions that have been a part of my experience. When I have been listened to and when I have been heard, I am able to reperceive my world in a new way and to go on. It is astonishing how elements that seem insoluble become soluble when someone listens, how confusions that seem irremediable turn into relatively clear flowing streams when one is heard. I have deeply appreciated

sensitive empathic concentrated

the times that I have experienced this sensitive, empathic, concentrated listening.

I dislike it in myself when I can't hear another, when I do not understand him. If it is only a simple failure of comprehension or a failure to focus my attention on what he is saying or a difficulty in understanding his words, then I feel only a very mild dissatisfaction with myself. But what I really dislike in myself is not being able to hear the other person because I am so sure in advance of what he is about to say that I don't listen. It is only afterward that I realize that I have heard what I have already decided he is saying; I have failed really to listen. Or even worse are those times when I catch myself trying to twist his message to make it say what I want him to say, and then only hearing that. This can be a very subtle thing, and it is surprising how skillful I can be in doing it. Just by twisting his words a small amount, by distorting his meaning just a little, I can make it appear that he is not only saying the thing I want to hear, but that he is the person I want him to be. Only when I realize through his protest or through my own gradual recognition that I am subtly manipulating him, do I become disgusted with myself. I know too, from being on the receiving end of this, how frustrating it is to be received for what you are not, to be heard as saying something which you have not said. This creates anger and bafflement and disillusion.

This last statement indeed leads into the next learning that I want to share with you: I am terribly frustrated and shut into myself when I try to express something which is deeply me, which is a part of my own private, inner world, and the other person does not understand. When I take the gamble, the risk, of trying to share something that is very personal with another individual and it is not received and not understood, this is a very deflating and a very lonely experience. I have come to believe that such an experience makes some individuals psychotic. It causes them to give up hoping that anyone can understand them. Once they have lost that hope, then their own inner world, which becomes more and more bizarre, is the only place where they can live. They can no longer live in any shared human experience. I can sympathize with them because I know that when I try to share some feeling aspect of myself which is private, precious, and tentative, and when this communication is met by evaluation, by reassurance, by distortion of my meaning, my very strong reaction is, "Oh, what's the use!" At such a time, one knows what it is to be alone.

So, as you can readily see from what I have said thus far, a creative, active, sensitive, accurate, empathic, nonjudgmental listening is for me terribly important in a relationship. It is important for me to provide it; it has been extremely important, especially at certain times in my life, to receive it. I feel that I have grown within myself when I have provided it; I am very sure that I have grown and been released and enhanced when I have received this kind of listening.

Let me move on to another area of my learnings.

I find it very satisfying when I can be real, when I can be close to whatever it is that is going on within me. I like it when I can listen to myself. To really know what I am experiencing in the moment is by no means an easy thing, but I feel somewhat encouraged because I think that over the years I have been improving at it. I am convinced, however, that it is a lifelong task and that none of us ever is totally able to be comfortably close to all that is going on within our own experience.

In place of the term "realness" I have sometimes used the word "congruence." By this I mean that when my experiencing of this moment is present in my awareness and when what is present in my awareness is present in my communication, then each of these three levels matches or is congruent. At such moments I am integrated or whole, I am completely in one piece. Most of the time, of course, I, like everyone else, exhibit some degree of incongruence. I have learned, however, that realness, or genuineness, or congruence—whatever term you wish to give it—is a fundamental basis for the best of communication.

What do I mean by being close to what is going on in me? Let me try to explain what I mean by describing what sometimes occurs in my work as a therapist. Sometimes a feeling "rises up in me" which seems to have no particular relationship to what is going on. Yet I have learned to accept and trust this feeling in my awareness and to try to communicate it to my client. For example, a client is talking to me and I suddenly feel an image of him as a pleading little boy, folding his hands in supplication, saying, "Please let me have this, please let me have this." I have learned that if I can be real in the relationship with him and express this feeling that has occurred in me, it is very likely to strike some deep note in him and to advance our relationship.

Let me give another example. It is often very hard for me, as for other writers, to get close to my self when I start to write. It is so easy to be distracted by the possibility of saying things which will catch approval or will look good to colleagues or make a popular appeal. How can I listen to the things that I really want to say and write? It is difficult. Sometimes I even have to trick myself to get close to what is in me. I tell myself that I am not writing for publication; I am just writing for my own satisfaction. I write on old scraps of paper so that I don't even have to reproach myself for wasting paper. I jot down feelings and ideas as they come, helter-skelter, with no attempt at coherence or organization. In this way I can sometimes get much closer to what I really am and feel and think. The writings that I have produced on this basis turn out to be ones for which I never feel apologetic and which often communicate deeply to others. So it is a very satisfying thing when I sense that I have gotten close to me, to the feelings and hidden aspects of myself that live below the surface.

Free association

I feel a sense of satisfaction when I can dare to communicate the realness in me to another. This is far from easy, partly because what I am experiencing keeps changing every moment. Usually there is a lag, sometimes of moments, sometimes of days, weeks, or months, between the experiencing and the communication: I experience something; I feel something, but only later do I dare to communicate it, when it has become cool enough to risk sharing it with another. But when I can communicate what is real in me at the moment that it occurs, I feel genuine, spontaneous, and alive.

The God in me touches the God in you

It is a sparkling thing when I encounter realness in another person. Sometimes in the basic encounter groups which have been a very important part of my experience these last few years, someone says something that comes from him transparently and whole. It is so obvious when a person is not hiding behind a facade but is speaking from deep within himself. When this happens, I leap to meet it. I want to encounter this real person. Sometimes the feelings thus expressed are very positive feelings; sometimes they are decidedly negative ones. I think of a man in a very responsible

sparkling

position, a scientist at the head of a large research department in a huge electronics firm. One day in such an encounter group he found the courage to speak of his isolation. He told us that he had never had a single friend in his life; there were plenty of people whom he knew but not one he could count as a friend. "As a matter of fact," he added, "there are only two individuals in the world with whom I have even a reasonably communicative relationship. These are my two children." By the time he finished, he was letting loose some of the tears of sorrow for himself which I am sure he had held in for many years. But it was the honesty and realness of his loneliness that caused every member of the group to reach out to him in some psychological sense. It was also most significant that his courage *chain reaction* in being real enabled all of us to be more genuine in our communications, to come out from behind the facades we ordinarily use.

I am disappointed when I realize—and of course this realization always comes afterward, after a lag of time—that I have been too frightened or too threatened *fear prevents congruency* to let myself get close to what I am experiencing, and that consequently I have not been genuine or congruent. There immediately comes to mind an instance that is somewhat painful to reveal. Some years ago I was invited to be a Fellow at the Center for Advanced Study in the Behavioral Sciences at Stanford. The Fellows are a group of brilliant and well-informed scholars. I suppose it is inevitable that there is a considerable amount of one-upmanship, of showing off one's knowledge and achievements. It seems important for each Fellow to impress the others, to be a little more assured, to be a little more knowledgeable than he really is. I found myself doing this same thing—playing

a role of having greater certainty and greater competence than I really possess. I can't tell you how disgusted with myself I felt as I realized what I was doing:
I was not being me, I was playing a part.

I regret it when I suppress my feelings too long and
they burst forth in ways that are distorted or attacking
or hurtful. I have a friend whom I like very much but
who has one particular pattern of behavior that thoroughly annoys me. Because of the usual tendency to
be nice, polite, and pleasant I kept this annoyance to
myself for too long and, when it finally burst its bounds,
it came out not only as annoyance but as an attack on
him. This was hurtful, and it took us some time to
repair the relationship.

I am inwardly pleased when I have the strength to
permit another person to be his own realness and to be
separate from me. I think that is often a very threatening possibility. In some ways I have found it an ultimate
test of staff leadership and of parenthood. Can I freely
permit this staff member or my son or my daughter to
become a separate person with ideas, purposes, and
values which may not be identical with my own? I think
of one staff member this past year who showed many
flashes of brilliance but who clearly held values different from mine and behaved in ways very different
from the ways in which I would behave. It was a real
struggle, in which I feel I was only partially successful,
to let him be himself, to let him develop as a person
entirely separate from me and my ideas and my values.
Yet to the extent that I was successful, I was pleased
with myself, because I think this permission to be a
separate person is what makes for the autonomous
development of another individual.

I am angry with myself when I discover that I have

been subtly controlling and molding another person in my own image. This has been a very painful part of my professional experience. I hate to have "disciples," students who have molded themselves meticulously into the pattern that they feel I wish. Some of the responsibility I place with them, but I cannot avoid the uncomfortable probability that in unknown ways I have subtly controlled such individuals and made them into carbon copies of myself, instead of the separate professional persons they have every right to become.

From what I have been saying, I trust it is clear that when I can permit realness in myself or sense it or permit it in another, I am very satisfied. When I cannot permit it in myself or fail to permit it in another, I am very distressed. When I am able to let myself be congruent and genuine, I often help the other person. When the other person is transparently real and congruent, he often helps me. In those rare moments when a deep realness in one meets a realness in the other, a memorable "I-thou relationship," as Martin Buber would call it, occurs. Such a deep and mutual personal encounter does not happen often, but I am convinced that unless it happens occasionally, we are not living as human beings.

I want to move on to another area of my learning in interpersonal relationships—one that has been slow and painful for me.

I feel warmed and fulfilled when I can let in the fact, or permit myself to feel, that someone cares for, accepts, admires, or prizes me. Because of elements in my past history, I suppose, it has been very difficult for me to do this. For a long time I tended almost automatically to brush aside any positive feelings aimed in my direction. My reaction was, "Who, me? You couldn't

cares for
accepts
admires
prizes

possibly care for me. You might like what I have done, or my achievements, but not me." This is one respect in which my own therapy helped me very much. I am not always able even now to let in such warm and loving feelings from others, but I find it very releasing when I can do so. I know that some people flatter me in order to gain something for themselves; some people praise me because they are afraid to be hostile. But I have come to recognize the fact that some people genuinely appreciate me, like me, love me, and I want to sense that fact and let it in. I think I have become less aloof as I have been able to take in and soak up those loving feelings.

I feel enriched when I can truly prize or care for or love another person and when I can let that feeling flow out to that person. Like many others, I used to fear being trapped by letting my feelings show. "If I care for him, he can control me." "If I love her, I am trying to control her." I think that I have moved a long way toward being less fearful in this respect. Like my clients, I too have slowly learned that tender, positive feelings are not dangerous either to give or to receive. To illustrate what I mean, I would like again to draw an example from a recent basic encounter group. A woman who described herself as "a loud, prickly, hyperactive individual" whose marriage was on the rocks, and who felt that life was just not worth living, said, "I had really buried under a layer of concrete many feelings I was afraid people were going to laugh at or stomp on which, needless to say, was working all kinds of hell on my family and me. I had been looking forward to the workshop with my last few crumbs of hope—it was really a needle of trust in a huge haystack of despair." She spoke of some of her experiences in the group and added, "The real turning point for me was a simple gesture on your part of putting your arm around my shoulder, one afternoon when I'd made some crack about you not really being a member of the group—that no one could cry on *your* shoulder. In my notes I had written, the night before, 'My God, there's no man in the world who loves me.' You seemed so genuinely concerned the day I fell apart, I was overwhelmed. . . . I received the gesture as one of the first feelings of acceptance—of me, just the dumb way I am, prickles and all—that I had ever experienced. I have felt needed, loving, competent, furious, frantic, anything and everything but just plain *loved*. You can imagine the flood of gratitude, humility, almost release, that swept over me. I wrote, with considerable joy, 'I actually felt love.' I doubt that I shall soon forget it."

This woman, of course, was speaking *to* me, and yet in some deep sense she was also speaking *for* me. I too have had similar feelings.

Another example concerns the experiencing and giving of love. I think of one governmental executive in a group in which I participated, a man with high responsibility and excellent technical training as an engineer. At the first meeting of the group he impressed me, and I think others, as being cold, aloof, somewhat bitter, resentful, and cynical. When he spoke of how he ran his office, it appeared that he administered it "by the book," without any warmth or human feeling. In one of the early sessions he was speaking of his wife, and a group member asked him, "Do you love your wife?" He paused for a long time and the questioner said, "O.K. That's answer enough." The executive said, "No. Wait a minute. The reason I didn't respond was that I was wondering, 'Have I ever loved anyone?' I don't really think I have ever *loved* anyone."

cold
aloof
& bitter
resentful
cynical

A few days later, he listened with great intensity as one member of the group revealed many personal feelings of isolation and loneliness and spoke of the extent to which he had been living behind a facade. The next morning the engineer said, "Last night I thought and thought about what he told us. I even wept quite a bit myself. I can't remember how long it has been since I have cried, and I really felt something. I think perhaps what I felt was love."

It is not surprising that before the week was over, he had thought through different ways of handling his growing son, on whom he had been placing very rigorous demands. He had also begun to really appreciate the love his wife had extended to him—love that he now felt he could in some measure reciprocate.

Because of having less fear of giving or receiving positive feelings, I have become more able to appreciate individuals. I have come to believe that this ability is rather rare; so often, even with our children, we love them to control them rather than loving them because we appreciate them. One of the most satisfying feelings I know—and also one of the most growth-promoting experiences for the other person—comes from my appreciating this individual in the same way that I appreciate a sunset. People are just as wonderful as sunsets if I can let them *be*. In fact, perhaps the reason we can truly appreciate a sunset is that we cannot control it. When I look at a sunset as I did the other evening, I don't find myself saying, "Soften the orange a little on the right hand corner, and put a bit more purple along the base, and use a little more pink in the cloud color." I don't do that. I don't *try* to control a sunset. I watch it with awe as it unfolds. I like myself best when

I can appreciate my staff member, my son, my daughter, my grandchildren, in this same way. I believe this is a somewhat Oriental attitude; for me it is a most satisfying one.

Another learning I would like to mention briefly is one of which I am not proud but which seems to be a fact. When I am not prized and appreciated, I not only *feel* very much diminished, but my behavior is actually affected by my feelings. When I am prized, I blossom and expand, I am an interesting individual. In a hostile or unappreciative group, I am just not much of anything. People wonder, with very good reason, how did he ever get a reputation? I wish I had the strength to be more similar in both kinds of groups, but actually the person I am in a warm and interested group is different from the person I am in a hostile or cold group. Thus, prizing or loving and being prized or loved is experienced as very growth enhancing. A person who is loved appreciatively, not possessively, blooms and develops his own unique self. The person who loves nonpossessively is himself enriched. This, at least, has been my experience.

I could give you some of the research evidence which shows that these qualities I have mentioned—an ability to listen empathically, a congruence or genuineness, an acceptance or prizing of the other—when they are present in a relationship make for good communication and for constructive change in personality. But I feel that, somehow, research evidence is out of place in a talk such as I have been giving.

I want to close instead with two statements drawn again from an intensive group experience. This was a one-week workshop, and the two statements I am quoting were written a number of weeks later by two members of the workshop. We had asked each individual to write about his current feelings and to address this to all the members of the group.

The first statement is written by a man who tells of the fact that he had some rather difficult experiences immediately after the workshop, including spending time with

a father-in-law who doesn't care much about me as a person but only in what I concretely accomplish. I was severely shaken. It was like going from one extreme to another. I again began to doubt my purpose and particularly my usefulness. But time and again I would hearken back to the group, to things you've said or done that gave me a feeling that I do have something to offer—that I don't have to demonstrate concretely to be worthwhile—and this would even the scale and lift me out of my depression. I have come to the conclusion that my experiences with you have profoundly affected me, and I am truly grateful. This is different from personal therapy. None of you had to care about me, none of you needed to seek me out and let me know of things you thought would help me, none of you had to let me know that I was of help to you—yet you did, and as a result, it has far more meaning than anything I have so far experienced. When I feel the need to hold back and not live spontaneously, for whatever reason, I remember that twelve persons, just like these before me, said to let go and be congruent, to be myself, and of all unbelievable things, they even loved me more for it. This has given me the courage to come out of myself many times since then. Often it seems, my very doing of this helps the others to experience similar freedom.

I have also been able to let others into my life more—to let them care for me and to receive their warmth. I remember the time in our group encounter when this change occurred. It felt like I had removed long-standing barriers—so much so that I

*deeply felt a new experience of openness toward you. I didn't
have to be afraid, I didn't have to fight or fearfully pull away
from the freedom this offered my own impulses—I could just
be and let you be with me.*

The second excerpt is taken from the report of a
woman who had come with her husband to this workshop in human relations, although she and her husband
were in separate groups. She talks at some length about
her experience in revealing her feelings to the group
and the results of taking that step.

*Taking the plunge was one of the hardest things I have ever
done. I have hidden my feelings of hurt and loneliness from
even my closest friends while I was feeling them. Only when I
had suppressed my feelings and could speak jokingly or casu-
ally could I share painful things at all, but that didn't help
me work through them. You knocked down the walls that were
holding back hurt, and it was good to be with you and hurt—
and not withdraw.*

*Also, before, it had been so painful to me to be misunder-
stood or criticized that I chose not to share truly meaningful
events, good or bad, most of my life. Only recently have I
dared risk the hurt. In the group I faced these fears and was
relieved beyond measure to find that my feelings in response
to your criticism and misunderstanding (so blessedly devoid
of hostility, I felt) were not deep hurt, but more curiosity,
regret, irritation, perhaps sadness, and [I felt] a deep sense of* mirror
*gratitude for the help I experienced in looking at part of me I
had not seen nor wanted to face before. I am sure my perception of your concern and respect for the person, even when my
behavior might irritate or alienate you, makes it possible for
me to accept all of this and find it helpful.*

*There were times I felt very afraid of the group, though
never of you individually. I needed very much at times to talk
with just an individual, but during the course of the week
discovered that most of you at some time or other were a real*

*help to me. What a release to find so many instead of just the
leaders. This experience opened me to a deeper trust in people, increased my ability to be open with others.*

*One of the nicest results is that now I can completely relax.
I didn't realize how much constant tension I was under until I
suddenly wasn't! I am now much more sensitive to the times
when my emotions or fatigue make me a poor listener, for I
find that my own inner hurts and anxiety, even suppressed,
interfered with my really listening to another. Since then I
have been able to listen better and to respond more helpfully
than ever before in my life. I have been far more aware of
what I was feeling and experiencing myself—an openness to
myself I never had before.*

*Congruence was more an ideal than reality to me. Frankly,
I found it disconcerting to experience and frightening to
express. This was the first really safe place I had found to see
what I was like, to experience and express myself. I now find
that a lack of congruence in myself is painful. The release
and joy in my being open to what I was experiencing within
and being able to keep this openness between us was new and
uplifting. I am deeply grateful to you who have made it possible for us to be so much more open with each other.*

I trust that you will see in these experiences some of
the elements of growth-promoting interpersonal communication that have had meaning for me. A sensitive
ability to hear, a deep satisfaction in being heard; an
ability to be more real, which in turn brings forth more
realness from others; and consequently a greater freedom to give and receive love—these, in my experience,
are the elements that make interpersonal communication enriching and enhancing.

My Philosophy of
Interpersonal Relationships
and How It Grew

This is a strictly autobiographical paper. I hope it will give some clues to the way my belief system has developed and altered, until it is now almost the antithesis of what I was taught—and believed—in my youth. It endeavors to point to the factors that have been responsible for the continual changingness of my views. Some of these factors are external, some internal, and some grew out of relationships. I first presented this paper at the August 1972 meeting of the Association for Humanistic Psychology in Honolulu, Hawaii. The audience seemed genuinely to be touched by it. I hope it will have meaning for you.

I wish to discuss the development and changes in my attitudes and approaches toward other persons. I will cover not only my professional approach, as it has changed over the years, but my personal approach as well.

Let me begin with my childhood. In a narrowly fundamentalist religious home, I introjected the value attitudes toward others that were held by my parents. Whether I truly believed in these I cannot be sure. I know that I acted on these values. I think the attitudes toward persons outside our large family can be summed up schematically in this way: "Other persons behave in dubious ways which we do not approve in our family. Many of them play cards, go to movies, smoke, dance, drink, and engage in other activities, some unmentionable. So the best thing to do is to be tolerant of them, since they may not know better, but to keep away from any close communication with them and to live your life within the family. 'Come ye out from among them and be ye separate' is a good Biblical text to follow."

To the best of my recollection this unconsciously arrogant separateness characterized my behavior all through elementary school. I certainly had no close friends. There were a group of boys and girls my age who rode bicycles together on the street behind our house. But I never went to their homes, nor did they come to mine.

As to the relations with the others in my family, I thoroughly enjoyed being with and playing with my younger brothers, was jealous of my next older brother, and greatly admired my oldest brother, although the age gap was too great for much communication. I knew my parents loved me, but it would never have occurred to me to share with them any of my personal or private thoughts or feelings, because I knew these would have been judged and found wanting. My thoughts, my fantasies, and the few feelings I was aware of I kept to myself.

I could sum up these boyhood years by saying that anything I would today regard as a close and communicative interpersonal relationship with another was completely lacking during that period. My attitude toward others outside my home was characterized by the distance and the aloofness that I had taken over from my parents.

I attended the same elementary school for seven years. From this point on, until I finished graduate work, I never attended any school for longer than two years, a fact that undoubtedly had its effect on me.

Beginning with high school, I believe my hunger for companionship came a little more into my awareness. But any satisfaction of that hunger was blocked first by the already mentioned attitudes of my parents, and second by circumstances. I attended three different high schools, none for more than two years, commuting long distances by train to each one, so that I never was able to put down any social roots and was never able to participate in any after-school or evening activities with other students. I respected and liked some of my fellow students, and some of them respected and probably liked me—perhaps partly because of my good grades— but there was never time enough to develop a friendship, and certainly I never had any close personal interaction with any of them. I had one date during high school—to attend a senior class dinner.

So, during the important years of adolescence I had no close friend and only superficial personal contact. I did express some feelings in my English themes during the two terms when I had reasonably understanding teachers. At home I felt increasingly close to my next younger brother, but an age difference of five years cut down on any deep sharing. I was now more consciously a complete outsider, an onlooker in anything involving personal relationships. I believe my intense scientific interest in collecting and rearing the great night-flying moths was without doubt a partial compensation for the lack of intimate sharing. I realized by now that I was peculiar, a loner, with very little place or opportunity for a place in the world of persons. I was socially incompetent in any but superficial contacts. My fantasies during this period were definitely bizarre, and probably would be classed as schizoid by a diagnostician, but fortunately I never came in contact with a psychologist.

College represented the first break in this solitary experience. I entered the college of agriculture at the University of Wisconsin, and almost immediately joined a group of fellows who met in a YMCA class. Starting with this narrow interest, we developed into an ongoing, self-directed group carrying on all sorts of activities. Here I first discovered what it meant to have comrades and even friends. There was lively, enjoyable, and interesting discussion of attitudes and ideas about moral and ethical issues. There was even some sharing of personal problems, especially on a one-to-one basis. For two years this group meant a great deal to me, until I shifted to majoring in history in the College of Letters and Science and gradually lost contact with them.

During this period, I suppose I could say that I began my first gropings toward a professional life. I was the leader of a boys' club, and enjoyed the experience. My concept of what to do was limited completely to *activities* in which we could engage—hikes, picnics, swimming, and the like. I don't recall that I ever encouraged, or that we had, any discussions on any matters of interest to the boys. The possibility of communication was evidently beginning to dawn on me so far as my peers were concerned, but I doubt if I ever dreamed of it as a possibility for these twelve-year-olds.

I was also a camp counselor in a camp for underprivileged youngsters during the summer, with eight counselors and one hundred boys under my supervision.

The cherry-picking work in which we engaged part-time and the athletic activities afterward constituted my idea of a suitable program. Here I have my first memory of a most dubious attempt at a "helping" relationship. Some articles and money had disappeared in our dormitory. The evidence pointed to one boy. So I and several of the counselors took him off by himself to get a confession from him. The term "brainwashing" had not then been invented, but we had real expertise at it. We cajoled, we argued, we persuaded, we were friendly, we were critical—some even prayed for him— but he withstood all our attempts, much to our disappointment. As I look back on this embarrassing scene, I gather that my concept of helping another person was to get him to confess his evil ways so that he might be instructed in the proper way to go.

In other directions, however, I was becoming more of a social being. I began dating girls, fearfully to be sure, but a start. I found I could express myself more freely with older girls, and as a freshman I dated several seniors. I also began going with Helen, the girl who later became my wife, and here an increasingly deep communication of hopes, ideals, and aims gradually began to take place. I discovered that private thoughts and dreams of the future could actually be shared on a mutual basis with another person. It was a very growing experience.

After two years of college we were separated by distance, but the courtship and frequent contacts continued for two more years before we were married. As I look back, I realize this was the first truly caring, close, sharing relationship I had ever formed with anyone. It meant the world to me. During the first two years of marriage we learned a vitally important lesson. We learned, through some chance help, that the elements

in the relationship that seemed impossible to share—
the secretly disturbing, dissatisfying elements—are the
most rewarding to share. This was a hard, risky,
frightening thing to learn, and we have relearned it
many, many times since. It was a rich and developing
experience for each of us.

 Meanwhile, in graduate school at Union Theological
Seminary in New York, we were sharing in several
courses as well as pursuing our own separate
directions—she becoming more of an artist until moth-
erhood occupied much of her time, while I continued
my studies. Although I became more and more turned
off by the academic courses in religion, there were two
experiences that helped to shape my way of relating to
others. The first was a self-organized, self-directed
seminar of students with no faculty leader. Here we
shared responsibility for the topics we considered and
the way we wanted to conduct the course. More important, we began to share our doubts, our personal problems with our work. We became a mutually trusting
group, discussing deep issues, and arriving at under-
standings which changed the lives of a number of us.
The second experience was a course on "Working with
Young People" conducted by Dr. Goodwin Watson,
who, before his death, was a prominent and active
NTL* trainer and a progressive leader in education.
While taking this course, I had my first clear realization
that working closely with individuals might be a profession. This possibility offered me a way out of religious
work, and as a result of these two experiences I shifted
"across the street" (literally) to Teachers College,
Columbia, where Goodwin Watson became my thesis
supervisor, and I began taking work in clinical psychol-

*National Training Laboratories, an organization of group leaders that is
especially active in business groups.

ogy. I was also exposed to the thinking of John Dewey, through William Heard Kilpatrick.

I had by this time made tentative steps toward understanding relationships with others. My learnings were to be important to me later. I had learned that deep sharing with others was possible and enriching. I had learned that in a close relationship the elements that "cannot" be shared are those that are most important and rewarding to share. I had found that a group could be trusted to move in the direction of highly significant and relevant personal learnings. I was even beginning to learn that an individual faculty sponsor could trust the student he was supervising, with only growthful effects. I had discovered that persons in trouble could be helped, but that there were very divergent ideas as to how this could be done.

In my graduate training in clinical psychology, I was learning two major ways of relating to individuals who come for help. At Teachers College the approach was to understand *about* the individual through testing, measurement, diagnostic interviews, and prescriptive advice as to treatment. This cold approach was, however, suffused with warmth by the personality of Dr. Leta Hollingworth, who taught us more by her person than by her lectures. Later, when I interned at the then new and affluent Institute for Child Guidance, I was exposed to a very different atmosphere. Dominated as it was by psychoanalysts, I learned more about the individual. I learned that he cannot be understood without an exhaustive case history seventy-five pages or more in length, going into all the personality dynamics of the grandparents, the parents, the aunts and uncles, and finally the "patient" himself—possible birth trauma, manner of weaning, degree of dependency, sibling relationships, and on and on. Then there was the elaborate testing, including the newly imported

Rorschach, and finally many interviews with the child before deciding what sort of treatment he should have. It nearly always came out the same: the child was treated psychoanalytically by the psychiatrist, the mother was dealt with in the same fashion by the social worker, and occasionally, the psychologist was asked to tutor the child. Yet I carried on my first therapy case there. It started with tutoring but developed into more and more personal interviews, and I discovered the thrill that comes from observing changes in a person's behavior. Whether those were due to my enthusiasm or my methods I cannot say.

As I look back, I realize that my interest in interviewing and in therapy certainly grew in part out of my early loneliness. Here was a socially approved way of getting really close to individuals and thus filling some of the hungers I had undoubtedly felt. The therapeutic interview also offered a chance of becoming close without having to go through what was to me a long and painful process of gradual and deepening acquaintance.

By the time I had completed my work in New York, I *knew*—with all the assurance of the newly trained—how to deal with people professionally. In spite of the wide differences between Teachers College and the Institute, they both helped me arrive at somewhat the same formula, which could be stated as follows: "I will gather an enormous amount of data about this individual: his history, his intelligence, his special abilities, his personality. Out of all this I can form an elaborate diagnostic formulation as to the causes of his present behavior, his personal and social resources for dealing with his situation, and the prognosis for his future. I will endeavor to interpret all this in simple language to the responsible agencies, to the parents, and to the child if he is capable of understanding it. I will make sound suggestions which, if carried out, will change the behavior, and I will reinforce those suggestions by repeated contact. In all of this I remain thoroughly objective, professional, and personally aloof from these persons in trouble, except insofar as personal warmth is necessary to build a satisfactory rapport."

This sounds a bit incredible to me now, but I know it is essentially true because I can recall the scorn I felt for one psychiatrist, not an analyst, who simply dealt with problem children as though he *liked* them. He even took them to his home. Clearly he had never learned the importance of being *professional*!

Thus when I went to Rochester, New York, as a member of the Child Study Department—really a child guidance clinic for delinquent children and those who were wards of the social agencies because of their poor home environment—I knew what to do. I was so sure, that I remember (painfully) telling PTA and community groups that our clinic was rather similar to a garage: you brought in a problem, received an expert diagnosis, and were advised how the difficulty could be corrected.

But my views were gradually eroded. Living in a stable community, I found I had to live with the consequences of my advice and recommendations—and they did *not* always work out. Many of the children I worked with were housed temporarily in the detention home next door, so I could see them day after day. I was astonished that sometimes, after a particularly "good" interview where I had interpreted to a boy all the causes of his misbehavior, he refused to see me the next day! So I had to win him back to find out what had gone wrong. I began to learn, experientially.

Then as director of the new and independent Rochester Guidance Center, which replaced the Child Study

Department, we had more self-referrals, where we had no authority whatsoever over child or parent and had to build a relationship if we were to be of help.

Then came a few incidents which markedly changed my approach; I shall tell you about the one that stands out most vividly in my mind. An intelligent mother brought her very seriously misbehaving boy to the clinic. I took the history from her myself. Another psychologist tested the boy. We decided in conference that the central problem was the mother's rejection of her son. I would work with her on this problem. The other psychologist would take the boy on for play therapy. In interview after interview I tried—much more softly and gently now, as a result of experience—to help the mother see the pattern of her rejection and its results in the boy. All to no avail. After about a dozen interviews I told her I thought we both had tried but were getting nowhere, and we should probably call it quits. She agreed. Then, as she was leaving the room, she turned and asked, "Do you ever take adults for counseling here?" Puzzled, I replied that sometimes we did. Whereupon she returned to the chair she had just left and began to pour out a story of the deep difficulties between herself and her husband and her great desire for some kind of help. I was bowled over. What she was telling me bore no resemblance to the neat history I had drawn from her. I scarcely knew what to do, but mostly I listened. Eventually, after many more interviews, not only did her marital relationship improve, but her son's problem behavior dropped away as she became a more real and free person. To jump ahead a bit, she was the first client I ever had who continued to keep in occasional touch with me for years afterward, until her boy was doing well in college.

This was a vital learning for me. I had followed *her* lead rather than mine. I had just *listened* instead of trying to nudge her toward a diagnostic understanding I had already reached. It was a far more personal relationship, and not nearly so "professional." Yet the results spoke for themselves.

At about this time came a brief two-day seminar with Otto Rank, and I found that in his therapy (not in his theory) he was emphasizing some of the things I had begun to learn. I felt stimulated and confirmed. I employed a social worker, trained in Rankian "relationship therapy" at the Philadelphia School of Social Work, and learned much from her. So my views shifted more and more. This transition is well captured in my book, *Clinical Treatment of the Problem Child*, written in 1937–1938, in which I devote a long chapter to relationship therapy, though the rest of the book is largely a diagnostic–prescriptive approach.

At Ohio State University, where I went in 1940, I was greatly enriched as I presented my views of clinical work to bright and questioning graduate students. Here too, I began to realize that I was saying something new, perhaps even original, about counseling and psychotherapy, and I wrote the book of that title. My dream of recording therapeutic interviews came true, helping to focus my interest on the effects of different responses in the interview. This led to a heavy emphasis on technique—the so-called nondirective technique.

But I was finding that this new-found trust in my client and his capacity for exploring and resolving his problems reached out uncomfortably into other areas. If I trusted my clients, why didn't I trust my students? If this was fine for the individual in trouble, why not for a staff group facing problems? I found that I had embarked not on a new *method* of therapy, but a sharply different *philosophy* of living and relationships.

Some of these issues I worked out while at Ohio State, and when I was given an opportunity to start a new Counseling Center at the University of Chicago, setting my own policies and selecting my own staff, I was ready to formulate and act on what was for me a new approach to human relationships. I think I can again state it in summarized fashion:

"I have come to trust the capacity of persons to explore and understand themselves and their troubles, and to resolve those problems, in any close, continuing relationship where I can provide a climate of real warmth and understanding.

"I am going to venture to put the same kind of trust in a staff group, endeavoring to build an atmosphere in which each is responsible for the actions of the group as a whole, and where the group has a responsibility to each individual. Authority has been given to me, and I am going to give it completely to the group.

"I am going to experiment with putting trust in students, in class groups, to choose their own directions and to evaluate their progress in terms of their own choosing."

Chicago was a time of great learning for me. I had ample opportunity to test out the hypotheses I have just stated. I greatly expanded the empirical testing of our therapeutic hypotheses, which we had begun earlier. By 1957 I had developed a rigorous theory of therapy and the therapeutic relationship. I had set forth the "necessary and sufficient conditions of therapeutic personality change" (Rogers, 1957), all of them personal attitudes, *not* professional training. This was a rather presumptuous paper, but it presented hypotheses to be tested and sparked much research over the next fifteen years, which has in general been confirming.

It was a period when, at the urging of my students, I became acquainted with Martin Buber (first in his writings and then personally) and with Sören Kierkegaard. I felt greatly supported in my new approach, which I found to my surprise was a home-grown brand of existential philosophy.

Finally, it was a period of great learning in my personal life. A badly bungled therapeutic relationship— really nontherapeutic—thrust me into a deep internal personal crisis, and finally into therapy with one of my colleagues. I now learned just what it was like to experience on one day a tremendous surge of fresh insight, only to seem to lose it all the next in a wave of despair. But as I slowly came out of this, I at last learned what many people, fortunately, learn first. I learned that not only could I trust clients and staff and students, but I could also trust myself. Slowly I learned to trust the feelings, the ideas, the purposes that continually emerge in *me*. It was not an easy learning, but a most valuable and continuing one. I found myself becoming much freer, more real, more deeply understanding, not only in my relationships with my clients but also with others.

All of these learnings I have mentioned carried over increasingly in my relationships with groups—first the workshops we started in Chicago as early as 1946, then in groups with which I have been so much involved in recent years. They have all been encounter groups, long before the term was coined.

I will quickly cover the years at the University of Wisconsin and in La Jolla. At Wisconsin I rediscovered what I had learned in Chicago—that by and large most psychologists are not open to new ideas. Perhaps this is true of me too, though I have struggled against that defensive tendency. But students, as before, were most responsive.

In one experience at Wisconsin, I violated one of the learnings I had so painfully acquired, and discovered what disaster that can bring. In the large research team assembled for the task of studying psychotherapy with schizophrenics, I gave over the authority and responsibility to the group. But I did not go far enough in establishing the climate of close, open, interpersonal communication which is fundamental for carrying such responsibility. Then, as serious crises developed, I made the even more fatal mistake of trying to draw back into my own hands the authority I had given the group. Rebellion and chaos were the very understandable results. It was one of the most painful lessons I have ever learned—a lesson in how *not* to carry on participative management of an enterprise.

In La Jolla, my experience has been much happier. A highly congenial group eventually formed the Center for Studies of the Person, a most unusual and exciting experiment. I will describe only its interpersonal aspects, because it would be impossible to describe all the activities of its members, which range from Kenya to Rome to Ireland, from New Jersey to Colorado to Seattle, from psychotherapy to writing to esoteric research, from consulting with organizations to leading groups of all kinds, from learning group facilitation to igniting revolutions in educational methods. Psychologically, we are a close community, supporting each other but criticizing each other just as openly. Although our director has routine responsibilities, no one is in authority over anyone else. Everyone can do as he wishes, alone or in concert with others. Everyone is responsible for his own support. Currently we have only one small grant, and that from a private foundation. We do not like the strings—often initially invisible—that are attached to large or government grants. There is absolutely nothing holding us together except a common interest in the dignity and capacity of persons and the continuing possibility of deep and real communication with each other. To me it is a great experiment in building a functioning group—a nonorganization really—entirely based on the strength of interpersonal sharing.

But I could easily go on too long in my enthusiasm. There has been one other input to my learning which I should like to mention. It was first brought to my attention many years ago by Leona Tyler, who, in a personal letter, pointed out to me that my thinking and action seemed to be something of a bridge between Eastern and Western thought. This was a surprising idea, but I find that in more recent years I have enjoyed some of the teachings of Buddhism, of Zen, and especially the sayings of Lao-tse, the Chinese sage who lived some twenty-five centuries ago. Let me quote a few lines of his thoughts to which I resonate very deeply:

It is as though he listened
and such listening as his enfolds us in a silence
in which at last we begin to hear
what we are meant to be.

One statement combines two of my favorite thinkers. Martin Buber endeavors to explain the Taoist principle of *wu-wei*, which is really the action of the whole being, but so effortless when it is most effective that it is often called the principle of "nonaction," a rather misleading term. Buber, in explaining this concept, says:

To interfere with the life of things means to harm both them and oneself. . . . He who imposes himself has the small, manifest might; he who does not impose himself has the great, secret might. . . .

The perfected man . . . does not interfere in the life of beings, he does not impose himself on them, but he "helps all beings to their freedom (Lao-tse)." Through his unity, he leads them too, to unity, he liberates their nature and their destiny, he releases Tao in them. (BUBER, 1957)

I suppose that my effort with people has increasingly been to liberate "their nature and their destiny."

Or, if one is seeking a definition of an effective group facilitator, one need look no further than Lao-tse:

*A leader is best
When people barely know that he exists,
Not so good when people obey and acclaim him,
Worst when they despise him. . . .
But of a good leader, who talks little,
When his work is done, his aim fulfilled,
They will all say, "We did this ourselves."*

(BYNNER, 1962)

But perhaps my favorite saying, which sums up many of my deeper beliefs, is another from Lao-tse:

*If I keep from meddling with people, they take care of themselves,
If I keep from commanding people, they behave themselves,
If I keep from preaching at people, they improve themselves,
If I keep from imposing on people, they become themselves.*

(FRIEDMAN, 1972)

I will admit that this saying is an oversimplification, yet for me it contains the sort of truth which we have not yet appreciated in our Western culture.

CONCLUSION

I trust I have made it clear that over the years I have moved a long way from some of the beliefs with which I started: that man was essentially evil; that professionally he was best treated as an object; that help was based on expertise; that the expert could advise, manipulate, and mold the individual to produce the desired result.

Let me, in contrast, try to summarize the learnings in which I currently believe and by which I would like to live. As I have indicated, I frequently fail to profit by these learnings, failing many times in small ways and occasionally in enormous blunders. I will list the learnings, not in the order in which they occurred in me but in what appears to be a more natural order.

I have come to prize each emerging facet of my experience, of myself. I would like to treasure the feelings of anger and tenderness and shame and hurt and love and anxiety and giving and fear—all the positive and negative reactions that crop up. I would like to treasure the ideas that emerge—foolish, creative, bizarre, sound, trivial—all part of me. I like the behavioral impulses—appropriate, crazy, achievement-oriented, sexual, murderous. I want to accept all of these feelings, ideas, and impulses as an enriching part of me. I don't expect to act on all of them, but when I accept them all, I can be more real; my behavior, therefore, will be much more appropriate to the immediate situation.

On the basis of my experience I have found that if I can help bring about a climate marked by genuineness, prizing, and understanding, then exciting things happen. Persons and groups in such a climate move away from rigidity and toward flexibility, away from static living toward process living, away from dependence toward autonomy, away from defensiveness toward self-acceptance, away from being predictable toward an unpredictable creativity. They exhibit living proof of an actualizing tendency.

When I am exposed to a growth-promoting climate, I am able to develop a deep trust in myself, in individuals, and in entire groups. I love to create such an environment, in which persons, groups, and even plants can grow.

I have learned that in any significant or continuing relationship, *persistent* feelings had best be expressed. If they are expressed as *feelings*, owned by *me*, the result may be temporarily upsetting but ultimately far more rewarding than any attempt to deny or conceal them.

I have found that for me interpersonal relationships best exist as a rhythm: openness and expression, and then assimilation; flow and change, then a temporary quiet; risk and anxiety, then temporary security. I could not live in a continuous encounter group.

For me, being transparently open is far more rewarding than being defensive. This is difficult to achieve, even partially, but enormously enriching to a relationship.

It is necessary for me to stay close to the earthiness of real experience. I cannot live my life in abstractions. So real relationships with persons, hands dirtied in the soil, observing the budding of a flower, or viewing the sunset, are necessary to my life. At least one foot must be in the soil of reality.

I like my life best when it faces outward most of the time. I prize the times when I am inward-looking—searching to know myself, meditating, and thinking. But this must be balanced by doing things—interacting with people, producing something, whether a flower or a book or a piece of carpentry.

Finally, I have a deep belief, which can only be a hypothesis, that the philosophy of interpersonal relationships which I have helped to formulate, and which is contained in this paper, is applicable to all situations involving persons. I believe it is applicable to therapy, to marriage, to parent and child, to teacher and student, to persons with high status and those with low status, to persons of one race relating to persons of another. I am even brash enough to believe that it could be effective in situations now dominated by the exercise of raw power—in politics, for example, especially in our dealings with other nations. I challenge, with all the strength I possess, the current American belief, evident in every phase of our foreign policy, and especially in our insane wars, that "might makes right." That, in my estimation, is the road to self-destruction. I go along with Martin Buber and the ancient Oriental sages: "He who imposes himself has the small, manifest might; he who does not impose himself has the great, secret might."

REFERENCES

BUBER, M. *Pointing the way.* New York: Harper & Row, 1957.

BYNNER, W. (Translator). *The way of life according to Laotzu.* New York: Capricorn Books, 1962.

FRIEDMAN, M. *Touchstones of reality.* New York: E. P. Dutton, 1972.

ROGERS, C. R. The necessary and sufficient conditions of therapeutic personality change. *Journal of Consulting Psychology,* 1957, *21*, 95–103.

In Retrospect:
Forty-Six Years

There is no such thing as a free lunch. This profound truth was the motivation for this paper. I was deeply honored to be awarded the Distinguished Professional Contribution Award by the American Psychological Association (APA), accompanied by a generous check. But along with the honor came the obligation to produce a paper for the convention, which was held in Montreal in August of the following year, 1973. I remember my perplexity as to a topic, and I recall writing another paper, then discarding it because it did not seem appropriate. Instead, I chose to review some of the threads of my professional life, looking back forty-six years to my fledgling experience as a Fellow ("Intern" would have been the more accurate term) at the Institute for Child Guidance in New York City. This Institute was lavishly supported by the privately run, New York–based Commonwealth Fund, to provide training for workers in child-guidance clinics, which were then rapidly gaining popularity. (Samuel Beck and I both learned the Rorschach that year, which had just been brought from Europe by Dr. David Levy, a psychiatrist.) At the end of the year, and the completion of my internship, I took a position in Rochester, New York, at the modest salary of $2,900 per year! This position is described in the chapter.

In what follows I mention a number of countries in which I have had influence. In the years since this was written I

would have to add many more, including a recent fascinating
workshop of ninety persons in Poland, my first experience
behind the so-called Iron Curtain.

This is a very subjective chapter—my picture of my professional life as seen from the inside. It is as I understand it.
I am sure a view from the outside would be quite different.

From 1927 to the present time I have been a practicing psychologist. I have made diagnostic studies of children and have developed recommendations for treatment of their problems; in 1928 I developed an inventory of the inner world of childhood which—may
Heaven forgive me—is still being sold by the thousands. I have counseled with parents, students, and
other adults; I have carried on intensive psychotherapy
with troubled individuals—normal, neurotic, and psychotic; I have engaged in and sponsored research in
psychotherapy and personality change; I have formulated a rigorous theory of therapy. I have had forty years
of teaching experience, fostering learning through both
cognitive and experiential channels. I have engaged in
facilitating personal development through the intensive
group experience; I have tried to make clear the processes of both individual therapy and the group experience through recordings, demonstrations, and films; I
have tried to communicate my experience through what
now seem to me to be countless writings, tapes, and
cassettes. I have played my part as a worker in professional associations of psychologists; I have had a continuous, varied, controversial, and richly rewarding
professional life.

So it has occurred to me that there might be some
interest in the question: What does such a psychologist

think about as he looks back on close to a half-century of study and work? It is to that question that I will address my remarks. What is my own current perspective on these years, thinking both about my professional life and its various periods of development and change?

AN ASTONISHING IMPACT

I believe the major element of my reaction as I look back on my work and its reception is *surprise*. Had I been told, thirty-five or forty years ago, of the impact it would have, I would have been absolutely unbelieving. The work that I and my colleagues have done has altered or made a difference in widely different enterprises, of which I will mention several. It turned the field of counseling upside down. It opened psychotherapy to public scrutiny and research investigation. It has made possible the empirical study of highly subjective phenomena. It has helped to bring some change in the methods of education at every level. It has been one of the factors bringing change in concepts of industrial (and even military) leadership, of social work practice, of nursing practice, and of religious work. It has been responsible for one of the major trends in the encounter group movement. It has, in small ways at least, affected the philosophy of science. It is beginning to have some influence in interracial and intercultural relationships. It has even influenced students of theology and of philosophy.

My work has, to my knowledge, changed the life directions and purposes of individuals in France, Belgium, Holland, Norway, Japan, Australia, New Zealand, and South Africa; in twelve foreign countries readers can find some of my work in their own language; if someone wishes to read a complete collection of everything I have written, he will find it—in Japanese. I look with utter astonishment at this long list of statements.

A Tentative Explanation

Why has my work had such a pervasive impact? I certainly do not attribute it to any special genius of my own, and most assuredly not to any far-sighted vision on my part. I give full credit to my younger colleagues throughout the years for their expansion and deepening of my thought and work, but even their efforts do not account for this far-reaching influence. In a number of the fields I have mentioned, neither I nor my colleagues have ever worked, or been involved in any way, except through our writings.

To me, as I try to understand the phenomenon, it seems that without knowing it I had expressed an idea whose time had come. It is as though a pond had become utterly still, so that a pebble dropped into it sent ripples out farther and farther and farther, having an influence that could not be understood by looking at the pebble. Or, to use a chemical analogy, as though a liquid solution had become supersaturated, so that the addition of one tiny crystal initiated the formation of crystals throughout the whole mass.

What was that idea, that pebble, that crystal? It was the gradually formed and tested hypothesis that the individual has within himself vast resources for self-understanding, for altering his self-concept, his attitudes, and his self-directed behavior—and that these resources can be tapped if only a definable climate of facilitative psychological attitudes can be provided.

This hypothesis, so new and yet in a way so old, was not an armchair theory. It had grown out of a number of very down-to-earth steps.

First, I had learned through hard and frustrating experiences that simply to listen understandingly to a client and to attempt to convey that understanding were potent forces for individual therapeutic change.

Second, I and my colleagues realized that this empathic listening provided one of the least clouded windows into the workings of the human psyche, in all its complex mystery.

Third, from our observations we made only low-level inferences and formulated testable hypotheses. We might have chosen to draw high-level inferences and to have developed abstract, untestable, high-level theory, but I think my own earthy agricultural background deterred me from that. (Freudian thinkers chose this second course, and this marks, in my estimation, one of the most fundamental differences between their approach and the client-centered approach.)

Fourth, in testing our hypotheses, we uncovered findings regarding persons and relationships between persons. These findings and the theory that embraced them were continually changing as new discoveries emerged, and this process continues to the present day.

Fifth, because our findings have to do with basic aspects of the way in which the person's own capacities for change can be released and with the way in which relationships can foster or defeat such self-directed change, it was discovered that they had wide applicability.

Sixth, situations involving persons, change in the behavior of persons, and the effects of different qualities of interpersonal relationships exist in almost every human undertaking. Hence, others began realizing that perhaps the testable hypotheses of this approach might have almost universal application, or might be retested or reformulated for use in an almost infinite variety of human situations.

Such is my attempt to explain an awesome and otherwise incomprehensible spread of ideas which began with a very simple question: Can I, by carefully observing and evaluating my experience with my clients, learn to be more effective in helping them to resolve their problems of personal distress, self-defeating behavior, and destructive interpersonal relationships? Who could have guessed that the groping and tentative answers would spread so far?

Psychology's Ambivalence

You may have noticed an omission in the listing of the areas of impact of my work. I did not say that I and my colleagues have affected academic, or so-called scientific, psychology. This was not an oversight. I believe an accurate statement would be that we have had very little influence on academic psychology, in the lecture hall, the textbook, or the laboratory. There is some passing mention of my thinking, my theories, or my approach to therapy, but, by and large, I think I have been a painfully embarrassing phenomenon to the academic psychologist. *I do not fit.* Increasingly I have come to agree with that assessment. Let me amplify.

The science and profession of psychology have, I believe, profoundly ambivalent feelings about me and my work. I am seen—and here I must rely mostly on hearsay—as softheaded, unscientific, cultish, too easy on students, full of strange and upsetting enthusiasms about ephemeral things like the self, therapist attitudes, and encounter groups. I have defamed the most holy mysteries of the academic—the professional lecture and the whole evaluation system—from the ABCs of course grades to the coveted hood of the doctor's degree. I can best be handled by most writers on psychology in one paragraph as the developer of a technique—the "nondirective technique." I am definitely not one of the ingroup of psychological academia.

The other side of the ambivalence is, however, even more striking. Psychology as a whole, science and profession together, has showered me with honors—many more, I believe, than I deserve. To my amazement I was awarded one of the first three awards for scientific contribution, and this was back in 1956 when I was much more controversial than I am at present. I had been chosen president of the American Association for Applied Psychology. I had been elected president of the American Psychological Association. I had been appointed or elected chairman of important committees and divisions, and these honors often touched me. Yet, never have I been so emotionally affected as I was by the scientific contribution award and its accompanying citation. When I was elected to an office it could have been partly due to my ambition, for I was ambitious to get ahead in my profession. But this award was to me, in some sense, the "purest" recognition I had ever received. For years I had been struggling to objectify knowledge in a potential field of science that no one else seemed to be concerned about. It was not ambition or hope of any reward that pushed me on. In the empirical research itself there was more than a little desire to prove something to others—clearly not a scientific goal. But in the basic phases of the work—the careful observation, the recorded interviews, the hunches as to hypotheses, the development of crude theories—I was as close to being a true scientist as I ever hope to be. But it was clear, I thought, that my colleagues and I were just about the only ones who knew or cared. So my voice choked and the tears flowed when I was called forth, at the 1956 APA Convention, to receive, with Wolfgang Köhler and Kenneth Spence, the first of the

nent in research, and fully equal in practice and in theory building, could not be challenged.

But when pushed into a corner, as on these two occasions, I can fight with all the effectiveness that one develops in a family of six children. People who know only my thoughtful or gentle side are astonished at my attitude and behavior in a situation of all-out war. I should, in warning, have raised the banner of the early Colonies, on which was emblazoned a rattlesnake and the motto, "Don't tread on me!"

In 1957 I went to the University of Wisconsin, where, I am happy to say, my joint appointment in psychology *and* psychiatry was a pleasant resolution of these struggles. Indeed, I initiated the formation of a group of psychologists and psychiatrists who gradually defused an incipient legal and legislative battle which was splitting the two professions in that state.

Struggle with Behavioristic Psychology

The other struggle of my professional life has been on the side of a humanistic approach to the study of human beings. The Rogers–Skinner debate of 1956 is one of the most reprinted writings in the psychological world. It would be absurd of me to try to review that continuing difference in any depth. I will simply make a few brief statements as I look back over these years.

To avoid misunderstanding, let me say immediately that I concur with the idea that the theory of operant conditioning, its development and its implementation, has been a creative achievement. It is a valuable tool in the promotion of certain types of learning. I do not denigrate the contribution it has made. But this is not the basis of divergence.

Let me also say that I have a great personal respect for Fred Skinner. He is an honest man, willing to carry his thinking through to its logical conclusions. Hence, we can differ sharply, without damaging my respect for him. I was invited by several periodicals to respond to *Beyond Freedom and Dignity* (Skinner, 1971) and declined primarily because I felt he had a right to his views. My one disappointment in regard to Skinner is his refusal to permit the nine-hour confrontation we held at the University of Minnesota in Duluth to be released. It was all taped and is the deepest exploration in existence of the issues between us. All of the other parties to the meeting had understood that it was agreed that the tapes, or transcripts of them, or both, would be released. After the meeting, Skinner refused his permission. I feel the profession was cheated.

I have come to realize that the basic difference between a behavioristic and a humanistic approach to human beings is a *philosophical* choice. This certainly can be discussed, but cannot possibly be settled by evidence. If one takes Skinner as of some years ago—and I believe this is his view today—then the environment, which is part of a causal sequence, is the sole determiner of the individual's behavior, which is thus again an unbreakable chain of cause and effect. All the things that I do, or that Skinner does, are simply inevitable results of our conditioning. As he has pointed out, man acts as he is forced to act, but as if he were not forced. Carried to its logical conclusion, this means, as John Calvin concluded earlier, that the universe was at some point wound up like a great clock and has been ticking off its inexorable way ever since. Thus, what we think are our decisions, choices, and values are all illusions. Skinner did not write his books because he had chosen to present his views, or to point to the kind of society he values, but simply because he was conditioned to make certain marks on paper. Amazingly to me, he admitted as much in one session in which we both participated.

My experience in therapy and in groups makes it impossible for me to deny the reality and significance of human choice. To me it is not an illusion that man is to some degree the architect of himself. I have presented evidence that the degree of self-understanding is perhaps the most important factor in predicting the individual's behavior. So for me the humanistic approach is the only possible one. It is for each person, however, to follow the pathway—behavioristic or humanistic—that he finds most congenial.

Saying that it is for the individual to decide is not synonymous with saying that it makes no difference. Choosing the humanistic philosophy, for example, means that very different topics are chosen for research and different methods for validating discoveries. It means an approach to social change based on the human desire and potentiality for change, not on conditioning. It leads to a deeply democratic political philosophy rather than management by an elite. So the choice does have consequences.

To me it is entirely logical that a technologically oriented society, with its steady emphasis on a greater control of human behavior, should be enamored of a behavioristic approach. Likewise, academic psychology, with its unwavering insistence that "the intellect is all," has greatly preferred it over the humanistic approach. If the university psychologist accepted the latter view, he would have to admit that he is involved, as a subjective person, in his choice of research topics, in his evaluation of data, in his relationship to students, in his professional work. The comfortable cloak of "objectivity" would necessarily be dropped, exposing him as a vulnerable, imperfect, subjective being, thoroughly engaged, intellectually *and* emotionally, objectively *and* subjectively, in all his activities. This is understandably too threatening.

Let me simply add that what is really at issue is the confrontation of two paradoxes. If the extreme behaviorist position is true, then everything an individual does is essentially meaningless, since he is but an atom caught in a seamless chain of cause and effect. On the other hand, if the thoroughgoing humanistic position is true, then choice enters in, and this individual subjective choice has some influence on the cause-and-effect chain. Then, scientific research, which is based on a complete confidence in an unbroken chain of cause and effect, must be fundamentally modified. I, as well as others, have attempted partially to explain away this dilemma—my own attempt was in a paper entitled "Freedom and Commitment" (Rogers, 1964)—but I believe we must wait for the future to bring about the full reconciliation of these paradoxes.

In all candor I must say that I believe that the humanistic view will, in the long run, take precedence. I believe that Americans are, as a people, beginning to refuse to allow technology to dominate our lives. Our culture, increasingly based on the conquest of nature and the control of man, is in decline. Emerging through the ruins is the new person, highly aware, self-directing, an explorer of inner, perhaps more than outer, space, scornful of the conformity of institutions and the dogma of authority. He does not believe in being behaviorally shaped, or in shaping the behavior of others. He is most assuredly humanistic rather than technological. In my judgment he has a high probability of survival.

Yet, this belief of mine is open to one exception. If we

were to permit one-man control, or a military take-over of our government—and it is obvious we have been (and are) perilously close to that—then another scenario would take place. A governmental–military–police–industrial complex would be more than happy to use scientific technology for military and industrial conquest and psychological technology for the control of human behavior. I am not being dramatic when I say that humanistic psychologists, emphasizing the essential freedom and dignity of the unique human person, and his capacity for self-determination, would be among the first to be incarcerated by such a government.

But enough of this issue. I have strayed into the future. Let me return to my retrospective look and to some less serious reflections.

TWO PUZZLEMENTS

There are two very different issues that have puzzled me: one of minor, the other of deeper concern.

Regarding Theory

By 1950, I wondered increasingly if my thinking could be put into a coherent theoretical form. At about this time came a request from Sigmund Koch to contribute to his monumental series of volumes, *Psychology: A Study of a Science* (1959–1963). This was just the slight nudge I needed, and for the next three or four years I worked harder on this theoretical formulation than on anything I have written before or since. It is, in my estimation, the most rigorously stated theory of the process of *change* in personality and behavior that has yet been produced. As one young psychologist with a background in mathematics said to me recently, "It is so precise! I could restate it in mathematical terms." I must confess this is close to my opinion.

I was very pleased that it would be in Koch's series, because I felt sure that these volumes would be studied by graduate students and psychologists for years to come. I do not have exact data, but I suspect these volumes are in fact very little used. Certainly my chapter "A Theory of Therapy, Personality, and Interpersonal Relationships as Developed in the Client-Centered Framework" is the most thoroughly ignored of anything I have written (Rogers, 1959). This does not particularly distress me, because I believe theories too often become dogma, but it has, over the years, perplexed me.

Regarding Creative Leadership

The second puzzlement is of a different order. In my younger years, although I was not a hero-worshiper, I definitely looked up to a number of men whom I felt were *"real* psychologists," whereas I existed on a poorly accepted fringe. I remember the community and professional furor when Leonard Carmichael was brought to the University of Rochester in 1936 as chairman of psychology: a special laboratory equipped to his specifications, a cluster of fellowships provided for his students, every acknowledgment paid to his brilliance and leadership. There was probably some envy in my attitude, as I labored away in a ramshackle frame building set aside for the Child Study Department of the Society for the Prevention of Cruelty to Children, but my feeling was mostly one of admiration and expectancy. I felt the same way toward perhaps a half-dozen others—better trained in psychology than I, in my judgment more brilliant, with books and research studies already to their credit. Here were the men who would produce the great ideas in psychology, who would exert the same kind of intellectual and world leadership as that of outstanding chemists, physicists, and astronomers. I had no doubt at all that I had picked those who, a generation later, would be the preeminently creative and productive leaders of our science.

In every case I have been mistaken. Carmichael, since I have mentioned his name, has gone on to become a revered administrator, operating in the highest levels of the establishment. The others I selected have also had perfectly reputable careers, some outside of and some in psychology. But the dazzling promise of their younger years has not been fulfilled. For some reason this has puzzled me very deeply, because they have one attribute in common. They have lost any truly vital *creative* interest in psychology. Why? Were their interests too narrow and unsatisfying as they grew older? Did they lack any basic conviction or philosophy which might have guided their work? Did their efforts come to seem to them irrelevant to the larger social scene, their contributions too picayune? Was their initial work done primarily to impress their fellow psychologists, a motive that declines in importance with age? Did they endeavor to stand on and defend their early work, thus inhibiting themselves from reaching out into the creative unknown? I do not know. It has thoroughly perplexed me and made me very wary indeed of trying to pick prospective leaders of creative thought.

THE SOURCES OF MY LEARNINGS

As I try to review all of the rich streams of thought and experience that have fed and are feeding my professional life, I can discriminate several of the most important sources.

Clients and Group Participants

First and overwhelmingly foremost are my clients in therapy and the persons with whom I have worked in groups. The gold mine of data that resides in interviews or group sessions staggers me. There is, first of all, the gut-level experience, which absorbs the statements, the feelings, and the gestures, providing its own complex type of learning, difficult to put into words. Then there is the listening to the interchanges in the tape recording. Here are the orderly sequences that were missed in the flow of the experience. Here, too, are the nuances of inflection, the half-formed sentences, the pauses, and the sighs, which were also partially missed. Then, if a transcript is laboriously produced, I have a microscope in which I can see, as I termed them in one paper, "the molecules of personality change." I know of no other way of combining the deepest experiential learning with the most highly abstract cognitive and theoretical learnings than the three steps I have mentioned: living the experience on a total basis, rehearing it on an experiential–cognitive basis, and studying it once more for every intellectual clue. As I said earlier, this type of interview is perhaps the most valuable and transparent window into the strange inner world of persons and relationships. I feel that if I subtracted from my work the learnings I have gained from deep relationships with clients and group participants, I would be nothing.

Younger Colleagues

The second most important source of stimulation for me is my symbiotic relationship with younger people. I do not understand this mutual attraction. I just feed upon it. In my youth I surely learned many things from my elders, and at times I have even learned from colleagues in my own age bracket, but certainly for the last thirty-five years any real learnings from professional sources have come from those who were younger. I feel a deep gratitude to all the graduate students, younger staff members, and inquiring youthful audiences who have educated and continue to educate me. I know that for many years, given the chance to associate with professional colleagues of my age, or with a younger group, I inevitably drift to the latter. They seem less stuffy, less defensive, more open in their criticism, more creative in suggestion. I owe them so much. I started to write down examples, but to give a few would be unfair to the hundreds who have so freely contributed their ideas and their feelings in a relationship which has also lighted sparks of creative thinking in me. They have excited me, and I have excited them. It has, I hope, been a fair exchange, though I often feel I have gained more than I have given. I feel a great pity for those persons I know who are growing into old age without the continuing stimulation of younger minds and younger lifestyles.

Scholarly Reading

Then, much farther down the scale, I would put what is often regarded as a major source of learning, the printed page. Reading, I fear, has most of its value for me in buttressing my views. I realize I am not a scholar, gaining my ideas from the writings of others. Occasionally, however, a book not only confirms me in what I am tentatively thinking, but lures me considerably further. Sören Kierkegaard, Martin Buber, and Michael Polanyi, for example, would fall in that category. But I must confess that when I wish to be scholarly, serendipity plays a very important part. Serendipity, in case you have forgotten, is "the faculty of making fortunate and unexpected discoveries by accident." I have an eerie feeling that I have that faculty. Let me give you the latest example. In preparing a current paper, "The Emerging Person: A New Revolution," I was aware of a few of the writers who were presenting similar views. But then Fred and Anne Richards (1973) sent me a copy of their book *Homonovus,* just off the press. It was most timely. John D. Rockefeller III (1973) likewise sent me a copy of his book *The Second American Revolution*, which was also highly pertinent. Then I was talking with a friend from northern California about my fantasies for my APA paper and he said, "Did you read the article by Joyce Carol Oates in the *Saturday Review?*" I had to confess complete ignorance not only of the article but of the author. His Xerox copy of the essay not only gave support to my view, but opened my eyes to a whole new facet of modern fiction. So, while one section of that paper may make it appear that I spent days or weeks researching in the library, at least half of that impression is due to serendipity. It has been a very frequent aid in my life.

MY CONCERN WITH COMMUNICATION

Still peering back—though my neck is getting stiff from that posture—I can see what is perhaps one overriding theme in my professional life. It is my caring about communication. From my very earliest years it has, for some reason, been a passionate concern of mine. I have been pained when I have seen others communicating past one another. I have wanted to communicate myself so that I could not be misunderstood. I have wanted to understand, as profoundly as possible, the communication of the other, be he a client or friend or family member. I have wanted to *be* understood. I have tried to facilitate clarity of communication between individuals of the most diverse points of view. I have worked for better communication between groups whose perceptions and experiences are poles apart: strangers, members of different cultures, representatives of different strata of society. To give adequate examples would compass the length of my career. I will cite only one. The filmed experience of a group involved in the drug scene included "straight" individuals, such as a narcotics agent, and "stoned" individuals, including a convicted drug pusher. There were blacks and whites, the young and middle-aged, people from the ghetto and members of the middle class. The group process by which communication and closeness became a living part of this diverse group is an experience I shall never forget. It is unfortunate that the film's title, *Because That's My Way*, chosen for us, catches so little of the vivid interchange that occurred (Station WQED, 1971).

This obsession with communication has had its own unexpected rewards. I held a half-hour interview with a young woman named Gloria (some of you may have seen the film [Shostrom, 1965]) and a deeply communicative contact was established. To my complete surprise, she has kept in occasional touch with me for eight years, primarily in appreciation for the closeness we achieved. With Randy, the convicted drug pusher in the drug film, I was in constant correspondence for more than a year. Mr. Vac, one of my clients in our complex research on psychotherapy with schizophrenics, tracked me down after eight years with a "Hi, Doc," to let me know that he was still doing well and had never returned to the state hospital, even for a day.

I think such rewards are savored more as the years go by.

IN SUM

So I can sum up my informal look at my professional past by saying:

I am amazed at the impact of our work;

I have a dim comprehension that the time was ripening for it;

I look with amusement and affection at the ambivalence I have created in psychology;

I see with satisfaction the war with psychiatry concluding;

I am pleased to have played a part in the continuing drama of the behavioristic versus the humanistic philosophy;

I am puzzled and humbled by the disregard of what I see as my theoretical rigor;

I am perplexed by the later careers of some of the truly shining lights I have seen;

I am especially grateful for the gift of vital learnings from the people whose development and growth I have endeavored to facilitate;

I have confidence in the young, from whom I have continuously learned;

I discern more sharply the theme of my life as having been built around the desire for clarity of communication, with all its ramifying results.

THE NOW—AND THE FUTURE

I should stop here, but I cannot. It is always a strain for me to look backward. It is still the present and the future that concern me most. I cannot close without a quick overview of my current interests and activities.

I am no longer actively engaged in individual therapy or empirical research. I am finding that after one passes the age of seventy, there are physical limitations on what one can do. I continue to engage in encounter groups when I believe they might have significant social impact. For example, I am involved in a program for the humanizing of medical education. Up to the present, more than two hundred high-status medical educators have been involved in intensive group experiences which appear to be more successful in facilitating change than we had dared hope. Perhaps more humanly sensitive physicians will be the result. Such group experiences certainly represent a new area of possible impact.

I have also helped to sponsor, and have taken some part in, interracial and intercultural groups, believing that better understanding between diverse groups is essential if our planet is to survive. The most difficult group was composed of citizens of Belfast, Northern Ireland. Represented in the group were militant and less militant Catholics, militant and less militant Protestants, and English. The film of that encounter portrays the participants' difficult and partial progress toward better understanding—a first step on a long road. I see this encounter group as a small test-tube attempt, which might be utilized in greater depth and much more widely.

I continue to write. I recognize that while my whole approach to persons and their relationships changes but slowly (and very little in its fundamentals), my interest in its application has shifted markedly. No longer am I primarily interested in individual therapeutic learning, but in broader and broader social implications. As I say this, the question arises in my mind, as it often has in the past, "Am I spreading myself too thin?" Only the judgment of others can answer that question at some future date.

And then I garden. Those mornings when I cannot find time to inspect my flowers, water the young shoots I am propagating, pull a few weeds, spray some destructive insects, and pour just the proper fertilizer on some budding plants, I feel cheated. My garden supplies the same intriguing question I have been trying to meet in all my professional life: What are the effective conditions for growth? But in my garden, though the frustrations are just as immediate, the results, whether success or failure, are more quickly evident. And when, through patient, intelligent, and understanding care I have provided the conditions that result in the production of a rare or glorious bloom, I feel the same kind of satisfaction that I have felt in the facilitation of growth in a person or in a group of persons.

REFERENCES

KOCH, S. (ED.). *Psychology: A study of a science* (6 vols.). New York: McGraw-Hill, 1959–1963.

RICHARDS, F., & RICHARDS, A. C. *Homonovus: The new man.* Boulder, Colo.: Shields, 1973.

ROCKFELLER, J. D., III. *The second American Revolution: Some personal observations.* New York: Harper & Row, 1973.

ROGERS, C. R. A theory of therapy, personality, and interpersonal relationships, as developed in the client-centered framework. In S. Koch (Ed.), *Psychology: A study of a science* (Vol. 3, *Formulations of the person and the social context*). New York: McGraw-Hill, 1959.

ROGERS, C. R. Freedom and commitment. *The Humanist,* 1964, *24*(2), 37–40.

ROGERS, C. R. The emerging person: A new revolution. In R. I. Evans (Ed.), *Carl Rogers: The man and his ideas.* New York: E. P. Dutton, 1975.

SHOSTROM, E. (ED.). *Three approaches to psychotherapy* (Film No. 1). Orange, California: Psychological Films, 1965.

SKINNER, B. F. *Beyond freedom and dignity.* New York: Knopf, 1971.

STATION WQED, PITTSBURGH. *Because that's my way* (60-minute color film). Lincoln: GPI Television Library, University of Nebraska, 1971.

Growing Old:
Or Older and Growing?

This chapter completes a trio of autobiographical papers. In Chapter 2, I present something of my own growth and the development of my thinking. Chapter 3 takes a backward look at my professional life. What follows tells of a recent decade in my life, from age sixty-five to age seventy-five. Since I am seventy-eight years old as I write this, I have written an "Update," which is placed at the end of this account.

This paper has gone through several stages. I presented one version early in 1977 to a large workshop in Brazil. A somewhat revised version was presented later to a small audience in San Diego. I gave the paper in the form that follows as part of a program entitled "Living Now: A Workshop on Life Stages" in La Jolla in July 1977.

I had been invited to give a talk on the older years. I realized, however, that I was poorly informed about aging in general, and that the only older person I really knew was myself. So I spoke about that person.

What is it like to be seventy-five years old? It is not the same as being fifty-five years old, or thirty-five, and yet, for me, the differences are not so great as you might imagine. I'm not sure whether my story will be of any use or significance to anyone else, because I have been so uniquely fortunate. It is mostly for myself that I am going to set down a few perceptions and reactions. I have chosen to limit myself to the decade from age sixty-five to seventy-five, because sixty-five marks, for many people, the end of a productive life and the beginning of "retirement," whatever that means!

THE PHYSICAL SIDE

I do feel physical deterioration. I notice it in many ways. Ten years ago I greatly enjoyed throwing a frisbee. Now my right shoulder is so painfully arthritic that this kind of activity is out of the question. In my garden I realize that a task which would have been easy five years ago, but difficult last year, now seems like too much, and I had better leave it for my once-a-week gardener. This slow deterioration, with various minor disorders of vision, heartbeat, and the like, informs me that the physical portion of what I call "me" is not going to last forever.

Yet I still enjoy a four-mile walk on the beach. I can lift heavy objects, do all the shopping, cooking, and dishwashing when my wife is ill, carry my own luggage without puffing. The female form still seems to me one of the loveliest creations of the universe, and I appreciate it greatly. I feel as sexual in my *interests* as I was at thirty-five, though I can't say the same about my ability to perform. I am delighted that I am still sexually alive, even though I can sympathize with the remark of Supreme Court Justice Oliver Wendell Holmes upon leaving a burlesque house at age eighty: "Oh to be seventy again!" Yes, or sixty-five, or sixty!

So, I am well aware that I am obviously old. Yet from the inside I'm still the same person in many ways, neither old nor young. It is that person of whom I will speak.

ACTIVITIES

New Enterprises

In the past decade I have embarked on many new ventures involving psychological or even physical risk. It puzzles me that in most instances my engagement in these enterprises was triggered by a suggestion or a remark made by someone else. This makes me realize that frequently there must be a readiness in me, of which I am not aware, which springs into action only when someone presses the appropriate button. Let me illustrate.

My colleague Bill Coulson, along with a few others, said to me in 1968, "Our group should form a new and separate organization." Out of that suggestion came the Center for Studies of the Person—the zaniest, most improbable, and most influential nonorganization imaginable. Once the idea of the Center had been suggested, I was very active in the group that brought it into being; I helped nurture it—and ourselves—during the first difficult years.

A niece of mine, Ruth Cornell, an elementary schoolteacher, asked, "Why is there no book of yours on our reading lists in Education?" This sparked the initial thinking that led to my book, *Freedom to Learn*.

I never would have considered trying to influence the status-conscious medical profession, had it not been for my colleague Orienne Strode's dream of having a humanizing impact on physicians through intensive group experiences. Skeptical but hopeful, I devoted energy to helping start the program. We ran a great risk of failure. Instead, the program has become widely influential. Nine hundred medical educators have participated in the encounter groups, along with many spouses and some physicians-in-training, who bring in the "worm's-eye-view" of medical education. It has been an exciting and rewarding development, now completely independent of any but the most minor assistance from me.

This summer we held our fifth sixteen-day intensive Workshop in the Person-Centered Approach. These workshops have taught me more than any other one venture in the past decade. I have learned and put into practice new ways of being myself. I have learned cognitively and intuitively about the group process and about group-initiated ways of forming a community. These have been tremendous experiences, involving a strong staff which has become a close professional family. We have done more and more risking as we try out new ways of being with a group. And how did I become involved in this large and time-consuming enterprise? Four years ago my daughter Natalie said to me, "Why don't we do a workshop together, perhaps around a client-centered approach?" Neither of us could have possibly guessed all that would grow out of that conversation.

My book *Carl Rogers on Personal Power* (1977) likewise found its initial spark in a conversation. Alan Nelson, a graduate student at the time, challenged me on my statement that there was no "politics" in client-centered therapy. This led me into a line of thought that I must have been very ready to pursue, because portions of the book simply wrote themselves.

Foolhardy or Wise?

The most recent and perhaps most risky venture was the trip that I and four other CSP members took to Brazil. In this case, the organizing efforts, the vision, and the persuasiveness of Eduardo Bandeira were the factors that caused me to agree to go. Some people believed the trip would be too long and hard for me at my age, and I had a few of these qualms myself about fifteen-hour plane flights and the like. And some felt it was arrogant to think that our efforts could in any way influence a vast country. But the opportunity to train Brazilian facilitators, most of whom had attended our workshops in the United States, in order that they could put on their own intensive workshops, was very attractive.

Then there was another opportunity. We were to meet audiences of six hundred to eight hundred people in three of Brazil's largest cities. These were two-day institutes, in which we would be together for a total of about twelve hours. Before we left the United States, we agreed that with meetings of such a large size and such a short duration, we would necessarily have to rely on giving talks. Yet, as the time approached, we felt more and more strongly that to talk *about* a person-centered approach, without sharing the control and direction of the sessions, without giving the participants a chance to express themselves and experience their own power, was inconsistent with our principles.

So we took some extremely far-out gambles. In addition to very short talks, we tried leaderless small groups, special-interest groups, a demonstration encounter group, dialogue between staff and audience. But the most daring thing was to form a large circle of eight hundred people (ten to twelve deep) and permit feelings and attitudes to be expressed. Microphones were handed about to those who wished to speak. Participants and staff took part as equals. There was no one person or group exercising leadership. It became a mammoth encounter group. There was much initial chaos, but then people began to listen to one another. There were criticisms—sometimes violent—of the staff and of the process. There were persons who felt they had never learned so much in such a short time. There were the sharpest of differences. After one person blasted the staff for not answering questions, not taking control and giving evidence, the next person said, "But when, if ever, have we all felt so free to criticize, to express ourselves, to say *anything?*" Finally, there was constructive discussion of what participants would do with their learnings in their back-home situations.

After the first evening in São Paulo, when the session had been extremely chaotic and I was keenly aware that we had but six hours more with the group, I remember refusing to talk with anyone about that meeting. I was experiencing enormous confusion. Either I had helped launch an incredibly stupid experiment doomed to failure, or I had helped to innovate a whole new way of permitting eight hundred people to sense their own potentialities and to participate in forming their own learning experience. There was no way to predict which it would prove to be.

Perhaps the greater the risk, the greater the satisfaction. In São Paulo, the second evening, there was a real sense of community, and persons were experiencing significant changes in themselves. Informal follow-up in the weeks and months since then bear out the worthwhileness of the experience for hundreds of people in each of the three cities.

Never have I felt an extended trip to have been so valuable. I learned a great deal, and there is no doubt that we managed to create a facilitative climate in which all kinds of creative things—at personal, interpersonal, and group levels—happened. I believe we left a mark on Brazil, and certainly Brazil changed all of us. Certainly we have extended our vision of what can be done in very large groups.

So those are some of the activities—all extremely profitable to me—into which I have been drawn during this period.

Risk Taking

In these activities there has been, in each case, an element of risk. Indeed it seems to me that the experiences I value most in my recent life all entail considerable risk. So I should like to pause for a moment and speculate as to the reasons behind my taking of chances.

Why does it appeal to me to try the unknown, to gamble on something new, when I could easily settle for ways of doing things that I know from past experience would work very satisfactorily? I am not sure I understand fully, but I can see several factors that have made a difference.

The first factor concerns what I think of as my support group, the loose cluster of friends and close associates, most of whom have worked with me in one or another of these endeavors. In the interactions of this group, there is no doubt that we actually or implicitly encourage one another to do the new or daring thing. For example, I am certain that, acting singly, no member of our Brazil group would have gone so far in experimentation as did the five of us working together. We could gamble because if we failed, we had colleagues who believed in us, who could help put the pieces back together. We gave each other courage.

A second element is my affinity for youth, and for the emerging lifestyle that younger people are helping to bring about. I cannot say why I have this affinity, but I know it exists. I have written about "the emerging person"of tomorrow, and I myself am drawn toward this newer way of being and living. I have wondered if I might simply be engaging in wishful thinking in describing such a person. But now I feel confirmed, for I have discovered that the Stanford Research Institute (1973) has completed a study in which it estimates that 45 million Americans are committed to "a way of living that reflects these inner convictions: first that it is better to have things on a human scale; second that it is better to live frugally, to conserve, recycle, not waste; and third that *the inner life*, rather than externals, is central" (Mitchell, 1977). I belong to that group, and trying to live in this new way is necessarily risky and uncertain.

Another factor: I am bored by safety and sureness. I know that sometimes when I prepare a talk or paper, it is very well received by an audience. This tells me that I could give the talk twenty times to twenty different audiences and I would be assured of a good reception. I simply cannot do this. If I give the same talk three or four times, I become bored with myself. I cannot bear to do it again. I could earn money, I could obtain a positive reaction, but I can't do it. I'm bored by knowing how it will turn out. I'm bored to hear myself saying the same things. It is necessary to my life to try something new.

But perhaps the major reason I am willing to take chances is that I have found that in doing so, whether I succeed or fail, I *learn*. Learning, especially learning from experience, has been a prime element in making my life worthwhile. Such learning helps me to expand. So I continue to risk.

WRITINGS

In thinking about this talk I asked myself, "What have I produced during this past decade?" I was utterly astonished at what I found. The list of my publications, which my secretary keeps up to date, tells me that I have turned out four books, some forty shorter pieces, and several films since I turned sixty-five! This is, I believe, more than I have published or produced during any previous decade. I simply cannot believe it!

Furthermore, each of the books is on a distinctively different subject, though they are all tied together by a common philosophy. *Freedom to Learn*, in 1969, concerns my unconventional approach to education. My book on encounter groups, published in 1970, expresses my accumulating learnings on this exciting development. In 1972, *Becoming Partners* was published; this book pictures many of the new patterns in relationships between men and women. And now, *Carl Rogers on Personal Power* explores the emerging politics of a person-centered approach, as applied to many fields.

Of the two-score papers, four stand out in my mind— two of them looking forward, two backward. [All four papers appear in this volume.] An article on empathy ("Empathic—An Unappreciated Way of Being") consolidates what I have learned about that extremely important way of being, and I think well of this paper. I also like the freshness of my statement on "Do We Need 'A'

Reality?" Then, two other papers reflect upon the development of my philosophy of interpersonal relationships ("My Philosophy of Interpersonal Relationships and How It Grew"), and my career as a psychologist ("In Retrospect: Forty-Six Years").

I look on this surge of writing with wonder. What is the explanation? Different persons in their later years have had very individual reasons for their writing. At age eighty, Arnold Toynbee asks himself the question, "What has made me work?" He responds, "*Conscience.* In my attitude toward work I am American-minded, not Australian-minded. To be always working and still at full stretch, has been laid upon me by my conscience as a duty. This enslavement to work for work's sake is, I suppose, irrational, but thinking so would not liberate me. If I slacked, or even just slackened, I should be conscience-stricken and therefore uneasy and unhappy, so this spur seems likely to continue to drive me as long as I have any working power left in me" (Toynbee, 1969). To live such a driven life seems very sad to me. It certainly bears little resemblance to my motivation.

I know that Abraham Maslow, in the years before his death, had a different urge. He experienced a great deal of internal pressure because he felt there was so much he had to say that was still unsaid. This urge to get it all down kept him writing to the end.

My view is quite different. My psychoanalyst friend, Paul Bergman, wrote that no person has more than one seminal idea in his or her lifetime; all writings by that person are simply further explications of that one theme. I agree. I think this describes my products.

Certainly, one reason for writing is that I have a curious mind. I like to see and explore the implications of ideas—mine and others'. I like to be logical, to pursue the ramifications of a thought. I am deeply involved in the world of feeling, intuition, nonverbal as well as verbal communication, but I also enjoy thinking and writing about that world. Conceptualizing the world clarifies its meaning for me.

Yet there is, I believe, a much more important reason for my writing. It seems to me that I am still—inside—the shy boy who found communication very difficult in interpersonal situations: who wrote love letters which were more eloquent than his direct expressions of love; who expressed himself freely in high school themes, but felt himself too "odd" to say the same things in class. That boy is still very much a part of me. Writing is my way of communicating with a world to which, in a very real sense, I feel I do not quite belong. I wish very much to be understood, but I don't expect to be. Writing is the message I seal in the bottle and cast into the sea. My astonishment is that people on an enormous number of beaches—psychological and geographical—have found the bottles and discovered that the messages speak to them. So I continue to write.

LEARNINGS

Taking Care of Myself

I have always been better at caring for and looking after others than I have in caring for myself. But in these later years I have made progress.

I have always been a very *responsible* person. If someone else is not looking after the details of an enterprise or the persons in a workshop, I must. But I have changed. In our 1976 Workshop on the Person-

Centered Approach in Ashland, Oregon, when I was not feeling well, and at the 1977 workshop in Arcozelo, Brazil, I shed all responsibility for the conduct of these complex undertakings and left it completely in the hands of others. I needed to take care of myself. So I let go of all responsibility except the responsibility—and the satisfaction—of being myself. For me it was a most unusual feeling: to be comfortably irresponsible with no feelings of guilt. And, to my surprise, I found I was more effective that way.

I have taken better care of myself physically, in a variety of ways. I have also learned to respect my psychological needs. Three years ago a workshop group helped me to realize how harried and driven I felt by outside demands—"nibbled to death by ducks" was the way one person put it, and the expression captured my feelings exactly. So I did what I have never done before: I spent ten days absolutley alone in a beach cottage which had been offered me, and I refreshed myself immensely. I found I thoroughly enjoyed being with me. I *like* me.

I have been more able to ask for help. I ask others to carry things for me, to do things for me, instead of proving that I can do it myself. I can also ask for personal help. When Helen, my wife, was very ill, and I was close to the breaking point from being on call as a 24-hour nurse, a housekeeper, a professional person in much demand, and a writer, I asked for help—and got it—from a therapist friend. I explored and tried to meet my own needs. I explored the strain that this period was putting on our marriage. I realized that it was necessary for my survival to live *my* life, and that this must come first, even though Helen was so ill. I am not quick to turn to others, but I am much more aware of the fact that I can't handle everything by myself. In these varied ways, I do a better job of prizing and looking after the person that is me.

Serenity?

It is often said or assumed that the older years are years of calm and serenity. I have found this attitude misleading. I believe I do have a longer perspective on events outside of myself, and hence I am often more of an objective observer than I once was. Yet, in contrast to this, events that touch me personally often evoke a stronger reaction than they would have years ago. When I am excited, I get very high. When I am concerned, I am more deeply disturbed. Hurts seem sharper, pain is more intense, tears come more easily, joy reaches higher peaks, even anger—with which I have always had trouble—is felt more keenly. Emotionally, I am more volatile than I used to be. The range from feeling depressed to feeling elated seems greater, and either state is more easily triggered.

Perhaps this volatility is due to my risk-taking style of living. Perhaps it comes from the greater sensitivity acquired in encounter groups. Perhaps it is a characteristic of the older years that has been overlooked. I do not know. I simply know that my feelings are more easily stirred, are sharper. I am more intimately acquainted with them all.

Opening Up to New Ideas

During these years I have been, I think, more open to new ideas. The ones of most importance to me have to do with inner space—the realm of the psychological powers and the psychic capabilities of the human person. In my estimation, this area constitutes the new frontier of knowledge, the cutting edge of discovery. Ten years ago I would not have made such a statement. But reading, experience, and conversation with some who are working in these fields have changed my view. Human beings have potentially available a tremendous range of intuitive powers. We are indeed wiser than our intellects. There is much evidence. We are learning how sadly we have neglected the capacities of the non-rational, creative "metaphoric mind"—the right half of our brain. Biofeedback has shown us that if we let ourselves function in a less conscious, more relaxed way, we can learn at some level to control temperature, heart rate, and all kinds of organic functions. We find that terminal cancer patients, when given an intensive program of meditation and fantasy training focused on overcoming the malignancy, experience a surprising number of remissions.

I am open to even more mysterious phenomena—precognition, thought transference, clairvoyance, human auras, Kirlian photography, even out-of-the-body experiences. These phenomena may not fit with known scientific laws, but perhaps we are on the verge of discovering new types of lawful order. I feel I am learning a great deal in a new area, and I find the experience enjoyable and exciting.

Intimacy

In the past few years, I have found myself opening up to much greater intimacy in relationships. I see this development as definitely the result of workshop experiences. I am more ready to touch and be touched, physically. I do more hugging and kissing of both men and women. I am more aware of the sensuous side of my life. I also realize how much I desire close psychological contact with others. I recognize how much I need to care deeply for another and to receive that kind of caring in return. I can say openly what I have always recognized dimly: that my deep involvement in psychotherapy was a cautious way of meeting this need for intimacy without risking too much of my person. Now I am more willing to be close in other relationships and to risk giving more of myself. I feel as though a whole new depth of capacity for intimacy has been discovered in me. This capacity has brought me much hurt, but an even greater share of joy.

How have these changes affected my behavior? I have developed deeper and more intimate relationships with men; I have been able to share without holding back, trusting the security of the friendship. Only during my college days—never before or after—did I have a group of really trusted, intimate men friends. So this is a new, tentative, adventurous development which seems very rewarding. I also have much more intimate communication with women. There are now a number of women with whom I have platonic but psychologically intimate relationships which have tremendous meaning for me.

With these close friends, men and women, I can share any aspect of my self—the painful, joyful, frightening, crazy, insecure, egotistical, self-deprecating feelings I have. I can share fantasies and dreams. Similarly, my friends share deeply with me. These experiences I find very enriching.

In my marriage of so many years, and in these friendships, I am continuing to learn more in the realm of intimacy. I am becoming more sharply aware of the times when I experience pain, anger, frustration, and rejection, as well as the closeness born of shared meanings or the satisfaction of being understood and accepted. I have learned how hard it is to confront with negative feelings a person about whom I care deeply. I have learned how expectations in a relationship turn very easily into demands made on the relationship. In my experience, I have found that one of the hardest things for me is to care for a person for whatever he or she *is*, at that time, in the relationship. It is so much easier to care for others for what I *think* they are, or *wish* they would be, or feel they *should* be. To care for this person for what he or she is, dropping my own expectations of what I want him or her to be for me, dropping my desire to change this person to suit my needs, is a most difficult but enriching way to a satisfying intimate relationship.

All of this has been a changing part of my life during the past decade. I find myself more open to closeness and to love.

PERSONAL JOYS AND DIFFICULTIES

In this period, I have had some painful and many pleasant experiences. The greatest stress revolves around coping with Helen's illness, which during the past five years has been very serious. She has met her pain and her restricted life with the utmost of courage. Her disabilities have posed new problems for each of us, both physical and psychological—problems that we continue to work through. It has been a very difficult period of alternating despair and hope, with currently much more of the latter.

She is making remarkable progress in fighting her way back, often by sheer force of will, to a more normal life, built around her own purposes. But it has not been easy. She first had to choose whether she wanted to live, whether there was any purpose in living. Then I have baffled and hurt her by the fact of my own independent life. While she was so ill, I felt heavily burdened by our close togetherness, heightened by her need for care. So I determined, for my own survival, to live a life of my own. She is often deeply hurt by this, and by the changing of my values. On her side, she is giving up the old model of being the supportive wife. This change brings her in touch with her anger at me and at society for giving her that socially approved role. On my part, I am angered at any move that would put us back in the old complete togetherness; I stubbornly resist anything that seems like control. So there are more tensions and difficulties in our relationship than ever before, more feelings that we are trying to work through, but there is also more honesty, as we strive to build new ways of being together.

So this period has involved struggle and strain. But it has also contained a wealth of positive experiences. There was our golden wedding celebration three years ago—several days of fun in a resort setting with our two children, our daughter-in-law, and all six of our grandchildren. It is such a joy to us that our son and daughter are now not only our offspring, but two of our best and closest friends, with whom we share our inner lives. There have been numerous intimate visits with them individually, and similar visits with close friends from other parts of the country. There is the continuing and growing closeness with our circle of friends here—all of them younger.

For me there have been the pleasures of gardening and of long walks. There have been honors and awards, more than I believe I deserve. The most touching was the honorary degree I received from Leiden University on the occasion of its four-hundredth anniversary, brought to me by a special emissary from this ancient Dutch seat of learning. There have been the dozens of highly personal letters from those whose lives have been touched or changed by my writings. These never cease to amaze me. That I could have had an important part in altering the life of a man in South Africa or a woman in the "outback" of Australia still seems a bit incredible—like magic, somehow.

THOUGHTS REGARDING DEATH

And then there is the ending of life. It may surprise you that at my age I think very little about death. The current popular interest in it surprises me.

Ten or fifteen years ago I felt quite certain that death was the total end of the person. I still regard that as the most likely prospect; however, it does not seem to me a tragic or awful prospect. I have been able to *live* my life—not to the full, certainly, but with a satisfying degree of fullness—and it seems natural that my life should come to an end. I already have a degree of immortality in other persons. I have sometimes said that, psychologically, I have strong sons and daughters all over the world. Also, I believe that the ideas and the ways of being that I and others have helped to develop will continue, for some time at least. So if I, as an individual, come to a complete and final end, aspects of me will still live on in a variety of growing ways, and that is a pleasant thought.

I think that no one can know whether he or she fears death until it arrives. Certainly, death is the ultimate leap in the dark, and I think it is highly probable that the apprehension I feel when going under an anesthetic will be duplicated or increased when I face death. Yet I don't experience a really deep fear of this process. So far as I am aware, my fears concerning death relate to its circumstances. I have a dread of any long and painful illness leading to death. I dread the thought of senility or of partial brain damage due to a stroke. My preference would be to die quickly, before it is too late to die with dignity. I think of Winston Churchill. I didn't mourn his death. I mourned the fact that death had not come sooner, when he could have died with the dignity he deserved.

My belief that death is the end has, however, been modified by some of my learnings of the past decade. I am impressed with the accounts by Raymond Moody (1975) of the experience of persons who have been so near death as to be declared dead, but who have come back to life. I am impressed by some of the reports of reincarnation, although reincarnation seems a very dubious blessing indeed. I am interested in the work of Elisabeth Kübler-Ross and the conclusions she has reached about life after death. I find definitely appealing the views of Arthur Koestler that individual consciousness is but a fragment of a cosmic consciousness, the fragment being reabsorbed into the whole upon the death of the individual. I like his analogy of the individual river eventually flowing into the tidal waters of the ocean, dropping its muddy silt as it enters the boundless sea.

So I consider death with, I believe, an openness to the experience. It will be what it will be, and I trust I can accept it as either an end to, or a continuation of life.

CONCLUSION

I recognize that I have been unusually fortunate in my health, in my marriage, in my family, in my stimulating younger friends, in the unexpectedly adequate income from my books. So I am in no way typical.

But for me, these past ten years have been fascinating—full of adventuresome undertakings. I have been able to open my self to new ideas, new feelings, new experiences, new risks. Increasingly I discover that being alive involves taking a chance, acting on less than certainty, engaging with life.

All of this brings change and for me the process of change *is* life. I realize that if I were stable and steady and static, I would be living death. So I accept confusion and uncertainty and fear and emotional highs and lows because they are the price I willingly pay for a flowing, perplexing, exciting life.

As I consider all the decades of my existence, there is only one other, the period at the Counseling Center at the University of Chicago, which can be compared to this one. It too involved risk, learning, personal growth and enrichment. But it was also a period of deep personal insecurity and strenuous professional struggle, much more difficult than these past years. So I believe I am being honest when I say that, all in all, this has been the most satisfying decade in my life. I have been increasingly able to be myself and have enjoyed doing just that.

As a boy, I was rather sickly, and my parents have told me that it was predicted I would die young. This prediction has been proven completely wrong in one sense, but has come profoundly true in another sense. I think it is correct that I will never live to be old. So now I agree with the prediction: I believe that I will die *young*.

UPDATE—1979

I choose to fill out this chapter by concentrating on one very full year—1979—in which pain, mourning, change, satisfaction, and risk were all markedly present.

Living the Process of Dying

In the eighteen months prior to my wife's death in March 1979, there were a series of experiences in which Helen and I and a number of friends were all involved, which decidedly changed my thoughts and feelings about dying and the continuation of the human spirit. The experiences were intensely personal, and some day I may write fully about them. For now, I can only hint. The following story is mostly about Helen, but I will concentrate on my portion of the experience.

Helen was a great skeptic about psychic phenomena and immortality. Yet, upon invitation, she and I visited a thoroughly honest medium, who would take no money. There, Helen experienced, and I observed, a "contact" with her deceased sister, involving facts that the medium could not possibly have known. The messages were extraordinarily convincing, and all came through the tipping of a sturdy table, tapping out letters. Later, when the medium came to our home and *my own table* tapped out messages in our living room, I could only be open to an incredible, and certainly non-fraudulent experience.

Helen also had visions and dreams of her family members, which made her increasingly certain that she would be welcomed "on the other side." As death came closer, she "saw" evil figures and the devil by her hospital bed. But when it was suggested by a friend that these might be creations of her own mind, she dismissed them, finally dismissing the devil by telling him he had made a mistake in coming, and she was not going with him. He never reappeared.

Also in these closing days, Helen had visions of an inspiring white light which came close, lifted her from the bed, and then deposited her back on the bed.

In this chapter, I mentioned that in these last years the distance between us had grown increasingly great. I wanted to care for her, but I was not at all sure that I loved her. One day, when she was very near death, I was in an internal frenzy which I could not understand at all. When I went to the hospital as usual to feed her her supper, I found myself pouring out to her how much I had loved her, how much she had meant in my life, how many positive initiatives she had contributed to our long partnership. I felt I had told her all these things before, but that night they had an intensity and sincerity they had not had before. I told her she should not feel obligated to live, that all was well with her family, and that she should feel free to live or die, as *she* wished. I also said I hoped the white light would come again that night.

Evidently I had released her from feeling that she had to live—for others. I later learned that when I left, she called together the nurses on the floor, thanked them for all they had done for her, and told them she was going to die.

By morning she was in a coma, and the following morning she died very peacefully, with her daughter holding her hand, several friends and I present.

That evening, friends of mine who had a long-standing appointment with the medium previously mentioned held a session with this woman. They were very soon in contact with Helen, who answered many questions: she had heard everything that was said while she was in a coma; she had experienced the white light and spirits coming for her; she was in contact with her family; she had the form of a young woman; her dying had been very peaceful and without pain.

All these experiences, so briefly suggested rather than described, have made me much more open to the possibility of the continuation of the individual human spirit, something I had never before believed possible. These experiences have left me very much interested in all types of paranormal phenomena. They have quite changed my understanding of the process of dying. I now consider it possible that each of us is a continuing spiritual essence lasting over time, and occasionally incarnated in a human body.

That all of these thoughts contrast sharply with some of the closing portions of the chapter, written only two years earlier, is obvious.

Activity and Risk

Perhaps partly in spite of, and partly because of, Helen's death, I have recently accepted more invitations than usual to participate with other staff members in workshops at home and abroad. The list includes: a workshop for educators in Venezuela; a large, turbulent workshop near Rome, with an international staff; a brief but deep experience with a Paris program for training group facilitators; a very rewarding regional person-centered workshop on Long Island (the second year with the same eastern staff); a person-centered workshop at Princeton, with many foreign participants; a fascinating workshop in Poland, held at a resort near Warsaw; and a beautifully flowing four-day workshop on "Life Transitions" in Pawling, New York. In addition to these activities, I have written some of the papers included in this volume.

I would like to comment on two of the programs mentioned above. The Princeton workshop, consisting of ninety persons, was probably the most difficult for me of any of the workshops in which I have participated. Yet, at least one of the staff feels it was the best such program we have ever conducted. For me, it was very painful, and the group only reached the edge, I felt, of becoming a community.

I perceive a number of factors as having made the workshop a painful experience. The staff had decided that this seventh annual person-centered workshop would be our last in this series; we felt very close to one another, but we were moving in different directions individually and we did not want these person-centered workshops to become a "routine" experience. The staff, from its long experience together, was probably more acceptant of negative, hostile, critical feelings than ever before—and they were expressed in abundance by participants, directed toward one another and toward the staff. There were a large number from foreign countries, and their scorn, contempt, and anger at the United States and at the American participants was freely voiced. There were two persons who knew exactly how the workshop should be conducted. (The two views were very different, but they both were strongly against our unstructured approach, and each attracted quite a following, though not enough to change the general direction of the workshop.) There were also several participants who showed evidence of deep personal disturbance.

When all these factors were added to the usual chaos of a large group trying to develop its own program and find its own way, the result was horrendous. Frustration and anger were very frequently expressed. When some members endeavored to move in creative and positive ways, they were blocked by others. It seemed genuinely uncertain whether the trust placed in these individuals to sense and use their own power constructively would be justified. We were all our own worst enemies. Only toward the end of the ten days did the faint beginnings of a unity in divergence, and a community built on diversity, show themselves. Yet, to my surprise, many participants wrote later to tell of their very positive learnings and changes, which emerged from the pain, the turbulence—and the closeness. I too learned, but it was difficult learning.

The Polish workshop was unusual for a number of reasons. I could hardly believe the degree of interest in my work, which drew together ninety people, both professional and nonprofessional. The Polish staff felt insecure, so the facilitation came largely from the four Americans who were present. This was a disappointment at the time, because I had hoped for more Polish leadership. In the middle of the week-long session, as individuals sensed their power and began to use it, many, especially the professionals, used it to hurt others. Hurtful labels and diagnoses, skillful putdowns, became quite prominent. To me, it resembled Princeton, and I thought, "Oh, no! Not again!" But largely due to a beautifully honest Polish woman, a staff member, people began to be aware of the consequences of such behavior, and it dropped away. By the end of the week, we were a close and loving community.

I was unaware of the full measure of what had occurred until I received a letter from a participant some months later, from which I quote: "People here talk of the 'historic event' that took place in Leskarzev—so many diverse people, so many professionals, psychiatrists and psychologists (each of them possessing the ultimate truth about the helping relationship), hating and putting each other down constantly on an everyday basis—all of them now integrated, and yes, without losing their own personality, without any imposing." I am happy that I did not know in advance of the professional rivalry and backbiting.

I found the group as a whole to be very sophisticated, intelligent, and often more scholarly than a similar

American group. Although they lived in a Socialist country, their problems, feelings, ways of coping, and their desire for openness and integrity seemed very similar to what I have found in every land.

Personal Matters

As the year drew to a close, I was increasingly aware of my capacity for love, my sensuality, my sexuality. I have found myself fortunate in discovering and building relationships in which these needs can find expression. There has been pain and hurt, but also joy and depth.

The year was capped on January 8, 1980, when a large group of friends came to my home, bringing food, drink, songs, and surprises to celebrate my seventy-eighth birthday. It was a wild, wonderful, hilarious party—full of love, caring, fellowship, and happiness—which I will never forget.

So I still feel I fit the second part of the title of this chapter. I sense myself as older and growing.

REFERENCES

MITCHELL, A. Quoted in *Los Angeles Times*, February 28, 1977.

MOODY, R. A., JR. *Life after life*. New York: Bantam Books, 1975.

STANFORD RESEARCH INSTITUTE. *Changing images of man*. Policy Research Report No. 3. Menlo Park, California, 1973.

TOYNBEE, A. Why and how I work. *Saturday Review*, April 5, 1969, p. 22.

Do We Need "A" Reality?

The paper that follows is one I enjoy because it brings back pleasant memories of the beach cottage (mentioned in the third paragraph) loaned me by a friend for a short while during the autumn of 1974. For ten precious days, I was completely alone—no phone or other contacts with persons, except for a few visits to the local grocery store. I promised myself that I would not attempt to achieve or produce anything during that period. I took with me some books I had wanted to read. I took long walks on the beach, made the acquaintance of a great blue heron, kept a journal, recorded my dreams, read, and let my mind wander where it would.

It was while I was sitting on the deck of the cottage one night that the germ of this paper arose in my mind. The paper turned out quite differently from anything I had written up to that time. It has a sort of dreamy quality that I like. None of the facts in it are new, but the implications of those facts are startling if taken seriously.

This is not a personal paper in the sense that the previous ones have been, but I include it in this section because it expresses a new and different facet of myself.

I believe most educators would agree that a high priority in education is to help individuals to acquire the learning, the information, and the personal growth that will enable them to deal more constructively with the "real world." This is often the theme of commencement addresses, in which one expresses hopes or fears concerning how the new graduates will face and cope with the "real world." It is often a topic in the final hours of intensive encounter groups, when individuals who have learned a great deal about themselves and about their interpersonal relationships are concerned about how they will behave when they return to their "real" lives outside.

What is this "real world"? It is this question that I want to explore, and I believe that the direction in which my thinking has inexorably led me will be best portrayed by giving a number of personal and commonplace examples.

A few weeks ago, I was sitting alone, late at night, on the deck of a beach cottage in northern California. As I sat there for several hours, a bright star on the horizon moved upward into clear view. A brilliant planet moved with the same slow, majestic speed from directly above me to a point well on my right. The star and the planet were accompanied in their movement by the Milky Way and all the other constellations. Obviously, I was the center of the universe, and the heavens were slowly revolving about me. It was a humbling experience (How small I am!) and an uplifting one (How marvelous to be such a focal point!). I was looking at the real world.

Yet, in another corner of my mind, I knew that I, and the earth beneath me, and the atmosphere surrounding me were moving at a breathless speed—faster than a modern jet plane—in the direction I called east, and that the stars and planets were, relative to the earth, comparatively motionless. Although I could not *see* what I've just described, I knew that this—not the more obvious perception—was *really* the real world.

At some other level, I was aware that I was an infinitesimal speck on an insignificant planet in one of the minor galaxies (of which there are millions) in the universe. I knew that each of these galaxies was moving at an incredible speed, often exploding away from the others. Was this reality, too? I was confused.

But at least there was one reality of which I could be sure: the hard wooden chair on which I sat, the solid earth on which the deck rested, the stainless steel pen I held in my hand. This was a reality that could not only be seen, but also felt and touched. These objects could sustain weight and pressure. They were solid.

But no, I knew enough of science to challenge all this. The chair is made up of formerly living cells, intricate in their composition, composed more of space than of matter. The earth is a slowly moving fluid mass, which shudders very frequently as it shrinks and cracks and crinkles. The road over which I drove yesterday had been a part of one of those shudders. One day in 1906, the earth shrugged a little and the road cracked, and the western side of the crack was carried twenty feet north of its continuation on the other side. Solid earth indeed!

And what about the reassuring hardness of my metal pen? They tell me it is composed of invisible atoms, moving at great speed. Each atom has a nucleus, and recent years have brought discoveries of more and more particles in those nuclei. Each particle is endowed with fantastically unbelievable characteristics; it moves in possibly random, possibly orderly trajectories in the great inner space of each atom. My pen is hardly the firm solid object that I so clearly feel and hold. The "real world" seems to be dissolving.

I am reassured, but also perplexed, by the statement of the great physical scientist, Sir James Jeans. He says: "The stream of human knowledge is impartially heading toward a nonmechanical reality: the Universe begins to look more like a great *thought* than a great machine." Try that on your practical friend, or your plumber, or your stockbroker. Tell them, "The real world is just a great thought." At any rate, the conception of a real world, obvious to anyone, is rapidly slipping completely out of my grasp.

But at least in the interpersonal world, I know my family and my friends; this knowledge is surely a solid basis on which I can act. But then my memories trip me up. One needs only the simple occasion of a softly facilitated encounter group, where permission is given to express oneself, to discover how shaky our interpersonal knowledge is. Individuals have discovered in their closest friends and family members great realms of hidden feelings. There are previously unknown fears, feelings of inadequacy, suppressed rages and resentments, bizarre sexual desires and fantasies, hidden pools of hopes and dreams, of joys and dreads, of creative urges and unbidden loves. This reality, too, seems as unsure, as full of unknowns, as any yet considered in this chapter.

So the individual is driven back to self: "At least I know who *I* am. I decide what I want to do, and I do it. *That's* for real." But is it? If I talk to the behaviorist, he tells me, "You are nothing but the sum of your stimulus inputs and the conditioned responses you emit. All the rest is illusion." Well, finally we have reality. I am nothing but a mechanical robot. Or is that all? Where do my dreams come from? Perhaps that can be explained too. Then I think of Jean, the woman who told me that her identical twin sister was driving back to her own home at night by a familiar route when Jean awoke in a panic of certainty. She phoned the highway police and told them, "There's been an accident on such-and-such a highway. It's a white car with this license and a lone woman driver." There was a pause, and then the officer said, in a puzzled and slightly suspicious voice, "But how did you know about that, lady? We only got the report of the accident two minutes ago." What do we make of *that* kind of reality?

That little episode opens up a whole train of thought about inner worlds and "separate realities." What do we make of the vision or dream that Carl Jung (1961) had at the age of three? He saw a large mysterious underground cavern, with all the light focused on a great pillar of flesh with something like a head on top, enthroned on a royal chair. Fifty years passed before he fully understood this experience, when he rediscovered this same vision in the phallic rituals of some primitive tribes. How had that vision come to him at the age of three? In what real world does this phenomenon belong?

Read the story of Robert Monroe (1971), a hard-headed businessman and engineer, who, after some puzzling experiences, found himself one night floating up to the ceiling of his room, looking down on his own body and that of his wife. His account of these experiences, in which he tells of his initial fright, then his increasing willingness to take journeys out of his body, is startling indeed, and often very convincing. One cannot help but ponder the question: What "reality" can encompass such experiences, as well as the "real" experiences I know?

How about Don Juan, the ageless Yaqui Indian, who opened whole new worlds to the stubbornly skeptical anthropologist, Carlos Castaneda? Worlds of magical events, of flights through the air, of a nonordinary reality where death is not different from life, where the "man of knowledge" has a spirit ally, where the impossible is experienced. Rubbish, you say? His own experiences were enough to force Castaneda (1969, 1971) to recognize that there exist separate realities completely alien to the thinking of the modern scientific mind.

I think of John Lilly (1973), a scientist trained at the California Institute of Technology, who went on to study neuroanatomy, medicine, and psychiatry, and who is perhaps best known for his twelve years of work with dolphins, trying to communicate with these animals, who he believes are at least as intelligent as human beings. To trace his path from his beginnings as a scientist who believed only in mechanical models of reality, to his present view that there are various levels of altered consciousness (which he has achieved and helped others to achieve), is mind-boggling. Along the way, he became convinced that the dolphins could read his thoughts. Lilly's experiences in a sensory-deprivation tank, where he floated in warm water with absolutely minimal input of sight, sound, touch, or taste—were fascinating. He discovered that the inner world, without any external stimuli, was incredibly rich, sometimes frightening, often bizarre. In trying to understand this inner world, he experimented with LSD, with both illuminating and terrifying results. This led to meditation, unbidden thought transmission, and higher and higher states of consciousness in which he—like many before him, who were called mystics— experienced the universe as a unity, a unity based on love. Quite a distance from his Caltech training!

These and other accounts cannot simply be dismissed with contempt or ridicule. The witnesses are too honest, their experiences too real. All these accounts indicate that a vast and mysterious universe—perhaps an inner reality, or perhaps a spirit world of which we are all unknowingly a part—seems to exist. Such a universe delivers a final crushing blow to our comfortable belief that "we all know what the real world is."

Where have my thoughts led me in relation to an objective world of reality?

It clearly does not exist in the objects we can see and feel and hold.

It does not exist in the technology we admire so greatly.

It is not found in the solid earth or the twinkling stars.

It does not lie in a solid knowledge of those around us.

It is not found in the organizations or customs or rituals of any one culture.

It is not even in our own known personal worlds.

It must take into account mysterious and currently unfathomable "separate realities," incredibly different from an objective world.

I, and many others, have come to a new realization. It is this: The only reality I can possibly know is the world as *I* perceive and experience it at this moment. The only reality you can possibly know is the world as *you* perceive and experience it at this moment. And the only certainty is that those perceived realities are different. There are as many "real worlds" as there are people! This creates a most burdensome dilemma, one never before experienced in history.

From time immemorial, the tribe or the community or the nation or the culture has agreed upon what constitutes the real world. To be sure, different tribes or different cultures might have held sharply different world views, but at least there was a large, relatively unified group which felt assured in its knowledge of the world and the universe, and knew that this perception was *true*. So the community frowned upon, condemned, persecuted, even killed those who did not agree, who perceived reality differently. Copernicus, even though he kept his findings secret for many years, was eventually declared a heretic. Galileo established proof of Copernicus's views, but in his seventies he was forced to recant his teachings. Giordano Bruno was burned at the stake in 1600 for teaching that there were many worlds in our universe.

Individuals who deviated in their perception of religious reality were tortured and killed. In the mid-1800s, Ignaz Semmelweis, an intense young Hungarian physician-scientist, was driven insane by his persecutors because he made the then absurd claim that childbed fever, that dread scourge of the maternity room, was carried from one woman to another by invisible germs on the hands and instruments of the doctors. Obvious nonsense, in terms of the reality of his day. In our own American Colonies, those who were even suspected of having psychic powers were considered witches and were hanged or crushed under great stones. History offers a continuing series of examples of the awful price paid by those who perceive a reality different from the agreed-upon real world. Although society has often come around eventually to agree with its dissidents, as in the instances I have mentioned, there is no doubt that this insistence upon a known and certain universe has been part of the cement that holds a culture together.

Today we face a different situation. The ease and rapidity of worldwide communication means that every one of us is aware of a dozen "realities"; even though we may think some of them absurd (like reincarnation) or dangerous (like communism), we cannot help but be aware of them. No longer can we exist in a secure cocoon, knowing that we all see the world in the same way.

Because of this change, I want to raise a very serious question: Can we today afford the luxury of having *"a"* reality? Can we still preserve the belief that there is a "real world" upon whose definition we all agree? I am convinced that this is a luxury we *cannot* afford, a myth we dare not maintain. Only once in recent history has this been fully and successfully achieved. Millions of people were in complete agreement as to the nature of social and cultural reality—an agreement brought about by the mesmerizing influence of Hitler. This agreement about reality nearly marked the destruction of Western culture. I do not see it as something to be emulated.

In Western culture during this century—especially in the United States—there has also been an agreed-upon reality of values. This gospel can be stated very briefly: "More is better, bigger is better, faster is better, and modern technology will achieve all three of these eminently desirable goals." But now that credo is a crumbling disaster in which few believe. It is dissolving in the smog of pollution, the famine of overpopulation, the Damocles' sword of the nuclear bomb. We have so successfully achieved the goal of "a bigger bang for a buck" that we are in danger of destroying all life on this planet.

Our attempts, then, to live in the "real world" which all perceive in the same way have, in my opinion, led us to the brink of annihilation as a species. I will be so bold as to suggest an alternative.

It appears to me that the way of the future must be to base our lives and our education on the assumption that

there are as many realities as there are persons, and
that our highest priority is to accept that hypothesis and
proceed from there. Proceed where? Proceed, each of
us, to explore openmindedly the many, many perceptions of reality that exist. We would, I believe, enrich
our own lives in the process. We would also become
more able to cope with the reality in which each one of
us exists, because we would be aware of many more
options. This might well be a life full of perplexity and
difficult choices, demanding greater maturity, but it
would be an exciting and adventurous life.

The question may well be raised, however, whether
we could have a community or a society based on this
hypothesis of multiple realities. Might not such a
society be a completely individualistic anarchy? That is
not my opinion. Suppose my grudging tolerance of your
separate world view became a full acceptance of you
and your right to have such a view. Suppose that
instead of shutting out the realities of others as absurd
or dangerous or heretical or stupid, I was willing to
explore and learn about those realities? Suppose you
were willing to do the same. What would be the social
result? I think that our society would be based not on a
blind commitment to a cause or creed or view of reality,
but on a common commitment to each other as right-
fully separate persons, with separate realities. The natural human tendency to care for another would no
longer be "I care for you because you are the same as
I," but, instead, "I prize and treasure you because you
are different from me."

Idealistic, you say? It surely is. How can I be so
utterly naive and "unrealistic" as to have any hope that
such a drastic change could conceivably come about? I
base my hope partly on the view of world history so
aptly stated by Charles Beard: "When the skies grow
dark, the stars begin to shine." So we may see the

emergence of leaders who are moving in this new direction.

I base my hope, even more solidly, on the view enunciated by Lancelot Whyte, the historian of ideas, in his final book before his death. It is his theory, in which he is not alone, that great steps in human history are anticipated, and probably brought about, by changes in the unconscious thinking of thousands and millions of individuals during the period preceding the change. Then, in a relatively short space of time, a new idea, a new perspective, seems to burst upon the world scene, and change occurs. He gives the example that before 1914, patriotism and nationalism were unquestioned virtues. Then began the faint unconscious questioning which built an unconscious tradition reversing a whole pattern of thought. This new perspective burst into the open between 1950 and 1970. "My country, right or wrong" is no longer a belief to live by. Nationalistic wars are out of date and out of favor, and even though they continue, world opinion is deeply opposed. Whyte (1974) points out that "at any moment the *unconscious levels are ahead of the conscious* in the task of unifying emotion, thought and action!" (p. 107)

For me, this line of thought is entirely congenial. I have stated that we are wiser than our intellects, that our organisms as a whole have a wisdom and purposiveness which goes well beyond our conscious thought. I believe that this idea applies to the concepts I have been presenting in this chapter. I think that men and women, individually and collectively, are inwardly and organismically rejecting the view of one single, culture-approved reality. I believe they are moving inevitably toward the acceptance of millions of separate, challenging, exciting, informative, *individual* perceptions of reality. I regard it as possible that this view—like the sudden and separate discovery of the principles of quantum mechanics by scientists in different countries—may begin to come into effective existence in many parts of the world at once. If so, we will be living in a totally new universe, different from any in history. Is it conceivable that such a change can come about?

Here lies the challenge to educators—probably the most insecure and frightened among any of the professions—battered by public pressures, limited by legislative restrictions, essentially conservative in their reactions. Can they possibly espouse such a view of multiple realities as I have been describing? Can they begin to bring into being the changes in attitudes, behaviors, and values that such a world view would demand? Certainly, by themselves they cannot. But with the underlying change in what Whyte calls "the unconscious tradition," and with the aid of the new person whom I and many others see emerging in our culture, it is just conceivable that they might succeed.

I conclude that if nations follow their past ways, then, because of the speed of world communication of separate views, each society will have to exert more and more coercion to bring about a forced agreement as to what constitutes the real world and its values. Those coerced agreements will differ from nation to nation, from culture to culture. The coercion will destroy individual freedom. We will bring about our own destruction through the clashes caused by differing world views.

But I have suggested an alternative. If we accept as a basic fact of all human life that we live in separate realities; if we can see those differing realities as the most promising resource for learning in all the history of the world; if we can live together in order to learn from one another without fear; if we can do all this, then a new age could be dawning. And perhaps—just perhaps—humankind's deep organic sensings are paving the way for just such a change.

REFERENCES

CASTANEDA, C. *The teachings of Don Juan: A Yaqui way of knowledge*. New York: Ballantine Books, 1969.

CASTANEDA, C. *A separate reality: Further conversations with Don Juan*. New York: Pocket Books, Division of Simon & Schuster, 1971.

JUNG, C. G. *Memories, dreams, reflections*. New York: Vintage Books, 1961.

LILLY, J. C. *The center of the cyclone*. New York: Doubleday, 1971.

MONROE, R. A. *Journeys out of the body*. New York: Bantam Books, 1973.

WHYTE, L. L. *The universe of experience*. New York: Harper Torchbooks, 1974.

Part II

ASPECTS OF A
PERSON-CENTERED
APPROACH

The Foundations of
a Person-Centered
Approach

This is a very basic chapter, which has roots in both the past and the present. In writing it, I have utilized a paper (1963) that marked an important clarification of my thinking at that time. The second source can be traced to a seed of thought that germinated at a conference on the theory of humanistic psychology, in the early 1970s, culminating in a paper on "The Formative Tendency" (1978). Although I acknowledged my indebtedness to the British historian of ideas, Lancelot Whyte, I was surprised to learn later that almost identical ideas are found in a much earlier book (1926) by Jan Christian Smuts, the legendary South African warrior, scholar, and prime minister. After a political defeat which ended his first term as prime minister, he wrote this book, whose theme was the "whole-making, holistic tendency . . . seen at all stages of existence . . . something fundamental in the universe . . ." Alfred Adler later (1933) used Smuts' concept of the holistic tendency in support of his view that "there can no longer be any doubt that everything we call a body shows a striving to become a whole." (My thanks go to Dr. Heinz Ansbacker, a professor at the University of Vermont and a follower of Adlerian theory, for calling my attention to these earlier thinkers.) It has been very confirming to find that this holistic force—almost totally ignored by scientists—was understood by these thinkers long ago.

The third basis for this paper comes from my reading of three men who are on the extreme cutting edge of present-day science: Fritjof Capra, a theoretical physicist; Magohah Murayama, a philosopher of science; and Ilya Prigogine, a Nobel Prize–winning chemist-philosopher.

Thus, this paper draws on many sources, integrating these ideas, old and new, into the structure of a person-centered way of being. What I have tried to do is put into simple language some profound concepts for which I am much indebted to others, whose generative thoughts come both from the past and from the immediate present.

I found real satisfaction in writing this chapter, and I am pleased to present it.

I wish to point to two related tendencies which have acquired more and more importance in my thinking as the years have gone by. One of these is an actualizing tendency, a characteristic of organic life. One is a formative tendency in the universe as a whole. Taken together, they are the foundation blocks of the person-centered approach.

CHARACTERISTICS OF THE PERSON-CENTERED APPROACH

What do I mean by a person-centered approach? It expresses the primary theme of my whole professional life, as that theme has become clarified through experience, interaction with others, and research. I smile as I think of the various labels I have given to this theme during the course of my career—nondirective counseling, client-centered therapy, student-centered teaching, group-centered leadership. Because the fields of application have grown in number and variety, the label "person-centered approach" seems the most descriptive.

The central hypothesis of this approach can be briefly stated. (See Rogers, 1959, for a complete statement.) Individuals have within themselves vast resources for self-understanding and for altering their self-concepts, basic attitudes, and self-directed behavior; these resources can be tapped if a definable climate of facilitative psychological attitudes can be provided.

There are three conditions that must be present in order for a climate to be growth-promoting. These conditions apply whether we are speaking of the relationship between therapist and client, parent and child, leader and group, teacher and student, or administrator and staff. The conditions apply, in fact, in any situation in which the development of the person is a goal. I have described these conditions in previous writings; I present here a brief summary from the point of view of psychotherapy, but the description applies to all of the foregoing relationships.

The first element could be called genuineness, realness, or congruence. The more the therapist is himself or herself in the relationship, putting up no professional front or personal facade, the greater is the likelihood that the client will change and grow in a constructive manner. This means that the therapist is openly being the feelings and attitudes that are flowing within at the moment. The term "transparent" catches the flavor of this condition: the therapist makes himself or herself transparent to the client; the client can see right through what the therapist *is* in the relationship; the client experiences no holding back on the part of the therapist. As for the therapist, what he or she is experiencing is available to awareness, can be lived in the relationship, and can be communicated, if appropriate.

experience
awareness
communication
congruence

Thus, there is a close matching, or congruence, between what is being experienced at the gut level, what is present in awareness, and what is expressed to the client.

2nd

The second attitude of importance in creating a climate for change is acceptance, or caring, or prizing—what I have called "unconditional positive regard." When the therapist is experiencing a positive, acceptant attitude toward whatever the client *is* at that moment, therapeutic movement or change is more likely to occur. The therapist is willing for the client to be whatever immediate feeling is going on—confusion, resentment, fear, anger, courage, love, or pride. Such caring on the part of the therapist is nonpossessive. The therapist prizes the client in a total rather than a conditional way.

The third facilitative aspect of the relationship is empathic understanding. This means that the therapist senses accurately the feelings and personal meanings that the client is experiencing and communicates this understanding to the client. When functioning best, the therapist is so much inside the private world of the other that he or she can clarify not only the meanings of which the client is aware but even those just below the level of awareness. This kind of sensitive, active listening is exceedingly rare in our lives. We think we listen, but very rarely do we listen with real understanding, true empathy. Yet listening, of this very special kind, is one of the most potent forces for change that I know.

How does this climate which I have just described bring about change? Briefly, as persons are accepted and prized, they tend to develop a more caring attitude toward themselves. As persons are empathically heard, it becomes possible for them to listen more accurately to the flow of inner experiencings. But as a person

how does
this
work

understands and prizes self, the self becomes more congruent with the experiencings. The person thus becomes more real, more genuine. These tendencies, the reciprocal of the therapist's attitudes, enable the person to be a more effective growth-enhancer for himself or herself. There is a greater freedom to be the true, whole person (Rogers, 1962).

EVIDENCE SUPPORTING THE PERSON-CENTERED APPROACH

There is a body of steadily mounting research evidence which by and large supports the view that when these facilitative conditions are present, changes in personality and behavior do indeed occur. Such research has been carried on from 1949 to the present. Studies have been made of the benefits of person-centered psychotherapy with troubled individuals and with schizophrenics; of the facilitation of learning in the schools; of the improvement in other interpersonal relationships. Some excellent and little-known research has been done by Aspy (1972), Aspy and Roebuck (1976), and others in the field of education, and by Tausch and colleagues in Germany in many different fields (Tausch, 1978, summary).

A DIRECTIONAL PROCESS IN LIFE

Practice, theory, and research make it clear that the person-centered approach rests on a basic trust in human beings, and in all organisms. There is evidence from many disciplines to support an even broader statement. We can say that there is in every organism, at whatever level, an underlying flow of movement toward constructive fulfillment of its inherent possibilities. In human beings, too, there is a natural tendency toward a more complex and complete development. The term that has most often been used for this is the "actualizing tendency," and it is present in all living organisms.

Whether we are speaking of a flower or an oak tree, of an earthworm or a beautiful bird, of an ape or a person, we will do well, I believe, to recognize that life is an active process, not a passive one. Whether the stimulus arises from within or without, whether the environment is favorable or unfavorable, the behaviors of an organism can be counted on to be in the direction of maintaining, enhancing, and reproducing itself. This is the very nature of the process we call life. This tendency is operative at all times. Indeed, only the presence or absence of this total directional process enables us to tell whether a given organism is alive or dead.

The actualizing tendency can, of course, be thwarted or warped, but it cannot be destroyed without destroying the organism. I remember that in my boyhood, the bin in which we stored our winter's supply of potatoes was in the basement, several feet below a small window. The conditions were unfavorable, but the potatoes would begin to sprout—pale white sprouts, so unlike the healthy green shoots they sent up when planted in the soil in the spring. But these sad, spindly sprouts would grow 2 or 3 feet in length as they reached toward the distant light of the window. The sprouts were, in their bizarre, futile growth, a sort of desperate expression of the directional tendency I have been describing. They would never become plants, never mature, never fulfill their real potential. But under the most adverse circumstances, they were striving to become. Life would not give up, even if it could not flourish. In dealing with clients whose lives have been terribly warped, in working with men and women on the back wards of state hospitals, I often think of those potato sprouts. So unfavorable have been the conditions in which these people have developed that their lives often seem abnormal, twisted, scarcely human. Yet, the directional tendency in them can be trusted. The clue to understanding their behavior is that they are striving, in the only ways that they perceive as available to them, to move toward growth, toward becoming. To healthy persons, the results may seem bizarre and futile, but they are life's desperate attempt to become itself. This potent constructive tendency is an underlying basis of the person-centered approach.

Some Confirming Examples of the Directional Process

I am not alone in seeing such an actualizing tendency as the fundamental answer to the question of what makes an organism "tick." Goldstein (1947), Maslow (1954), Angyal (1941, 1965), Szent-Gyoergyi (1974), and others have held similar views and have influenced my own thinking. I (1963) have pointed out that this tendency involves a development toward the differentiation of organs and functions; it involves enhancement through reproduction. Szent-Gyoergyi says that he cannot explain the mysteries of biological development "without supposing an innate 'drive' in living matter to perfect itself" (p. 17). The organism, in its normal state, moves toward its own fulfillment, toward self-regulation and an independence from external control.

But is this view confirmed by other evidence? Let me point to some of the work in biology that supports the concept of the actualizing tendency. One example, replicated with different species, is the work of Hans Driesch with sea urchins many years ago. Driesch learned how to tease apart the two cells that are formed after the first division of the fertilized egg. Had they been left to develop normally, it is clear that each of these two cells would have grown into a portion of a sea urchin larva, the contributions of both being needed to form a whole creature. So it seems equally obvious that when the two cells are skillfully separated, each, if it grows, will simply develop into some portion of a sea urchin. But this assumption overlooks the directional and actualizing tendency characteristic of all organic growth. It is found that each cell, if it can be kept alive, now develops into a whole sea urchin larva—a bit smaller than usual, but normal and complete.

I have chosen this example because it seems so closely analogous to my experience in dealing with individuals in one-to-one therapeutic relationships, in facilitating intensive groups, in providing "freedom to learn" for students in classes. In these situations, I am most impressed with the fact that each human being has a directional tendency toward wholeness, toward actualization of his or her potentialities. I have not found psychotherapy or group experience effective when I have tried to create in another individual something that is not already there; I have found, however, that if I can provide the conditions that allow growth to occur, then this positive directional tendency brings about constructive results. The scientist with the divided sea urchin egg was in the same situation. He could not cause the cell to develop in one way or another, but when he focused his skill on providing the conditions that permitted the cell to survive and grow, the tendency for growth and the direction of growth were evident, and came from within the organism. I cannot think of a better analogy for therapy or the group experience, where, if I can supply a psychological amniotic fluid, forward movement of a constructive sort will occur.

I would like to add one comment which may be clarifying. Sometimes this growth tendency is spoken of as though it involved the development of all the potentialities of the organism. This is clearly not true. As one of my colleagues pointed out, the organism does not tend toward developing its capacity for nausea, nor does it actualize its potentiality for self-destruction, nor its ability to bear pain. Only under unusual or perverse circumstances do these potentialities become actualized. It is clear that the actualizing tendency is selective and directional—a constructive tendency, if you will.

Support from Modern Theory and Experience

Pentony (unpublished paper, 1978) points out forcefully that those who favor the view of an actualizing tendency "do not need to be inhibited by the belief that it is in conflict with modern science or theories of knowledge" (p. 20). He describes the differing recent epistemologies, particularly that of Murayama (1977). It is now theorized that the "genetic code" does not contain all the information necessary to specify the characteristics of the mature organism. Instead, it contains a *set of rules* determining the interactions of the dividing cells. Much less information is needed to codify the rules than to guide every aspect of maturing development. "Thus information can be generated within the organism system—information can *grow*" (Pentony, p. 9, emphasis added). Hence, Driesch's sea urchin cells are doubtless following the coded rules and, consequently, are able to develop in original, not previously or rigidly specified ways.

All this goes deeply against the current (and possibly outdated) epistemology of the social sciences, which holds that a "cause" is followed in a one-way direction by an "effect." In contrast, Murayama and others believe that there are *mutual* cause-effect interactions, which amplify deviations and permit new information and new forms to develop. This "morphogenetic epistemology" appears to be basic to an understanding of all living systems, including all growth processes in organisms. Murayama (1977) states that an understanding of biology "lies in the recognition that the biological processes are reciprocal causal processes, not random processes" (p. 130). On the other hand, as he points out elsewhere, an understanding of biology does *not* emerge from an epistemology based on one-way cause-effect systems. Thus, there is great need to rethink the stimulus-response, cause-effect basis on which most of social science rests.

The work in the field of sensory deprivation shows how strong is the organismic tendency to amplify diversities and create new information and new forms. Certainly, tension reduction, or the absence of stimulation, is a far cry from being the desired state of the organism. Freud (1953) could not have been more wrong in his postulate that "The nervous system is . . . an apparatus which would even, if this were feasible, maintain itself in an altogether unstimulated condition" (p. 63). On the contrary, when deprived of external stimuli, the human organism produces a flood of internal stimuli, sometimes of the most bizarre sort. Lilly (1972) was one of the first to tell of his experiences when suspended weightless in a soundproof tank of water. He speaks of trancelike states, mystical experiences, the sense of being tuned in on communication networks not available to ordinary consciousness, and even experiences that can only be called hallucinatory. It is very clear that when a person is receiving an absolute minimum of external stimuli, he or she is opened to a flood of experiencing at a level far beyond that of everyday living. The individual most certainly does not lapse into homeostasis, into a passive equilibrium. This occurs only in diseased organisms.

A Trustworthy Base

Thus, to me it is meaningful to say that the substratum of all motivation is the organismic tendency toward fulfillment. This tendency may express itself in the widest range of behaviors and in response to a wide variety of needs. To be sure, certain basic wants must be at least partially met before other needs become urgent. Consequently, the tendency of the organism to actualize itself may at one moment lead to the seeking of food or sexual satisfaction, and yet, unless these needs are overpoweringly great, even these satisfactions will be sought in ways that enhance, rather than diminish, self-esteem. And the organism will also seek other fulfillments in its transactions with the environment. The need for exploration of and producing change in the environment, the need for play and for self-exploration—all of these and many other behaviors are basically expressions of the actualizing tendency.

In short, organisms are always seeking, always initiating, always "up to something." There is one central source of energy in the human organism. This source is a trustworthy function of the whole system rather than of some portion of it; it is most simply conceptualized as a tendency toward fulfillment, toward actualization, involving not only the maintenance but also the enhancement of the organism.

A BROADER VIEW:
THE FORMATIVE TENDENCY

There are many who criticize this point of view. They regard it as too optimistic, not dealing adequately with the negative element, the evil, the dark side in human beings.

Consequently, I would like to put this directional tendency in a broader context. In doing so, I shall draw heavily on the work and thinking of others, from disciplines other than my own. I have learned from many scientists, but I wish to mention a special indebtedness to the works of Albert Szent-Gyoergyi (1974), a Nobel Prize–winning biologist, and Lancelot Whyte (1974), a historian of ideas.

My main thesis is this: there appears to be a formative tendency at work in the universe, which can be observed at every level. This tendency has received much less attention than it deserves.

Physical scientists up to now have focused primarily on "entropy," the tendency toward deterioration, or disorder. They know a great deal about this tendency. Studying closed systems, they can give it a clear mathematical description. They know that order tends to deteriorate into randomness, each stage less organized than the last.

We are also very familiar with deterioration in organic life. The system—whether plant, animal, or human—eventually deteriorates into a lesser and lesser degree of functioning organization, or order, until decay reaches a stasis. In one sense, this is what one aspect of medicine is all about—a concern with the malfunctioning or deterioration of an organ or the organism as a whole. The complex process of the death of the physical organism is increasingly well understood.

So a great deal is known of the universal tendency of systems at all levels to deteriorate in the direction of less and less orderliness, more and more randomness. When this system operates, it is a one-way street: the world seems to be a great machine, running down and wearing out.

But there is far less recognition of, or emphasis on, the even more important formative tendency which can be equally well observed at every level of the universe. After all, every form that we see or know emerged from a simpler, less complex form. This a a phenomenon which is at least as significant as entropy. Examples could be given from every form of inorganic or organic being. Let me illustrate with just a few.

It appears that every galaxy, every star, every planet, including our own, was formed from a less organized whirling storm of particles. Many of these stellar objects are themselves formative. In the atmosphere of our sun, hydrogen nuclei collide to form molecules of helium, which are more complex in nature. It is hypothesized that in other stars, even heavier molecules are formed by such interactions.

I understand that when the simple materials of the earth's atmosphere which were present before life began—hydrogen, oxygen, and nitrogen, in the form of water and ammonia—are infused by electrical charges or by radiation, heavier molecules begin to form first, followed by the more complex amino acids. We seem only a step away from the formation of viruses and the even more complex living organisms. A creative, not a disintegrative process, is at work.

Another fascinating example is the formation of crystals. In every case, from less ordered and less symmetrical fluid matter there emerges the startlingly unique, ordered symmetrical and often beautiful crystalline form. All of us have marveled at the perfection and complexity of the snowflake. Yet it emerged from formless vapor.

When we consider the single living cell, we discover that it often forms more complex colonies, as in coral reefs. Even more order enters the picture as the cell emerges into an organism of many cells with specialized functions.

I do not need to portray the whole gradual process of organic evolution. We are all familiar with the steadily increasing complexity of organisms. They are not always successful in their ability to cope with the changing environment, but the trend toward complexity is always evident.

Perhaps, for most of us, the process of organic evolution is best recognized as we consider the development of the single fertilized human ovum through the simplest stages of cell division, then the aquatic gill stage, and on to the vastly complex, highly organized human infant. As Jonas Salk has said, there is a manifest and increasing order in evolution.

Thus, without ignoring the tendency toward deterioration, we need to recognize fully what Szent-Gyoergyi terms "syntropy" and what Whyte calls the "morphic tendency," the ever operating trend toward increased order and interrelated complexity evident at both the inorganic and the organic level. The universe is always building and creating as well as deteriorating. This process is evident in the human being, too.

THE FUNCTION OF CONSCIOUSNESS
IN HUMAN BEINGS

What part does our awareness have in this formative function? I believe that consciousness has a small but very important part. The ability to focus conscious attention seems to be one of the latest evolutionary developments in our species. This ability can be described as a tiny peak of awareness, of symbolizing capacity, topping a vast pyramid of nonconscious organismic functioning. Perhaps a better analogy, more indicative of the continual change going on, is to think of the pyramid as a large fountain of the same shape. The very tip of the fountain is intermittently illuminated with the flickering light of consciousness, but the constant flow of life goes on in the darkness as well, in nonconscious as well as conscious ways. It seems that the human organism has been moving toward the more complete development of awareness. It is at this level that new forms are invented, perhaps even new directions for the human species. It is here that the reciprocal relationship between cause and effect is most demonstrably evident. It is here that choices are made, spontaneous forms created. We see here perhaps the highest of the human functions.

Some of my colleagues have said that organismic choice—the nonverbal, subconscious choice of way of being—is guided by the evolutionary flow. I agree; I will even go one step further. I would point out that in psychotherapy we have learned something about the psychological conditions that are most conducive to increasing this highly important self-awareness. With greater self-awareness, a more informed choice is possible, a choice more free from introjects, a *conscious* choice that is even more in tune with the evolutionary flow. Such a person is more potentially aware, not only of the stimuli from outside, but of ideas and dreams, and of the ongoing flow of feelings, emotions, and physiological reactions that he or she senses from within. The greater this awareness, the more surely the person will float in a direction consonant with the directional evolutionary flow.

When a person is functioning in this way, it does not mean that there is a self-conscious awareness of all that is going on within, like the centipede whose movements were paralyzed when it became aware of each of its legs. On the contrary, such a person is free to live a feeling subjectively, as well as be aware of it. The individual might experience love, or pain, or fear, or just live in these experiences subjectively. Or, he or she might abstract self from this subjectivity and realize in awareness, "I am in pain;" "I am afraid;" "I do love." The crucial point is that when a person is functioning fully, there are no barriers, no inhibitions, which prevent the full experiencing of whatever is organismically present. This person is moving in the direction of wholeness, integration, a unified life. Consciousness is participating in this larger, creative, formative tendency.

ALTERED STATES OF CONSCIOUSNESS

But some go even further in their theories. Researchers such as Grof and Grof (1977) and Lilly (1973) believe that persons are able to advance beyond the ordinary level of consciousness. Their studies appear to reveal that in altered states of consciousness, persons feel they are in touch with, and grasp the meaning of, this evolutionary flow. They experience it as tending toward a transcending experience of unity. They picture the individual self as being dissolved in a whole area of higher values, especially beauty, harmony, and love. The person feels at one with the cosmos. Hard-headed research seems to be confirming the mystic's experience of union with the universal.

For me, this point of view is confirmed by my more recent experience in working with clients, and especially in dealing with intensive groups. I described earlier those characteristics of a growth-promoting relationship that have been investigated and supported by research. But recently, my view has broadened into a new area which cannot as yet be studied empirically.

When I am at my best, as a group facilitator or as a therapist, I discover another characteristic. I find that when I am closest to my inner, intuitive self, when I am somehow in touch with the unknown in me, when perhaps I am in a slightly altered state of consciousness, then whatever I do seems to be full of healing. Then, simply my *presence* is releasing and helpful to the other. There is nothing I can do to force this experience, but when I can relax and be close to the transcendental core of me, then I may behave in strange and impulsive ways in the relationship, ways which I cannot justify rationally, which have nothing to do with my thought processes. But these strange behaviors turn out to be *right*, in some odd way: it seems that my inner spirit has reached out and touched the inner spirit of the other. Our relationship transcends itself and becomes a part of something larger. Profound growth and healing and energy are present.

This kind of transcendent phenomenon has certainly been experienced at times in groups in which I have worked, changing the lives of some of those involved. One participant in a workshop put it eloquently: "I found it to be a profound spiritual experience. I felt the oneness of spirit in the community. We breathed together, felt together, even spoke for one another. I felt the power of the 'life force' that infuses each of us—whatever that is. I felt its presence without the usual barricades of 'me-ness' or 'you-ness'—it was like a meditative experience when I feel myself as a center of consciousness, very much a part of the broader, universal consciousness. And yet with that extraordinary sense of oneness, the separateness of each person present has never been more clearly preserved."

Again, as in the description of altered states of consciousness, this account partakes of the mystical. Our experiences in therapy and in groups, it is clear, involve the transcendent, the indescribable, the spiritual. I am compelled to believe that I, like many others, have underestimated the importance of this mystical, spiritual dimension.

SCIENCE AND THE MYSTICAL

Here many readers, I am sure, will part company with me. What, they will wish to know, has become of logic, of science, of hard-headedness? But before they leave me entirely, I would like to adduce some surprising support for such views, from the most unexpected quarters.

Fritjof Capra (1975), a well-known theoretical physicist, has shown how present-day physics has almost completely abolished any solid concepts of our world, with the exception of energy. In a summarizing statement, he says, "In modern physics the universe is thus experienced as a dynamic, inseparable whole which always includes the observer in an essential way. In this experience the traditional concepts of space and time, of isolated objects, and of cause and effect lose their meaning. Such an experience, however, is very similar to that of the Eastern mystics" (p. 81). He then goes on to point out the astonishing parallels of Zen, Taoism, Buddhism, and other Oriental views. His own conviction is that physics and Eastern mysticism are separate but complementary roads to the same knowledge, supplementing each other in providing a fuller understanding of the universe.

Recently, the work of chemist-philosopher Ilya Prigogine (Ferguson, 1979) offers a different perspective, which also throws new light on what I have been discussing.

In trying to answer the basic question of how order and complexity emerge from the process of entropy, he has originated an entirely new theoretical system. He has developed mathematical formulas and proofs which demonstrate that the world of living nature is probabilistic, rather than solely deterministic. His views apply to all open systems in which energy is exchanged with the environment. This obviously includes the human organism.

Briefly, the more complex the structure—whether a chemical or a human—the more energy it expends to maintain that complexity. For example, the human brain, with only 2 percent of body weight, uses 20 percent of the available oxygen! Such a system is unstable, has fluctuations or "perturbations," as Prigogine calls them. As these fluctuations increase, they are amplified by the system's many connections, and thus drive the system—whether chemical compound or human individual—into a new, altered state, *more* ordered and coherent than before. This new state has still greater complexity, and hence, even more potential for creating change.

The transformation from one state to another is a sudden shift, a nonlinear event, in which many factors act on one another at once. It is especially interesting to me that this phenomenon has already been demonstrated by Don (1977–1978) in his investigation of Gendlin's concept of "experiencing" in psychotherapy (Gendlin,

1978). When a hitherto repressed feeling is fully and acceptantly experienced in awareness during the therapeutic relationship, there is not only a definitely felt psychological shift, but also a concomitant physiological change, as a new state of insight is achieved.

Prigogine's theory appears to shed light on meditation, relaxation techniques, and altered states of consciousness, in which fluctuations are augmented by various means. It gives support to the value of fully recognizing and expressing one's feelings—positive or negative—thus permitting the full perturbation of the system.

Prigogine recognizes the strong resemblance between his "science of complexity" and the views of Eastern sages and mystics, as well as the philosophies of Alfred North Whitehead and Henri Bergson. His view points, he says, toward "a deep collective vision." Rather amazingly, the title of his latest book is *From Being to Becoming* (1979), a strange label for a volume by a chemist-philosopher. His conclusion can be stated very briefly: "The more complex a system, the greater its potential for self-transcendence: its parts cooperate to reorganize it" (Ferguson, 1979).

Thus, from theoretical physics and chemistry comes some confirmation of the validity of experiences that are transcendent, indescribable, unexpected, transformational—the sort of phenomena that I and my colleagues have observed and felt as concomitants of the person-centered approach.

A HYPOTHESIS FOR THE FUTURE

As I try to take into account the scope of the various themes I have presented, along with some of the available evidence that appears to support them, I am led to formulate a broad hypothesis. In my mind, this hypothesis is very tentative. But, for the sake of clarity, I will state it in definite terms.

I hypothesize that there is a formative directional tendency in the universe, which can be traced and observed in stellar space, in crystals, in microorganisms, in more complex organic life, and in human beings. This is an evolutionary tendency toward greater order, greater complexity, greater interrelatedness. In humankind, this tendency exhibits itself as the individual moves from a single-cell origin to complex organic functioning, to knowing and sensing below the level of consciousness, to a conscious awareness of the organism and the external world, to a transcendent awareness of the harmony and unity of the cosmic system, including humankind.

It seems to me just possible that this hypothesis could be a base upon which we could begin to build a theory for humanistic psychology. It definitely forms a base for the person-centered approach.

humanistic psych in future.

CONCLUSIONS

What I have been saying is that in our work as person-centered therapists and facilitators, we have discovered the attitudinal qualities that are demonstrably effective in releasing constructive and growthful changes in the personality and behavior of individuals. Persons in an environment infused with these attitudes develop more self-understanding, more self-confidence, more ability to choose their behaviors. They learn more significantly, they have more freedom to be and become.

The individual in this nurturing climate is free to choose *any* direction, but actually selects positive and constructive ways. The actualizing tendency is operative in the human being.

It is still further confirming to find that this is not simply a tendency in living systems but is part of a strong formative tendency in our universe, which is evident at all levels.

Thus, when we provide a psychological climate that permits persons to *be*—whether they are clients, students, workers, or persons in a group—we are not involved in a chance event. We are tapping into a tendency which permeates all of organic life—a tendency to become all the complexity of which the organism is capable. And on an even larger scale, I believe we are tuning in to a potent creative tendency which has formed our universe, from the smallest snowflake to the largest galaxy, from the lowly amoeba to the most sensitive and gifted of persons. And perhaps we are touching the cutting edge of our ability to transcend ourselves, to create new and more spiritual directions in human evolution.

This kind of formulation is, for me, a philosophical base for a person-centered approach. It justifies me in engaging in a life-affirming way of being.

REFERENCES

ADLER, A. *Social interest: A challenge to mankind.* New York: Capricorn Books, 1964. (Originally published in 1933.)

ANGYAL, A. *Foundations for a science of personality.* New York: Commonwealth Fund, 1941.

ANGYAL, A. *Neurosis and treatment.* New York: John Wiley & Sons, 1965.

ASPY, D. *Toward a technology for humanizing education.* Champaign, Illinois: Research Press, 1972.

ASPY, D., & ROEBUCK, F. M. *A lever long enough.* Washington, D.C.: National Consortium for Humanizing Education, 1976.

CAPRA, F. *The Tao of physics.* Boulder, Colorado: Shambala, 1975.

DON, N. S. The transformation of conscious experience and its EEG correlates. *Journal of Altered States of Consciousness,* 1977–1978, p. 147.

FERGUSON, M. Special issue: Prigogine's science of becoming. *Brain/Mind Bulletin,* May 21, 1979, 4(13).

FREUD, S. Instincts and their vicissitudes. In *Collected papers* (Vol. 4). London: Hogarth Press and Institute of Psychoanalysis, 1953, pp. 60–83.

GENDLIN, E. T. *Focusing.* New York: Everest House, 1978.

GOLDSTEIN, K. *Human nature in the light of psychopathology.* Cambridge: Harvard University Press, 1947.

GROF, S., & GROF, J. H. *The human encounter with death.* New York: E. P. Dutton Co., 1977.

LILLY, J. C. *The center of the cyclone.* New York: Bantam Books, 1973. (Originally Julian Press, 1972.)

MASLOW, A. H. *Motivation and personality.* New York: Harper and Brothers, 1954.

MURAYAMA, M. Heterogenetics: An epistemological restructuring of biological and social sciences. *Acta biotheretica,* 1977, *26,* 120–137.

PENTONY, P. Rogers' formative tendency: an epistemological perspective. Unpublished manuscript, University of Canberra, Australia, 1978.

PRIGOGINE, I. *From being to becoming.* San Francisco: W. H. Freeman, 1979.

ROGERS, C. R. A theory of therapy, personality and interpersonal relationships. In S. Koch (Ed.), *Psychology: A study of a science* (Vol. 3). New York: McGraw-Hill, 1959, pp. 184–256.

ROGERS, C. R. Toward becoming a fully functioning person. In *Perceiving, behaving, becoming,* 1962 Yearbook, Association for Supervision and Curriculum Development. Washington, D.C.: National Education Association, 1962, pp. 21–23.

ROGERS, C. R. The actualizing tendency in relation to "motives" and to consciousness. In M. Jones (Ed.), *Nebraska Symposium on Motivation*, Lincoln: University of Nebraska Press, 1963, pp. 1–24.

ROGERS, C. R. The formative tendency. *Journal of Humanistic Psychology*, 1978, *18*(1), 23–26.

SMUTS, J. C. *Holism and evolution*. New York: Viking Press, 1961. (Originally published 1926.)

SZENT-GYOERGYI, A. Drive in living matter to perfect itself. *Synthesis*, Spring, 1974, pp. 12–24.

TAUSCH, R. Facilitative dimensions in interpersonal relations: Verifying the theoretical assumptions of Carl Rogers. *College Student Journal*, 1978, *12*(1), 2–11.

WHYTE, L. *The universe of experience*. New York: Harper & Row, 1974.

Empathic: An Unappreciated Way of Being

It is my thesis in this paper that we should re-examine and re-evaluate that very special way of being with another person which has been called "empathic." I believe we tend to give too little consideration to an element that is extremely important both for the understanding of personality dynamics and for effecting changes in personality and behavior. It is one of the most delicate and powerful ways we have of using ourselves. In spite of all that has been said and written on this topic, it is a way of being that is rarely seen in full bloom in a relationship. I start with my own somewhat faltering history in relation to this topic.

PERSONAL VACILLATIONS

Very early in my work as a therapist, I discovered that simply listening to my client, very attentively, was an important way of being helpful. So when I was in doubt as to what I should do in some active way, I listened. It seemed surprising to me that such a passive kind of interaction could be so useful.

A little later a social worker, who had a background of Rankian training, helped me to learn that the most effective approach was to listen for the feelings, the emotions, whose patterns could be discerned through the client's words. I believe she was the one who suggested that the best response was to "reflect" these feelings back to the client—"reflect" becoming in time a word that made me cringe. But at that time, it improved my work as therapist, and I was grateful.

Then came my transition to a full-time position at Ohio State University, where, with the help of students, I was at last able to scrounge equipment for recording my and my students' interviews. I cannot exaggerate the excitement of our learnings as we clustered about the machine that enabled us to listen to ourselves, playing over and over some puzzling point at which the interview clearly went wrong, or those moments in which the client moved significantly forward. (I still regard this as the one best way of learning to improve oneself as a therapist.) Among many lessons from these recordings, we came to realize that listening to feelings and "reflecting" them was a vastly complex process. We discovered that we could pinpoint which response of the therapist caused a fruitful flow of significant expression to become superficial and unprofitable. Likewise, we were able to spot the remark that turned a client's dull and desultory talk into a focused self-exploration.

In such a context of learning, it became quite natural to lay more stress upon the content of the therapist's response than upon the empathic quality of the listening. To this extent, we became heavily conscious of the techniques that the counselor or therapist was using. We became expert in analyzing, in very minute detail, the ebb and flow of the process in each interview, and we gained a great deal from that microscopic study.

But this tendency to focus on the therapist's

responses had appalling consequences. I had met hostility, but these reactions were worse. The whole approach came, in a few years, to be known as a technique. "Nondirective therapy," it was said, "is the technique of reflecting the client's feelings." Or an even worse caricature was simply that "in nondirective therapy you repeat the last words the client has said." I was so shocked by these complete distortions of our approach that for a number of years I said almost nothing about empathic listening, and when I did it was to stress an empathic attitude, with little comment as to how this might be implemented in the relationship. I preferred to discuss the qualities of positive regard and therapist congruence, which, together with empathy, I hypothesized as promoting the therapeutic process. They, too, were often misunderstood, but at least they were not caricatured.

THE CURRENT NEED

Over the years, however, the research evidence has kept piling up, and it points strongly to the conclusion that a high degree of empathy in a relationship is possibly *the* most potent factor in bringing about change and learning. And so I believe it is time for me to forget the caricatures and misrepresentations of the past and take a fresh look at empathy.

For still another reason it seems timely to do this. In the United States during the past decade or two, many new approaches to therapy have held center stage. Gestalt therapy, psychodrama, primal therapy, bioenergetics, rational-emotive therapy, and transactional analysis are some of the best known, but there are more. Part of their appeal lies in the fact that in most instances, the therapist is clearly the expert, actively manipulating the situation, often in dramatic ways, for the client's benefit. If I am reading the signs correctly, I believe there is a decrease in the fascination with such expertise in guidance. With behavior therapy, another approach based on expertise, I believe interest and fascination are still on the increase. A technological society has been delighted to have found a technology by which people's behavior can be shaped, even without their knowledge or approval, toward goals selected by therapists or by society. Yet even in this case, much questioning by thoughtful individuals is springing up as the philosophical and political implications of "behavior mod" become more clearly visible. So I have seen a willingness on the part of many to take another look at ways of being with people that locate power in the person, not the expert, and this brings me again to examine carefully what is meant by the term "empathy" and what we have come to know about it. Perhaps the time is ripe for its value to be appreciated.

EARLY DEFINITIONS

Many definitions have been given of the term, and I myself have set forth several. More than twenty years ago, I (Rogers, 1959) attempted to give a highly rigorous definition as part of a formal statement of my concepts and theory. It went as follows:

The state of empathy, or being empathic, is to perceive the internal frame of reference of another with accuracy and with the emotional components and meanings which pertain thereto as if one were the person, but without ever losing the "as if" condition. Thus it means to sense the hurt or the pleasure of another as he senses it and to perceive the causes thereof as he perceives them, but without ever losing the

recognition that it is as if *I were hurt or pleased and so forth.
If this "as if" quality is lost, then the state is one of identification. (pp. 210–211. See also Rogers, 1957.)*

EXPERIENCING AS A USEFUL CONSTRUCT

In formulating my current description, I have drawn on
the concept of "experiencing" as formulated by
Gendlin (1962). This concept has enriched my thinking
in various ways, as will be evident in this paper. Briefly,
it is his view that at all times there is going on in the
human organism a flow of experiencings to which the
individual can turn again and again as a referent in
order to discover the meaning of those experiences. An
empathic therapist points sensitively to the "felt meaning" which the client is experiencing in this particular
moment, in order to help him or her to focus on that
meaning and carry it further to its full and uninhibited
experiencing.

An example may clarify both the concept and its
relation to empathy. A man in an encounter group has
been making vaguely negative statements about his
father. The facilitator says, "It sounds as though you
might be angry at your father." The man replies, "No, I
don't think so." "Possibly dissatisfied with him?"
"Well, yes, perhaps" (said rather doubtfully). "Maybe
you're disappointed in him." Quickly the man
responds, "That's it! I *am* disappointed that he's not a
strong person. I think I've always been disappointed in
him ever since I was a boy."

Against what is the man checking these terms for
their correctness? Gendlin's view, with which I concur,
is that he is checking them against the ongoing psycho-
physiological flow within himself to see if they fit. This
flow is a very real thing, and people are able to use it as

a referent. In this case, "angry" doesn't match the felt meaning at all; "dissatisfied" comes closer, but is not really correct; "disappointed" matches it exactly, and encourages a further flow of the experiencing, as often happens.

A CURRENT DEFINITION

With this conceptual background, let me attempt a description of empathy that would seem satisfactory to me today. I would no longer be terming it a "state of empathy," because I believe it to be a process, rather than a state. Perhaps I can capture that quality.

An empathic way of being with another person has several facets. It means entering the private perceptual world of the other and becoming thoroughly at home in it. It involves being sensitive, moment by moment, to the changing felt meanings which flow in this other person, to the fear or rage or tenderness or confusion or whatever that he or she is experiencing. It means temporarily living in the other's life, moving about in it delicately without making judgments; it means sensing meanings of which he or she is scarcely aware, but not trying to uncover totally unconscious feelings, since this would be too threatening. It includes communicating your sensings of the person's world as you look with fresh and unfrightened eyes at elements of which he or she is fearful. It means frequently checking with the person as to the accuracy of your sensings, and being guided by the responses you receive. You are a confident companion to the person in his or her inner world. By pointing to the possible meanings in the flow of another person's experiencing, you help the other to focus on this useful type of referent, to experience the meanings more fully, and to move forward in the experiencing.

To be with another in this way means that for the time being, you lay aside your own views and values in order to enter another's world without prejudice. In some sense it means that you lay aside your self; this can only be done by persons who are secure enough in themselves that they know they will not get lost in what may turn out to be the strange or bizarre world of the other, and that they can comfortably return to their own world when they wish.

Perhaps this description makes clear that being empathic is a complex, demanding, and strong—yet also a subtle and gentle—way of being.

OPERATIONAL DEFINITIONS

The foregoing description is hardly an operational definition, suitable for use in research. Yet such operational definitions have been formulated and widely used. For example, the Barrett-Lennard Relationship Inventory, to be filled out by the parties to the relationship, defines empathy operationally by the items used. Some of the items from this instrument, indicating the range from empathic to nonempathic, follow:

He appreciates what my experience feels like to me.
He understands what I say from a detached, objective point of view.
He understands my words but not the way I feel.

Barrett-Lennard (1962) also has a specific conceptual formulation of empathy, upon which he based his items. While it definitely overlaps with the definition given above, it is sufficiently different to warrant its quotation.

Qualitatively it (emphatic understanding) is an active process of desiring to know the full, present and changing awareness of another person, of reaching out to receive his communication and meaning, and of translating his words and signs into experienced meaning *that matches* at least *those aspects of his awareness that are most important to him at the moment. It is an experiencing of the consciousness "behind" another's outward communication, but with continuous awareness that this consciousness is originating and proceeding in the other.*

Then there is the Accurate Empathy Scale, devised by Truax (1967) and others for use by raters. Even small portions of recorded interviews can be reliably rated by this scale. The nature of the scale may be indicated by giving the definition of Stage 1, which is the lowest level of empathic understanding, and Stage 8, which is a very high (though not the highest) degree of empathy. Here is Stage 1:

Therapist seems completely unaware of even the most conspicuous of the client's feelings. His responses are not appropriate to the mood and content of the client's statements and there is no determinable quality of empathy, hence, no accuracy whatsoever. The therapist may be bored and disinterested or actively offering advice, but he is not communicating an awareness of the client's current feelings. (pp. 556–557)

Stage 8 is defined as follows:

Therapist accurately interprets all the client's present acknowledged feelings. He also uncovers the most deeply shrouded of the client's feeling areas, voicing meanings in the client's experience of which the client is scarcely aware. He moves into feelings and experiences that are only hinted at by the client and does so with sensitivity and accuracy. The content that comes to life may be new but is not alien. While the therapist in Stage 8 makes mistakes, mistakes do not have a jarring note but are covered by the tentative character of the response. Also the therapist is sensitive to his mistakes and quickly alters or changes his responses in midstream, indicating that he more clearly knows what is being talked about and

what is being sought after in the client's own explorations.
The therapist reflects a togetherness with the [client] in ten-
tative trial and error exploration. His voice tone reflects the
seriousness and depth of his empathic grasp. (p. 566)

I have wished to indicate by these examples that the
empathic process can be defined in theoretical, conceptual, subjective, and operational ways. Even so, we
have not reached the limits of its base.

A DEFINITION FOR CONTEMPORARY
PERSONS

Eugene Gendlin and others (Gendlin & Hendricks,
undated) have recently been involved in a helping-com-
munity enterprise called "Changes," which has many
implications for dealing with the alienated and counter-
culture members of the chaos which we call urban living. Of particular interest is the "Rap Manual," which
has been developed to aid the ordinary person in learning "how to help with the other person's process."

The Manual starts out with a section on "Absolute
Listening." Some excerpts give the flavor:

This is not laying trips on people. You only listen and say
back the other person's thing, step by step, just as that person
seems to have it at that moment. You never mix into it any of
your own things or ideas, never lay on the other person any-
thing that person didn't express. . . . To show that you under-
stand exactly, make a sentence or two which gets exactly at
the personal meaning this person wanted to put across. This
might be in your own words, usually, but use that person's
own words for the touchy main things.

It continues in this same vein, with many detailed
suggestions, including ideas on "how to know when
you're doing it right."

So it seems clear that an empathic way of being, although highly subtle conceptually, can also be described in terms which are perfectly understandable by contemporary youth or citizens of a beleaguered inner city. It is a broad-ranging conception.

GENERAL RESEARCH FINDINGS

What have we come to know about empathy through research based on the instruments mentioned above, as well as others which have been devised? We have learned a great deal, and I will present some of these learnings, giving first some of the interesting general findings. I will reserve until later an analysis of the effects of an empathic climate on the dynamics of the behavior of the recipient. Here, then, are some of the general statements which can be made with assurance:

The ideal therapist is, first of all, empathic. When psychotherapists of many different orientations describe their concept of the ideal therapist—the therapist they would like to become—they are in high agreement in giving empathy the highest ranking out of twelve variables. This statement is based on a study by Raskin (1974) of eighty-three practicing therapists with at least eight different therapeutic approaches. The definition of the empathic quality was very similar to that used in this paper. Raskin's study corroborates and strengthens an earlier research by Fiedler (1950b). So we may conclude that therapists recognize that the most important factor in *being* a therapist is "trying, as sensitively and as accurately as [one] can, to understand the client, *from the latter's own point of view*" (Raskin, 1974).

Empathy is correlated with self-exploration and process movement. It has been learned that a high degree of empathy in the therapeutic relationship is associated with various aspects of process and progress in the therapy. Such a climate is definitely related to a high degree of self-exploration in the client (Bergin & Strupp, 1972; Kurtz & Grummon, 1972; Tausch, Bastine, Friese, & Sander, 1970).

Empathy early in the relationship predicts later success. The degree of empathy that exists and will exist in the relationship can be determined very early, by the fifth or even the second interview. Such early measurements are predictive of the later success or lack of success in therapy (Barrett-Lennard, 1962; Tausch, 1973). The implication of these findings is that we could avoid a great deal of unsuccessful therapy by measuring the therapist's empathy early on.

In successful cases, the client comes to perceive more empathy. In successful cases, the client's perception of the empathic quality in the relationship increases over time, although the increase is not very great; objective judges are found to have the same perceptions as the clients (Cartwright & Lerner, 1966; van der Veen, 1970).

Empathic understanding is provided freely by the therapist, not drawn from him or her. Empathy is something *offered* by the therapist, and not simply elicited by some particular type of client (Tausch et al., 1970; Truax & Carkhuff, 1967). There have been speculations to the contrary: that an appealing or seducing client might be responsible for drawing understanding from the therapist. The evidence does not support this. Indeed, the degree of empathy in a relationship can be rather accurately inferred simply by listening to the therapist's responses, without any knowledge of the client's statements (Quinn, 1953). So, if an empathic climate exists in a relationship, the probability is high that the therapist is responsible for it.

The more experienced the therapist is, the more likely he or she is to be empathic. Experienced therapists offer a higher degree of empathy to their clients than those less experienced, whether this quality is being assessed through the client's perception or through the ears of qualified judges (Barrett-Lennard, 1962; Fiedler, 1949, 1950a; Mullen & Abeles, 1972). Evidently, therapists do learn, as the years go by, to come closer to their ideal of a therapist and to be more sensitively understanding.

Empathy is a special quality in a relationship, and therapists offer definitely more of it than even helpful friends (van der Veen, 1970). This is reassuring.

The better integrated the therapist is, the higher the degree of empathy he or she exhibits. Personality disturbance in the therapist goes along with a lower empathic understanding. Therapists who are free from discomfort and confident in interpersonal relationships can offer more of understanding (Bergin & Jasper, 1969; Bergin & Solomon, 1970). As I have considered this evidence and also my own experience in the training of therapists, I come to the somewhat uncomfortable conclusion that the more psychologically mature and integrated the therapist is, the more helpful is the relationship that he or she provides. This puts a heavy demand on the therapist as a person.

Experienced therapists often fall short of being empathic. In spite of what has been said of experienced therapists, they differ sharply in the degree of empathy they offer. Raskin (1974) showed that when the recorded interviews of six experienced therapists were rated by eighty-three other experienced therapists, the differences on twelve variables were significant at the .001 level, and empathy was second in the extent of difference. The outstanding characteristic of the client-centered therapist was his empathy. Other types of therapeutic approaches had as their outstanding characteristic their cognitive quality, their therapist-directedness, and the like. So, although therapists regarded empathic listening as the most important element in their *ideal*, in their actual *practice* they often fell far short of this. In fact, the ratings of the recorded interviews of these six expert therapists by other therapists turned up a surprising finding. In only two cases did the ratings of the work of the experts correlate positively with the collective description of the ideal therapist. In four cases the correlation was negative, the most extreme being a −.66! So much for therapy as it is practiced!

Clients are better judges of the degree of empathy than are therapists. Perhaps, then, it is not too surprising that therapists prove to be rather inaccurate in assessing their own degree of empathy in a relationship. The client's perception of this quality agrees rather well with that of unbiased judges listening to the recordings, but the agreement between clients and therapists, or judges and therapists, is low (Rogers, Gendlin, Kiesler, & Truax, 1967, chaps. 5, 8). Perhaps, if we wish to become better therapists, we should let our clients tell us whether we are understanding them accurately!

Brilliance and diagnostic perceptiveness are unrelated to empathy. It is important to know that the degree to which therapists create an empathic climate is not related to their academic performance or intellectual competence (Bergin & Jasper, 1969; Bergin & Solomon, 1970). Neither is it related to the accuracy of their perception of individuals or their diagnostic competence. In fact, it may be negatively related to the latter (Fiedler, 1953). This is a most important finding. If

neither academic brilliance nor diagnostic skill is significant, then clearly an empathic quality belongs in a different realm of discourse from most clinical thinking—
psychological and psychiatric. I believe that therapists
are reluctant to accept the implications.

*An empathic way of being can be learned from
empathic persons.* Perhaps the most important statement of all is that the ability to be accurately empathic
is something that can be developed by training. Therapists, teachers, and parents can be helped to become
empathic. This is especially likely to occur if their own
supervisors, teachers, and parents are individuals of
sensitive understanding (Aspy, 1972; Aspy & Roebuck,
1975; Guerney, Andronico, & Guerney, 1970). It is most
encouraging to know that this subtle, elusive quality, of
utmost importance in therapy, is not something one is
"born with"; rather, it can be learned, and learned
most rapidly in an empathic climate. Perhaps only two
basic elements of therapeutic effectiveness can profit
from cognitive and experiential training: empathy and
congruence.

THE CONSEQUENCES OF AN
EMPATHIC CLIMATE

So much for the knowledge that has been gained *about*
empathy. But what effects do a series of deeply
empathic responses have upon the recipient? Here the
evidence is quite overwhelming. *Empathy is clearly
related to positive outcome.* From schizophrenic
patients in psychiatric hospitals to pupils in ordinary
classrooms, from clients of a counseling center to
teachers in training, from neurotics in Germany to neurotics in the United States, the evidence is the same: it
indicates that the more sensitively understanding is the

therapist or teacher, the more likely are constructive learning and change to take place (Aspy, 1972, chap. 4; Aspy & Roebuck, 1975; Barrett-Lennard, 1962; Bergin & Jasper, 1969; Bergin & Strupp, 1972; Halkides, 1958; Kurtz & Grummon, 1972; Mullen & Abeles, 1972; Rogers et al., 1967, chaps. 5, 9; Tausch, Bastine, Bommert, Minsel, Nickel, & Langer, 1972; Truax, 1966). As stated by Bergin and Strupp (1972), various studies "demonstrate a positive correlation between therapist empathy, patient self-exploration, and independent criteria of patient change" (p. 25).

Yet, I believe that far too little attention has been given these findings. This deceptively simple empathic interaction has many profound consequences. I want to discuss these at some length.

First, empathy dissolves alienation. For the moment, at least, the recipient finds himself or herself a connected part of the human race. Although it may not be articulated clearly, the experience goes something like this: "I have been talking about hidden things, partly veiled even from myself, feelings that are strange— possibly abnormal—feelings I have never communicated to another, nor even clearly to myself. And yet, another person has understood, understood my feelings even more clearly than I do. If someone else knows what I am talking about, what I mean, then to this degree I am not so strange, or alien, or set apart. I make sense to another human being. So I am in touch with, even in relationship with, others. I am no longer an isolate."

Perhaps this explains one of the major findings of our study of psychotherapy with schizophrenics. We found that those patients receiving from their therapists a high degree of accurate empathy as rated by unbiased judges, showed the sharpest reduction in schizophrenic pathology as measured by the Minnesota Multiphasic

Personality Inventory (Rogers et al., 1967, p. 85). This suggests that the sensitive understanding by another may have been the most potent element in bringing the schizophrenics out of their estrangement, and into the world of relatedness. Carl Jung has said that schizophrenics cease to be schizophrenic when they meet other persons by whom they feel understood. Our study provides empirical evidence in support of that statement.

Other studies, both of schizophrenics and of counseling center clients, show that a low level of empathy is related to a slight worsening in adjustment and pathology. Here, too, the findings make sense. It is as though the individual concludes: "If no one understands me, if no one can grasp what these experiences are like, then I am indeed in a bad way—more abnormal than I thought." One of R. D. Laing's patients states this feeling vividly in describing earlier contacts with psychiatrists:

> It's a most terrifying feeling to realize that the doctor can't see the real you, that he can't understand what you feel and that he's just going ahead with his own ideas. I would start to feel that I was invisible or maybe not there at all. (Laing, 1965, p. 166)

A second consequence of empathic understanding is that the recipient feels valued, cared for, accepted as the person that he or she is. It might seem that we have here stepped into another area, and that we are no longer speaking of empathy. But this is not so. It is impossible to accurately sense the perceptual world of another person unless you value that person and his or her world—unless you, in some sense, care. Hence, the message comes through to the recipient that "this other individual trusts me, thinks I'm worthwhile. Perhaps I

am worth something. Perhaps *I* could value *myself.*
Perhaps I could care for myself."

A vivid example of this comes from a young man who
has been a recipient of much sensitive understanding
and who is now in the later stages of his therapy:

CLIENT *I could even conceive of it as a possibility that I could
have a kind of tender concern for me. Still, how could I be
tender, be concerned for* myself, *when they're one and the
same thing? But yet I can* feel *it so clearly—you know, like
taking care of a child. You want to give it this and give it that.
I can kind of clearly see the purposes for somebody else, but I
can never see them for myself, that I could do this for me, you
know. Is it possible that I can really want to take care of
myself, and make that a major purpose of my life? That
means I'd have to deal with the whole world as if I were
guardian of the most cherished and most wanted possession,
that this I was between this precious* me *that I wanted to take
care of and the whole world. It's almost as if I* loved *myself;
you know, that's strange—but it's true.*
THERAPIST *It seems such a strange concept to realize. It would
mean I would face the world as though a part of my primary
responsibility was taking care of this precious individual who
is me—whom I love.*
CLIENT *Whom I care for—whom I feel so* close to. *Woof!
That's another* strange *one.*
THERAPIST *It just seems* weird.
CLIENT *Yeah. It hits rather close somehow. The idea of my
loving me and taking care of me. (His eyes grow moist.) That's
a very nice one—very nice.*

It is, I believe, the therapist's caring understanding—exhibited in this excerpt as well as previously—
which has permitted this client to experience a high
regard, even a love, for himself.

Still a third impact of a sensitive understanding
comes from its nonjudgmental quality. The highest
expression of empathy is accepting and nonjudgmental.

This is true because it is impossible to be accurately perceptive of another's inner world if you have formed an evaluative opinion of that person. If you doubt this statement, choose someone you know with whom you deeply disagree and who is, in your judgment, definitely wrong or mistaken. Now try to state that individual's views, beliefs, and feelings so accurately that he or she will agree that you have sensitively and correctly described his or her stance. I predict that nine times out of ten you will fail, because your judgment of the person's views creeps into your description of them.

Consequently, true empathy is always free of any evaluative or diagnostic quality. The recipient perceives this with some surprise: "If I am not being judged, perhaps I am not so evil or abnormal as I have thought. Perhaps I don't have to judge myself so harshly." Thus, the possibility of self-acceptance is gradually increased.

There comes to mind a psychologist whose interest in psychotherapy started as a result of his research in visual perception. In this research, many students were interviewed and asked to relate their visual and perceptual history, including any difficulties in seeing or reading, their reaction to wearing glasses, and so forth. The psychologist simply listened with interest, made no judgments on what he was hearing, and completed the gathering of his data. To his amazement, a number of these students returned spontaneously to thank him for all the help he had given them. He had, in his opinion, given them no help at all. But it forced him to recognize that interested nonevaluative listening is a potent therapeutic force, even when directed at a narrow sector of life, and with no intent of being helpful.

Perhaps another way of putting some of what I have been saying is that a finely tuned understanding by another individual gives the recipient a sense of personhood, of identity. Laing (1965) has said that "the sense of identity requires the existence of another by whom one is known" (p. 139). Buber has also spoken of the need to have our existence confirmed by another. Empathy gives that needed confirmation that one does exist as a separate, valued person with an identity.

Let us turn to a more specific result of the empathic interaction, in which individuals feel understood. Persons begin revealing material that they have never communicated before, in the process discovering previously unknown elements in themselves. Such an element may be "I never knew before that I was angry at my father," or "I never realized that I am afraid of succeeding." Such discoveries are unsettling but exciting. To perceive a new aspect of oneself is the first step toward changing the concept of oneself. The new element is, in an understanding atmosphere, owned and assimilated into a now altered self-concept. This is the basis, in my estimation, of the behavior changes that can come about as a result of psychotherapy. Once the self-concept changes, behavior changes to match the freshly perceived self.

If we think, however, that empathy is effective only in the one-to-one relationship called psychotherapy, we are greatly mistaken. Even in the classroom it makes an important difference. When teachers show evidence that they understand the meaning of classroom experiences for students, learning improves. In studies made by Aspy and colleagues, it was found that children's reading improved significantly more when teachers exhibited a high degree of understanding than in classrooms where such understanding did not exist. This finding has been replicated in many classrooms (Aspy, 1972, chap. 4; Aspy & Roebuck, 1975). Just as clients in psychotherapy find that empathy provides a climate for learning more of themselves, so students in the classroom find themselves in a climate for learning subject matter when they are in the presence of an understanding teacher.

Thus far, I have spoken of the more obvious change-producing effects of empathy. I should like to turn to an aspect having to do with the dynamics of personality.

When persons are perceptively understood, they find themselves coming in closer touch with a wider range of their experiencing. This gives them an expanded referent to which they can turn for guidance in understanding themselves and in directing their behavior. If the empathy has been accurate and deep, they may also be able to unblock a flow of experiencing and permit it to run its uninhibited course.

What is meant by these statements? I believe they will be clearer if I present an excerpt from a recorded interview with Mrs. Oak, a middle-aged woman in the later stages of therapy. She is exploring some of the complex feelings that have been troubling her.

CLIENT *I have the feeling it isn't guilt. (Pause. She weeps.) Of course, I mean, I can't verbalize it yet. (Then, with a rush of emotion.) It's just being terribly hurt!*

THERAPIST *Mm-hmm. It isn't guilt except in the sense of being very much wounded somehow.*

CLIENT *(Weeping.) It's—you know, often I've been guilty of it myself, but in later years when I've heard parents say to their children, "Stop crying!" I've had a feeling, a hurt, as though, well, why should they tell them to stop crying? They feel sorry for themselves, and who can feel more adequately sorry for himself than the child? Well, that is sort of what I mean, as though I mean, I thought that they should let him cry. And . . . feel sorry for him too, maybe. In a rather objective kind of way. Well, that's . . . something of the kind of thing I've been experiencing. I mean, now—just right now. And in—in—*

THERAPIST *That catches a little more of the flavor of the feeling, that it's almost as if you're really weeping for yourself.*

CLIENT *Yeah. And again, you see, there's conflict. Our culture is such that . . . I mean, one doesn't indulge in self-pity. But this isn't—I mean, I feel it doesn't quite have that connotation. It may have.*

THERAPIST *You sort of think there is a cultural objection to feeling sorry about yourself. And yet you feel the feeling you're experiencing isn't quite what the culture objects to either.*

CLIENT *And then of course, I've come to . . . to see and to feel that over this—see, I've covered it up. (Weeps.) But I've covered it up with so much bitterness, which in turn I had to cover up. (Weeping.) That's what I want to get rid of! I almost don't care if I hurt.*

THERAPIST *(Softly, and with an empathic tenderness toward the hurt she is experiencing.) You feel that here at the basis of it as you experience it, is a feeling of real tears for yourself. But that you can't show, mustn't show, so that's been covered by bitterness that you don't like, that you'd like to be rid of. You almost feel you'd rather absorb the hurt than to—than to feel the bitterness. (Pause.) And what you seem to be saying quite strongly is, "I do hurt, and I've tried to cover it up."*

CLIENT *I didn't know it.*

THERAPIST *Mm-hmmm. Like a new discovery, really.*

CLIENT *(Speaking at the same time.) I never really did know. But it's—you know, it's almost a physical thing. It's—it's sort of as though I were looking within myself at all kinds of— nerve endings and bits of things that have been sort of mashed. (Weeping.)*

THERAPIST *As though some of the most delicate aspects of you, physically almost, have been crushed or hurt.*

CLIENT *Yes. And you know, I do get the feeling, "Oh you poor thing."*

Here it is clear that empathic therapist responses encourage her in the wider exploration of, and closer acquaintance with, the visceral experiencing going on within. She is learning to listen to her guts (to use an inelegant term). She has expanded her knowledge of the flow of her experiencing.

Here, too, we see how this unverbalized visceral flow is used as a referent. How does she know that "guilt" is not the word to describe her feeling? She knows by turning within, taking another look at this reality, this palpable process that is taking place, this experiencing. And so she can test the word "hurt" against this referent, and she finds it closer. Only when she tries on the phrase, "Oh you poor thing," does it really fit the inner felt meaning of compassion and sorrow for herself. In my judgment, she has not only used this aspect of her experiencing as a referent, but has also learned something about this process of checking with her total physiological being—a learning she can apply again and again. And empathy has helped to make it possible.

We can also find in this slice of therapy what it means to let an experiencing run its course. This is clearly not a new feeling. She has often felt it before, yet it has never been lived out. It has been blocked in some way. I am quite clear as to the reality and vividness of the unblocking that follows, because I have many times been a party to its occurrence, but I am not sure how it may best be described. It seems to me that only when a gut-level experience is fully accepted and accurately labeled in awareness can it be completed. Then the person can move beyond it. Again, it is the sensitively empathic climate that helps to move the experiencing forward to its conclusion, which, in this case, is the uninhibited experiencing of the pity she feels for herself.

CONCLUSIONS

I wish now to back off and give a rather different perspective on the significance of empathy. We can say that when persons find themselves sensitively and accurately understood, they develop a set of growth-promoting or therapeutic attitudes toward themselves. Let me explain:

1. The nonevaluative and acceptant quality of the empathic climate enables persons, as we have seen, to take a prizing, caring attitude toward themselves.

2. Being listened to by someone who understands makes it possible for persons to listen more accurately to themselves, with greater empathy toward their own visceral experiencing, their own vaguely felt meanings.

3. The individuals' greater understanding of and prizing of themselves opens to them new facets of experience which become part of a more accurately based self-concept.

The self is now more congruent with the experiencing. Thus, the persons have become, in their attitudes toward themselves, more caring and acceptant, more empathic and understanding, more real and congruent. But these three elements are the very ones that both experience and research indicate are the attitudes of an effective therapist. So we are perhaps not overstating the total picture if we say that an emphatic understanding by another enables a person to become a more effective growth enhancer, a more effective therapist, for himself or herself.

Consequently, whether we are functioning as therapists, as encounter-group facilitators, as teachers, or as parents, we have in our hands, if we are able to take an empathic stance, a powerful force for change and growth. Its strength needs to be appreciated.

Finally, I want to put all that I have said into a larger context. Because I have been speaking only of the empathic process, it may seem that I regard this as the *only* important factor in growthful relationships. I would not wish to leave that impression. I would like briefly to state my views on the significance of what I see as the three attitudinal elements making for growth, and their relationship to one another.

In the ordinary interactions of life—between marital and sex partners, between teacher and student, employer and employee, or between colleagues or friends—congruence is probably the most important element. Congruence, or genuineness, involves letting the other person know "where you are" emotionally. It may involve confrontation and the straightforward expression of personally owned feelings—both negative and positive. Thus, congruence is a basis for living together in a climate of realness.

But in certain other special situations, caring, or prizing, may turn out to be the most significant element. Such situations include nonverbal relationships—between parent and infant, therapist and mute psychotic, physician and very ill patient. Caring is an attitude that is known to foster creativity—a nurturing climate in which delicate, tentative new thoughts and productive processes can emerge.

Then, in my experience, there are other situations in which the empathic way of being has the highest priority. When the other person is hurting, confused, troubled, anxious, alienated, terrified, or when he or she is doubtful of self-worth, uncertain as to identity—then understanding is called for. The gentle and sensitive companionship offered by an empathic person (who must, of course, possess the other two attitudes) provides illumination and healing. In such situations deep understanding is, I believe, the most precious gift one can give to another.

REFERENCES

ASPY, D. *Toward a technology for humanizing education.* Champaign, Illinois: Research Press, 1972.

ASPY, D., & ROEBUCK, F. From humane ideas to humane technology and back again, many times. *Education,* 1974, *95*(2), 163–171.

BARRETT-LENNARD, G. T. Dimensions of therapist response as causal factors in therapeutic change. *Psychological Monographs,* 1962, *76*(43, Whole No. 562).

BERGIN, A. E., & JASPER, L. G. Correlates of empathy in psychotherapy: A replication. *Journal of Abnormal Psychology,* 1969, *74,* 477–481.

BERGIN, A. E., & SOLOMON, S. Personality and performance correlates of empathic understanding in psychotherapy. In J. T. Hart & T. M. Tomlinson (Eds.), *New directions in client-centered therapy.* Boston: Houghton Mifflin, 1970.

BERGIN, A. E., & STRUPP, H. H. *Changing frontiers in the science of psychotherapy.* Chicago: Aldine-Atherton, 1972.

BLOCKSMA, D. D. *An experiment in counselor learning.* Unpublished doctoral dissertation, University of Chicago, 1951.

CARTWRIGHT, R. D., & LERNER, B. Empathy, need to change, and improvement in psychotherapy. In G. E. Stollak, B. G. Guerney, Jr., & M. Rothberg (Eds.), *Psychotherapy research: Selected readings.* Chicago: Rand McNally, 1966.

FIEDLER, F. E. *A comparative investigation of early therapeutic relationships created by experts and non-experts of the psychoanalytic, non-directive, and Adlerian schools.* Unpublished doctoral dissertation, University of Chicago, 1949.

FIEDLER, F. E. A comparison of therapeutic relationships in

psychoanalytic, non-directive and Adlerian therapy. *Journal of Consulting Psychology*, 1950, *14*, 436–445. (a)

FIEDLER, F. E. The concept of the ideal therapeutic relationship. *Journal of Consulting Psychology*, 1950, *14*, 239–245. (b)

FIEDLER, F. E. Quantitative studies on the role of therapists' feelings toward their patients. In O. H. Mowrer (Ed.), *Psychotherapy theory and research*. New York: Ronald Press, 1953.

GENDLIN, E. T. *Experiencing and the creation of meaning*. New York: The Free Press of Glencoe, 1962.

GENDLIN, E. T., & HENDRICKS, M. Rap manual, *Changes*. Chicago, Illinois, mimeographed document, undated.

GUERNEY, B. G., JR., ANDRONICO, M. P., & GUERNEY, L. F. Filial therapy. In J. T. Hart & T. M. Tomlinson (Eds.), *New directions in client-centered therapy*. Boston: Houghton Mifflin, 1970.

HALKIDES, G. *An experimental study of four conditions necessary for therapeutic change*. Unpublished doctoral dissertation, University of Chicago, 1958.

KURTZ, R. R., & GRUMMON, D. L. Different approaches to the measurement of therapist empathy and their relationship to therapy outcomes. *Journal of Consulting and Clinical Psychology*, 1972, *39*(1), 106–115.

LAING, R. D. *The divided self*. London: Tavistock, 1960. Pelican edition, 1965.

MULLEN, J., & ABELES, N. Relationship of liking, empathy, and therapist's experience to outcome of therapy. In *Psychotherapy, 1971, an Aldine annual*. Chicago: Aldine-Atherton, 1972.

QUINN, R. D. Psychotherapists' expressions as an index to the quality of early therapeutic relationships established by representatives of the non-directive, Adlerian and psychoanalytic schools. In O. H. Mowrer (Ed.), *Psychotherapy theory and research*. New York: Ronald Press, 1953.

RASKIN, N. Studies on psychotherapeutic orientation: Ideology in practice. *AAP Psychotherapy Research Monographs*, Orlando, Florida: American Academy of Psychotherapists, 1974.

ROGERS, C. R. The necessary and sufficient conditions of therapeutic personality change. *Journal of Consulting Psychology*, 1957, *21*, 95–103.

ROGERS, C. R. A theory of therapy, personality and interpersonal relationships as developed in the client-centered framework. In S. Koch (Ed.), *Psychology: A study of a science* (Vol. 3, *Formulations of the person and the social context)*. New York: McGraw-Hill, 1959.

ROGERS, C. R., GENDLIN, E. T., KIESLER, D. J., & TRUAX, C. B. (EDS.) *The therapeutic relationship and its impact: A study of psychotherapy with schizophrenics*. Madison, Wisconsin: University of Wisconsin Press, 1967.

TAUSCH, R. Personal communication, 1973.

TAUSCH, R., BASTINE, R., BOMMERT, H., MINSEL, W-R., NICKEL, H., & LANGER, I. Weitere Untersuchung der Auswirkung und der Prozesse klientenzentrierter Gesprächpsychotherapie. *Zeitschrift für Klinische Psychologie*, 1972, 1(3), 232–250.

TAUSCH, R., BASTINE, R., FRIESE, H., & SANDER, K. Variablen und Ergebnisse bei Psychotherapie mit alternierenden Psychotherapeuten. *Verlag für Psychologie*, 1970, *XXI/I*, Göttingen.

TRUAX, C. B. Effective ingredients in psychotherapy: An approach to unraveling the patient-therapist interaction. In G. E. Stollak, B. G. Guerney, Jr., & M. Rothberg (Eds.), *Psychotherapy research: Selected readings*. Chicago: Rand McNally, 1966.

TRUAX, C. B. A scale for the rating of accurate empathy. In C. R. Rogers, E. T. Gendlin, D. J. Kiesler, & C. B. Truax (Eds.), *The therapeutic relationship and its impact: A study of psychotherapy with schizophrenics*. Madison, Wisconsin: University of Wisconsin Press, 1967.

TRUAX, C. B., & CARKHUFF, R. R. *Toward effective counseling and psychotherapy: training and practice*. Chicago: Aldine-Atherton, 1967.

VAN DER VEEN, F. Client perception of therapist conditions as a factor in psychotherapy. In J. T. Hart & T. M. Tomlinson (Eds.), *New directions in client-centered therapy*. Boston: Houghton Mifflin, 1970.

Ellen West—
And Loneliness

This chapter has a long history. Rollo May's book *Existence*, a presentation of an existential point of view, was published in 1958. It contained a chapter by Dr. Ludwig Binswanger on a famous case in which he and Dr. Eugen Bleuler were involved, which was first reported in German (Binswanger, 1944–1945). Obviously, the treatment methods were in the early days of psychiatry and psychoanalysis.

In the autumn of 1958, a conference was held by the newly formed American Academy of Psychotherapists, which included both psychiatrists and psychologists. Dr. May organized a symposium at the conference to discuss the case of Ellen West. Taking part in the symposium were three psychiatrists, two psychologists (I was one), an anthropologist, and a social historian. The meeting was an all-day session, and the case was discussed from many angles. It has never been reported in full.

As I studied the case in preparation for the symposium, I became more and more angry at the many and serious "mistakes" that were made in the treatment of Ellen. I felt she was dealt with by her parents, her various physicians, her psychiatrists, and her two analysts in ways that could not possibly help her—ways that would, in fact, certainly worsen her psychological health. Intellectually, I could forgive these errors, knowing that Ellen had lived many, many years ago and that psychotherapy

164

and psychiatric treatment were in a primitive stage. But my forgiving thoughts did nothing to change the anger I felt.

Consequently, in my presentation at the symposium I not only presented the dynamics of the interactions as I saw them, but I also speculated on what the dynamics would be if Ellen entered my office, or that of any client-centered therapist today, seeking help. The outcome, as I saw it, would have been very different.

Some years later I expanded the paper, presenting the major events in Ellen's life, summarizing Binswanger's account, and relating Ellen's life to the isolation and loneliness that exist in modern society. The expanded paper is able to stand alone; it is not just one commentary in a symposium.

Even though the initial commentary was written long ago and the expanded paper is far from new, I still stand by it, and am pleased to present it as illustrating additional facets of a client-centered, person-centered approach to a human being in distress.

I would like to give my view of the basic isolation felt by modern man. I will then indicate the way in which I see Ellen West as an illustration of the development of this loneliness to a tragic point.

There are many ways of looking at loneliness, but I wish to focus on two elements of the sense of aloneness which we so often see in our clients and in others. The first is the estrangement of man from himself, from his experiencing organism. In this fundamental rift, the experiencing organism senses one meaning in experience, but the conscious self clings rigidly to another, since that is the way it has found love and acceptance from others. Thus, we have a potentially fatal division, with most behavior being regulated in terms of meanings perceived in awareness, but with other meanings

estranged from self & other

sensed by the physiological organism being denied and ignored because of an inability to communicate freely within oneself.

The other element in our loneliness is the lack of any relationship in which we communicate our real experiencing—and hence our real self—to another. When there is no relationship in which we are able to communicate both aspects of our divided self—our conscious façade and our deeper level of experiencing—then we feel the loneliness of not being in real touch with any other human being.

Is this loneliness contemporary only? Perhaps. In earlier times, the individual also distrusted or ignored his experiencing in order to keep the regard of significant others. But the façade he adopted, the meaning he now felt he had found in his experiences, became a unified and strongly supportive set of beliefs and meanings. His whole social group tended to perceive life and experience in the same way, so that while he had unwittingly given up his deepest self, at least he had taken on a consistent, respected, approved self by which he could live. An early Puritan, for example, must have experienced much inward strain as he denied vast areas of his organismic experiencing. It is doubtful, however, if he experienced as much isolation and aloneness as our clients today.

Modern man, like the members of earlier and more homogeneous groups, deserts his own experiencing to take on the way of being that will bring love. But the façade he adopts is taken over only from parents or a few others, and he is continually exposed to the knowledge that although that façade is approved by some, others see life in very different fashions. There is no security in any single façade. Hence, to a degree probably unknown before, modern man *experiences* his

yet still not part of a large group, no cohesive group view

loneliness, his cut-off-ness, his isolation both from his own deeper being and from others.

In the remainder of this paper I will discuss this very fundamental present-day type of isolation, using as an example the highly informative history of a young woman known as Ellen West.

I am pleased that this case was chosen as the basis of this symposium. First, Ellen West's diaries and letters add much personal richness to the account. There are also included observations and reports by physicians, therapists, and diagnosticians, further adding to the completeness. Second, the full account of the case is available in both German (1944–1945) and English (1958). Finally, the case illustrates the way in which some of the best-known persons in the psychiatric and psychotherapeutic field thought and worked as of a generation or more ago.

I cannot possibly give the whole tragic history of Ellen West—which in its published form covers more than thirty closely packed pages—but I shall choose and comment on a few of the crucial events of her life.

First, her youth. Up to the age of twenty I see her as being as whole, as integrated, as the average person. It is easy for clinicians to read pathology into a history, especially with the advantages of hindsight, but I do not see pathology here. Ellen is a girl who is lively, head-strong, sensitive, defiant, questioning, competitive, emotional, expressive, variable—in short, a living person. She is devoted to her father. She wants very much to be a boy—until she meets a boy she likes. She wonders what life is for. She has idealistic dreams of great achievement for herself. None of these characteristics necessarily portends a black future. On the contrary, she seems to be a richly variable and sensitive adolescent, with much promise.

"Her twentieth year is full of happiness, yearning and hopes."* She is eager to find a vital, serious, loving man. She takes pleasure in eating and drinking. But during this year there occurs a significant estrangement from herself. "She becomes engaged to a romantic foreigner, but at her father's wish breaks the engagement." Our facts are meager, but I suspect, from the lack of any protest on her part, that she adopts her father's feelings as if they were her own. If we put this episode in schematic form, her realization would be something like this: "I thought my feelings meant that I was in love. I felt I was doing the positive and meaningful thing to get engaged. But my experiencing cannot be trusted. I was not in love. My engagement was not a meaningful commitment. I cannot be guided by what I experience. To do so would be to act wrongly, and to lose my father's love."

Within a few weeks of this time she is eating too much and growing fat—the first appearance of what was to become her major symptom. It is perhaps indicative of the beginnings of her lack of trust in herself that she begins to diet only when teased by her companions. She feels an increasing need to live her life in terms of the expectations of others, since her own impulses are unreliable.

It is not difficult to see why she begins to despise herself shortly after this time, and even to perceive death as "a glorious woman." After all, she is an untrustworthy organism, a misleading cluster of experiencings, deserving to be despised. Her diary reports "shadows of doubt and of dread," which soon translate into a dread of getting fat. Nor is it surprising that she is

*This quotation and those that follow are taken from the chapter in May (1958).

frightened at the "evil spirits" in her—the unaccepted
and denied feelings that haunt her.

I am sure this was not the first real estrangement
between her self and her underlying feelings, but there
seems little doubt but that it was a deeply significant
one. It went a long way in destroying her confidence in
herself as a being capable of autonomy. Even though
her good spirits return, and she has happy periods, she
has given up a part of her self and introjected as her
own the feelings of her father.

During this period she is full of fluctuations. She
wants to do something great; she hopes for a social
revolution; she works very hard as a student; she
establishes reading rooms for children. But at times she
is "a timid, earthly worm"; she longs for death and has
her tutor reread the sentence, "The good die young."
Occasionally, "life has triumphed again." She has an
"unpleasant affair with a riding teacher." She has a
"breakdown." She is very overconcerned with her
weight.

When she is twenty-four, there is another point at
which she even more fully loses confidence in herself.
Though she still is unsure enough of herself to need her
old governess with her, she is nevertheless happy in her
studies. "The diary breathes joy of life and sensuality."
She falls in love with a student. This was evidently a
deep commitment, judging by its lasting and pervasive
qualities. She becomes engaged, but again her parents
insist that her experiencing is erroneous. They demand
a temporary separation. So to her it must seem that the
relationship is not real, is not wise, is better given up.
Once more, she distrusts and disregards her own experience and introjects her parents' feelings. She gives up
the relationship and, with it, any trust in herself as
capable of wise self-direction. Only the experience of

others can be trusted. At this time, she turns to her doctor for help.

Had she rebelled at this point, had she possessed the strength to fight for her own experiencing of her own world, she would have been true to her deeper feelings and would, quite literally, have saved her potentially autonomous self. But instead of rebellion there is only a terrible depression and a hatred of her body, which is obviously a totally untrustworthy organism for dealing with life. The extent to which she has surrendered her self is indicated by her terrific dieting. As she says later, "Something in me rebels against becoming fat. Rebels against becoming healthy, having plump red cheeks, becoming a simple, robust woman, as corresponds to my true nature."

In other words, if she were to trust her own feelings, desires, experiences, she would become a robust, plump, young woman and marry the student she loves. But her feelings have been proven completely unreliable, her desires and experiences totally untrustworthy guides. So she must not only deny her feelings for her loved one; she also must starve and coerce her body into a form approved by others but completely opposite from her own tendencies. She has lost, completely, her trust in her own experiencing as the basis for living.

I shall comment briefly on one other episode. She finds her cousin to be a possible mate, and this choice is approved by her family. They plan to marry. But for two more years, until age twenty-eight, she vacillates between her cousin and the student she has loved. She goes to see the student and breaks off with him, leaving, in her words, an "open wound." We know nothing of the content of this most crucial interaction, but I would speculate that her psychological life hung in the balance here. Should she trust her own experiencing and choose the person she loves, or should she choose her cousin? Her own feelings are cooler toward the cousin, but for him she *should* feel all the approved feelings she is supposed to feel. I suspect that she realized dimly that if she chose the student, she would be choosing the uncharted path of autonomous selfhood. If she chose her cousin, she would be living the life expected of her by others, but it would be a safe and approved pretense. She chose her cousin and married him, thus renouncing still further any trust in her self.*

By the age of thirty-two, she is totally obsessed with the idea that she *must* make herself thin. To this end she starves herself and takes sixty laxative pills a day! Not surprisingly, she has little strength. She tries psychoanalysis but feels she is not helped. She says, "I analyzed with my mind, but everything remained theory"; and, "The analyst can give me discernment, but not healing." However, when the analysis is broken off by circumstances, she becomes worse.

During this period she speaks of her ideal love, the student. She says to her husband in a letter, "At that time you were the life I was ready to accept and to give up my ideal for. But it was . . . a forced resolve." She appears to be trying desperately to have the feelings that others want her to have, but she has to force herself.

From here on, the estrangement within herself leads to more estrangement and to more and more feelings of isolation from others. It is not surprising that her first attempt at suicide comes at a point when her second

---

*To show how differently the same episode can be viewed, here is Dr. Binswanger's comment, as he contrasts the struggle she feels between the "ideal" and the "real" parts of herself. He compares "the blonde beloved who is part of the ethereal (ideal) world and the other (the cousin) who stands with both feet firmly on the ground. . . . Life on the earth wins out again." I fear this indicates—both for Dr. Binswanger and for me—that our values show through even when we are trying to make "objective" observations!

analyst, working with her in the hospital to which she was sent, repeats the now familiar pattern. Her husband wants to be with her in the hospital—and she wants him to be with her. But the father-figure, the analyst, knows better, and he sends the husband away. He destroys still further any lingering confidence she might have in herself as a self-directing person.

From this point on, the isolation is ever greater, and the tragedy closes in. She goes to more doctors, to more psychiatrists, becoming increasingly an object in the eyes of those dealing with her. She is finally placed in Dr. Binswanger's sanitarium, where she remains for a number of months.

During this period there are continuing differences over her diagnosis. Emil Kraepelin, the noted psychiatrist, diagnoses her during one of her depressed periods as a victim of melancholia. Her second analyst diagnoses her as having a "severe obsessive neurosis combined with manic-depressive oscillations." A consulting psychiatrist says that her problem is a "psychopathic constitution progressively unfolding." He says she is not schizophrenic, because there is no intellectual defect. But Drs. Bleuler and Binswanger are in agreement that her situation is "progressive schizophrenic psychosis (schizophrenia simplex)." They see little hope for her and say, "It was clear that a release from the institution meant certain suicide."

Since Ellen was aware of a number of these discussions, she must have come to seem to herself not a person but some strange abnormal mechanism, completely out of her control, going its own way to destruction. One looks in vain through all these "diagnoses" for any trace of recognition that the doctors were dealing with a human person! It is not hard to understand Ellen's words: "I confront myself as a strange person. I am afraid of myself." Or, at another time: "On this one point I am insane—I am perishing in the struggle against my nature. Fate wanted to have me fat and strong, but I want to be thin and delicate." Indeed, she is perishing in the struggle with her nature. Her organism wants to be healthy and strong, but the introjected "I"—the false self she has taken on to please others—wants to be, as she says at one point, thin and "intellectual."

The wise doctors, in spite of the risk of suicide, come to the following conclusion: "No definitely reliable therapy is possible. We therefore resolved to give in to the patient's demand for discharge." She left the hospital. Three days later, she seemed well and happy, ate well for the first time in years, and then took a lethal dose of poison. She was thirty-three. Her epitaph might well be her own words: "I feel myself, quite passively, the stage on which two hostile forces are mangling each other."

What went so fatally wrong in the life of Ellen West? I hope I have indicated my belief that what went wrong is something that occurs to some degree in the life of every one of us, but that in her case was exaggerated. As infants, we live in our experience; we trust it. When the baby is hungry, he neither doubts his hunger nor questions whether he should make every effort to get food. Without being in any way conscious of it, he is a self-trusting organism. But at some point, parents or others say to him, in effect, "If you feel *that* way, I won't love you." And so he feels what he *should* feel, not what he *does* feel. To this degree, he builds up a self that feels what it should feel, only occasionally seeing frightening glimpses of what his organism, of which the self is a part, is actually experiencing. In Ellen's case, this process operated in an extreme fashion. In some of the most significant moments of life, she was made to feel that her own experiencing was invalid, erroneous, wrong, and unsound, and that what she *should* be feeling was something quite different. Unfortunately for her, her love for her parents, especially her father, was so strong that she surrendered her own capacity for trusting her experience and substituted theirs, or his. She gave up being her self. This observation, made by one of her doctors during her last year, is no surprise: "Though as a child she was wholly independent of the opinion of others, she is now completely dependent on what others think." She no longer has any way of knowing what she feels or what her opinion is. This is the loneliest state of all—an almost complete separation from one's autonomous organism.

What went wrong with her treatment? Here is an intelligent, sensitive young woman, seeking help. The prognosis, by modern standards, would seem very favorable. Why such complete failure? I am sure opinions differ, but I should like to state mine.

The greatest weakness in her treatment was that no one involved seems to have related to her as a *person*— a person worthy of respect, a person capable of autonomous choice, a person whose inner experiencing is a precious resource to be drawn upon and trusted.

Rather, she seems to have been dealt with as an object. Her first analyst helps her to *see* her feelings but not to experience them. This only makes her more of an object to herself and still further estranges her from living in and drawing upon her experience. Wisely, she says that the "analyst can give me discernment, but not healing." The analyst points out to her that she is an individual with such and such dynamics. She agrees with him, though surely not on the basis of experiencing these dynamic feelings. She is simply following the pattern which has already isolated her—distrusting her own experiencing and trying to believe and feel what she should feel, what the expert tells her she feels.

Then comes the comic-tragic argument over her diagnosis, of which she was evidently quite aware. The doctors disagree as to what type of object she is: She is manic-depressive. She is obsessive-compulsive. She is a case of melancholia. She is treatable. She is not. Then comes the final, incredible decision: She is suicidal, schizophrenic, and hopeless for treatment; therefore, we will discharge her and let her commit suicide. This at least was one prediction that was fulfilled.

"I scream but they do not hear me." Ellen's words ring in my ears. No one *did* hear her as a person. Beyond her childhood years—and perhaps not even then—neither her parents, nor her two analysts, nor her physicians ever seem to have respected her enough to hear her deeply. They did not deal with her as a person capable of meeting life, a person whose experiencing is trustworthy, whose inner feelings are worthy of acceptance. How, then, could she listen to herself or respect the experiencing going on within her?

"I am isolated. I sit in a glass ball, I see people through a glass wall. I scream, but they do not hear me." What a desperate cry for a relationship between two persons. She never experienced what Buber has called "healing through meeting." There was no one who could meet her, accept her, as she was.

Reading this tragic case angers me (as will have been evident), but it also encourages me. I feel angry at the tragic waste of a human being, encouraged because I feel that we have learned enough during the intervening years that if Ellen West came today to my office, or to the offices of many therapists I know, she would be helped. Let me try to sketch this possibility. To do it most vividly, I will assume that she came to my office at about the age of twenty-four. This is the time when she did seek medical help, so it is reasonable to assume that today she would have sought psychological help. It is just after she has separated, at the insistence of her parents, from the student whom she loves.

Even from just a reading of the case I feel sure I would find no barrier to feeling acceptant toward this depressed, unhappy, emaciated, self-starved young woman. I would sense both what she is and what her potentialities are, and I would be willing for her to be both, or either.

I feel sure that our contacts would start with themes such as the following: "I am very depressed, with no reason for my depression." "I can't bear to be alone, but I don't know why." "I hate myself when I'm fat, and I *have* to be thin, but again I don't know the reason for this." "I did love this student, but I don't believe it would have been a wise match. My father and mother felt he was not the man for me." As I understood each of these feelings and accepted her right to *be* these feelings, other attitudes would tentatively and fearfully appear: her disappointment at the separation from her fiancé; the strong feelings that she had, and still has for him; her resentment (a very frightening feeling) toward her father. Slowly, gradually, she would discover that she could experience and be both love and resentment toward her father, both love and resentment toward me, both fear of independent living and eagerness for independent living, both the desire to be a man and the desire to be a woman, both the desire to be a plump, robust, contented wife and the desire to be a slim, brilliant, competitive achiever of social reform. She could experience both her hunger and desire to eat and be plump and her fear of being fat, ugly, and disapproved of by friends. She could say, as she did say, "I am afraid of myself, of the feelings to which I am defenselessly delivered over every minute." Little by little, she could freely experience all of these feelings, all of these elements of herself.

She would discover that some of these feelings are very frightening indeed. To explore and to *experience* both the risk and the excitement of being an independent person is one of those fearful elements. Another person, a client of mine, expressed this realization in a statement which Ellen would be likely to make. She said:

> *I have all the symptoms of fright. . . . It really seems like I'm cut loose and very vulnerable. . . . Still, I have a feeling of* strength. . . . *I'm feeling it internally now, a sort of surging up, or force . . . something really big and strong. And yet at first it was almost a physical feeling of just being out* alone, *and sort of cut off from a support I have been carrying around. . . . (pause) . . . I have the feeling that now I am going to begin to* do *more things.*

This is an example of what I mean by experiencing a feeling fully and acceptantly, in a safe relationship. It represents, in my judgment, a moment of change— probably physiological, irreversible change. As Ellen experienced, in a similar way, these different hidden facets of herself, she would find herself changing. This time the changed self that emerged would be based on her organismic reactions, her inner experiencing, and not on the values and expectations of others.

She would find that she did not have to struggle against her nature, against her feelings. Rather, she would find that when she could be open to all her experiencing—both her inner experiencing, and her

experiencing of the demands and attitudes of others—
she would have a basis by which to live. She would
discover that her experiencing, if she could be open to
it and could listen sensitively for its meaning, would
provide a constructive guide for her behavior and for
her life.

This is not to say that the process would be smooth or
comfortable. To be a person—sometimes opposing her
parents, sometimes standing against social pressures,
often choosing to act even though uncertain of the
outcome—this would be painful, costly, sometimes
even terrifying. But it would be *very* precious: to be
oneself is worth a high price. It would also have many
other valuable aspects.

In the therapeutic relationship, where all of herself
was accepted, she could discover that it was safe to
communicate her self more completely. She would discover that she did not need to be lonely and isolated,
that another could understand and share the meaning
of her experience. She would discover, too, that in this
process she had made friends with herself—that her
body, her feelings, and her desires were not enemy
aliens but friendly and constructive parts of herself. It
would be unnecessary for her to utter those desperate
words, "I am perishing in the struggle against my
nature." Her two essential estrangements would have
been assuaged. She would be in a good and communicative relationship with herself. She would also have
found it safe to *be* her full self in a relationship. As a
consequence, she would find herself relating with more
of herself to others, and again discovering that it is not
dangerously unsafe, but rather far more satisfying, to
be one's real self in relating to others.

It is by such a process, in my judgment, that the
glass wall would have dissolved. She would have found

life adventurous, often painful. It would be a never-ending puzzlement to discover the behavior that would best harmonize with her complex and contradictory feelings. But she would be vital and real and in relationship to herself and others. She would have resolved for herself the great loneliness of contemporary man.

I cannot apologize for having stated with confidence and optimism the probable outcome of therapeutic events for Ellen, had she had the opportunity to participate in person-centered therapy. My experience justifies no other conclusion. I am not sure she would move as far as I have indicated, but that she would move in this direction I have no doubt, providing I had been able to create a person-to-person therapeutic relationship.

For myself, I draw certain lessons from this case of Ellen West. The first is that in every respect in which we make an object of the person—whether by diagnosing him, analyzing him, or perceiving him impersonally in a case history—we stand in the way of our therapeutic goal. To make an object of a person has been helpful in treating physical ills; it has not been successful in treating psychological ills. We are deeply helpful only when we relate as persons, when we risk ourselves as persons in the relationship, when we experience the other as a person in his own right. Only then is there a meeting at a depth that dissolves the pain of aloneness in both client and therapist.

REFERENCES

BINSWANGER, L. Der Fall Ellen West. *Schweizer Archiv für Neurologie and Psychiatrie*, 1944, *53*, 255–277; 54, 69–117, 330–360; 1945, *55*, 16–40.

BINSWANGER, L. The case of Ellen West. In May, R., Angel, E., & Ellenberger, H. F. (Eds.), *Existence: A new dimension in psychiatry and psychology.* New York: Basic Books, 1958.

MAY, R., ANGEL, E., & ELLENBERGER, H. F. (EDS.) *Existence: A new dimension in psychiatry and psychology.* New York: Basic Books, 1958.

Building Person-Centered Communities: The Implications for the Future

The two preceding chapters have pointed to different aspects of working with individuals. This chapter presents my and my colleagues' most recent learnings in working with groups, and some of the exciting possibilities for the future. The workshops we have conducted in recent years have provided the basis for the learnings and the speculations in this chapter. In the writings and thoughts that make up this chapter, I am indebted to many people, but especially to Maria Bowen, Joanne Justyn, Jared Kass, Maureen Miller, Natalie Rogers, and John K. Wood.

Although small intensive groups—encounter groups or special-interest groups—are nearly always important experiences for the participants, I will make no effort to describe them or their dynamics. My thinking on this topic has been quite fully presented in my book on encounter groups (Rogers, 1970).

I and my colleagues have become increasingly interested in the powerful forces operating during the meetings of all the participants in a workshop. Though we often refer to these as "community meetings," they actually do not involve a true sense of community in the early sessions. It is often only toward the end of the workshop that the participants, including the staff, genuinely feel part of a community.

Curiously enough, much the same dynamics occur in a four-day workshop as in one of seventeen days or more. It is my belief that the group, in its wisdom, uses the time available to reach goals that are possible within the particular limit. This wisdom of the group is to me, in many ways, awesome.

For those whose interest in such workshops makes them wish for a more detailed and living description, they can find such an account in my most recent book (Rogers, 1977, chap. 8).

THE FORMING OF COMMUNITY

For the past fifteen years I have been involved, with many different colleagues from the United States and other countries, in what I have come to think of as the building of community. We have worked with small groups, then with larger groups of fifty to two hundred, and occasionally with very large groups of six hundred to eight hundred. We have taken real personal risks. We have been changed by our learnings. We have made many mistakes. We have often been deeply puzzled by the process in which we have become involved. We have tried out different formulations of what we have observed and experienced but we feel very tentative about coming to any conclusions.

Yet one central element stands out. We have, at some fundamental level, become more effective in facilitating the formation of temporary communities. In these communities, most of the members feel both a keen sense of their own power and a sense of close and respectful union with all of the other members. The ongoing process includes increasingly open interpersonal communication, a growing sense of unity, and a collective harmonious psyche, almost spiritual in nature.

In these groups we have come to focus our efforts on providing a climate in which the participant can make his or her own choices, can participate equally with others in planning or carrying out activities, can become more aware of personal strengths, can become increasingly autonomous and creative as the architect of his or her own life. Because of this total focus on empowering the individual, we have come to think of our way as a person-centered approach.

The Context

I would point out that this philosophical approach, the foundation stone of what I shall be describing, is not the only possible basis for forming communities. Communities began in the prehistoric past, when our ancient ancestors banded together for the common purpose of hunting, or later for agriculture. The communities of the American Indians have patterns based in philosophy and ritual from which we could profit today. The earliest communities in civilization formed around rivers or harbors, whose commerce bound the citizens together. In the United States, idealistic communities formed around charismatic leaders or religious ideologies. One has only to think of the Amish to realize that some of these communities have had remarkable survival strength. In China, groups have for centuries been a part of village life. To some extent historically, and certainly since the founding of the People's Republic in 1949, these communities have been notable for their emphasis on the collective purpose. The welfare of the total organism, the state or nation, is paramount. Individual autonomy is de-emphasized, and each person is helped to become conscious of being but one cell in a great organic structure.

In Western culture, however, there has been a different trend, a stress on the importance of the individual. The philosophy of democracy, of human rights, the right of self-determination—these are the elements that have come to be stressed. Out of such a soil has developed a particular philosophical way of being—the person-centered approach which I have mentioned. I am, for the moment, ignoring all the other possible bases for forming community, and will be speaking only of experiences based on and growing out of this person-centered philosophy.

Person-centered communities of various kinds have formed in different settings. Teachers have been able to create such entities in their classrooms. Staff groups in a number of organizations grow and function in a person-centered way. Some church groups function in this fashion. To a very limited degree, industry has experimented with such communities quite success-fully—until a point is reached where the goal of personal growth confronts the goal of profit-making. In short, there has been a ferment at work in our culture which has brought about many efforts to give more prominence to the dignity and strength and self-determination of the individual. As a culture, we are groping for future forms of community.

Person-Centered Workshops

Out of this general direction, the experiences that have come closest to being pure social experiments, carefully implementing an articulated philosophy and theory, are the workshops that I and many colleagues have conducted in recent years. In these workshops, we have had the opportunity to experience and observe the formation of communities in which the dynamics of the process stand out because there are relatively few factors extraneous to the experiment. These workshops have not been carried out within the framework of established institutions. They are not under university or government or foundation sponsorship. They are not profit-making. They are free from any conditions except those that they establish themselves. They thus become worthy of close scrutiny.

It is for reasons of this sort that the following discussion deals entirely with our experiences in these workshops. I hope, by describing these activities, which are also social experiments, that the basic organic form and process can emerge more clearly.

We have been fortunate to have had the opportunity to work with groups very diverse in nature and widely scattered in geography. In trying to think about the process, I am drawing on experiences with groups of varying sizes, from groups held in various parts of the United States, especially the two coasts, and from groups in Mexico, Brazil, Venezuela, Japan, England, and Spain, where 170 participants came to an exciting intercultural workshop from 22 different countries.

I will describe the processes that go on in these groups, but first I should speak of the way in which the staff has learned to prepare itself in the days before a group gathers.

A Way of Being in the Staff*

My learnings about the way in which the staff functions have been sharpest and most vivid in working with colleagues in six summer workshops in the person-centered approach, beginning in 1974. These have been held in six different locations—three in California and one each in Oregon, the Adirondacks, and Nottingham, England. The numbers of participants have

---

*In this section especially, and to some extent in other portions of the chapter, I have drawn on material produced by the staff of the person-centered approach workshops (Bowen et al., 1978).

ranged from 65 to 135. (For a detailed description of one of these workshops, see Rogers, 1977.)

The staff of these workshops has been relatively constant. The membership has ranged in number from five to seven, and there have been a few changes, but the feeling is one of continuity. During the year we work separately, but we come together before each workshop. The way we function and the way we meet one another's needs have changed over time.

Initially, we saw our function in somewhat traditional ways. In meetings held prior to the workshop, we spent much time in making alternative plans and designs for the program—for example, by providing small-group and other special activities. We wished to "give" as much freedom of choice as possible (as though it were ours to give). We saw ourselves primarily as specialists having different interests and skills to offer, as teachers and facilitators. We endeavored to be prepared and to offer a wide variety of resources for learning.

Staff members also spent time working through interpersonal frictions and differences, which we did not wish to expose to the participants.

Gradually we have come to see our function as a staff in a very different way. Briefly, we believe that our major task is to *be ourselves*. To this end, we spend several days together before the workshop convenes so that, insofar as we are capable:

we are fully open—first to one another, and later to the whole group;

we are prepared to explore new and unknown areas of our own lives;

we are truly acceptant of our own differences;

we are open to the new learnings we will receive from our fresh inward journeys, all stimulated by our staff and group experiences.

Thus it can be said that we now prepare *ourselves*, with much less emphasis on plans or materials. We value our staff process and want that to be available to the group. We have found that by being as fully ourselves as we are able—creative, diverse, contradictory, present, open, and sharing—we somehow become tuning forks, finding resonances with those qualities in all the members of the workshop community.

In the relationships we form with the group and its members, the power is shared. We let ourselves "be"; we let others "be." At our best, we have little desire to judge or manipulate the other's thoughts or actions. When persons are approached in this way, when they are accepted as they are, we discover them to be highly creative and resourceful in examining and changing their own lives.

While we do not persuade, interpret, or manipulate, we are certainly not laissez-faire in our attitude. Instead we find that we can share ourselves, our feelings, our potentialities, and our skills in active ways. We are each free to be as much of ourselves as it is possible for us to be.

Part of that way of being has become ingrained: it is our desire to *hear*. During periods of chaos, or criticism of staff, or expression of deep feelings, we listen intently, acceptantly, occasionally voicing our understanding of what we have heard. We listen especially to the contrary voices, the soft voices, those that are expressing unpopular or unacceptable views. We make a point of responding to a person if he or she spoke openly, but no one responded. We thus tend to validate each person.

We do not stop here. We as a staff are continually exploring new facets of our own experience as individuals. Recently, this has meant uncovering the learnings we are gaining from our intimate relationships in our differing lifestyles. It has meant facing openly the increasingly intuitive and psychic aspects of our lives. As we push on into these unknown inner areas, we seem better able to help each new workshop community—individually and collectively—to probe more deeply into their own worlds of shadow and mystery. In turn, each workshop has brought us learnings we did not anticipate.

One striking example is that the workshop community has an almost telepathic knowledge of where the staff *is*, in its own process. One year, in meetings of the staff, we discussed in depth the sexual overtones and sexual behaviors which appear to be a part of workshops, and we openly shared these same sexual aspects in ourselves. In the workshop that followed, this topic, without any suggestion from the staff, was for the first time openly talked about and considered. As one staff member put it, "The mystery that remains for me is the uncanny way the community seemed to live out the ideas we generated in our staff meetings (right down to the psychic happenings)."

One final statement about the way we function: We are a thoroughly open staff, with no leader and no hierarchical organization. Leadership and responsibility are shared. We have become a very close team, living our relationship in the most person-centered manner we know.

My Own Learnings

I have found this way of being with a staff a most nourishing experience.

It has, first, enabled me to take risks I would never have dared to take alone. I know that if I behave in stupid ways in a large workshop group, or try something new that fails, the staff still believes in me and accepts me. This situation enables me to dare to do the new and the impossible.

This way of being with the staff has also helped me to feel that I have no special responsibility for the workshop, that that responsibility is completely shared. No longer does my gut tighten up when I sense something going "wrong" in a group. I can relax and simply *be* whatever I am at the moment. My trust in the collective wisdom of the staff has now become a deep trust in the collective wisdom of the whole workshop community.

Finally, I have felt tremendously released by having a human environment where I can completely let go. In the three or four days of staff meetings prior to a workshop, I pour out my problems, my predicaments, my feelings. I can moan and groan. I can brag and rejoice. I can be utterly baffled and hopeless. I can be full of creative ideas. I can be critical of others in the group. I can be close and loving. This goes for each of us: we share as deeply as we are able. This process is restorative, therapeutic; it gives an incredible security. During the workshop, this kind of sharing continues in our staff meetings and makes it possible for us also to share deeply with the larger community. We give one another helpful feedback. We astonish one another with our creativity and ingeniousness. We anger one another by the way we have handled relationships and situations. We are sometimes critical of one another, and at other times, proud. We learn from one another and we work out feelings together. We are a marvelous support group for one another. We have become a catalytic force.

THE PROCESS OF THE GROUP

So complex is the process within these workshop groups that I despair of doing more than hinting at its multifaceted aspects. Yet, there are elements that I think are significant and characteristic.

Unity Out of Separateness

The sense of community does not arise out of collective movement, nor from conforming to some group direction. Quite the contrary. Each individual tends to use the opportunity to become all that he or she *can* become. Separateness and diversity—the uniqueness of being "me"—are experienced. This very characteristic of a marked separateness of consciousness seems to raise the group level to a oneness of consciousness.

We have found that each person not only perceives the workshop as a place to meet personal needs, but actively forms the situation to meet those needs. One individual finds new ways of meeting a difficult transition in marriage or career. Another gains insights that enable inner growth. Another learns new ways of building community. Still another gains improved skills in interpersonal relationships. Others find new means of spiritual, artistic, and aesthetic renewal and refreshment. Many move toward more informed and effective action for social change. Others experience combinations of these learnings. The freedom to be individual, to work toward one's own goals in a harmony of diversity, is one of the most prized aspects of the workshop.

One participant catches beautifully, in poetic form, both the separateness and the closeness that develop.

For the first time in my life,
I feel I am a truly special person.
For the first time in my life,
I feel that who I am
                    is all I need to be.

It is the knowledge that at the tender core
                  and naked center,
                  where I am,
There need be no more.
There is enough.
I have never felt so validated,
                  or so affirmed,
                  as a person.
I have never known real self-esteem.
You . . . have empowered me to live
                  in openness,
                  to touch your realness.
I have never known myself before.
I have never known another human being,
                  before this week.
I have never known such peace, or strength.
                  Nor have I ever grown so fast,
                  or learned so much.
I have never felt so rich
                  in love of self
                  and love of you.

Another participant, writing at a point some months following the workshop, states very well the way in which community develops out of separateness.

Each moment of the nine days seemed to add more threads to a kind of complicated tapestry that was unfolding before our eyes and being woven by participants . . . some using strong threads, others bold colors, others delicate touches. For me it became so awesome, so complicated a masterpiece of artwork, that until I could stand back from a distance and view the entire tapestry against an uncluttered background, it could not be fully understood or appreciated. Even then, in its fullness, it would still appear to change each day and never be completely finished. The still unfinished part is all the insights that are hitting me at the most unexpected times.

The diversity of the threads in this tapestry can be explained by the incredible variety that exists among the participants: a youth of eighteen and a woman of seventy-five in the same group; ardent Marxists and conservative business and professional people in the Spanish workshop; devoutly religious persons of many faiths, and those who scoff at religion; athletic men and women, and paralyzed persons whose lives are spent in wheelchairs. All of these differing persons have been active participants, and each has contributed his or her distinctive self in the process.

The Chaotic, Painful Aspects

I would not want it to appear that the group develops smoothly. The initial sessions are often chaotic. Usually there is disbelief that the workshop plan is to arise from all of us together. Participants are suspicious of the staff. (In the international workshop in Spain, persons expressed a general dislike of the United States and its economic imperialism—a dislike that extended to American staff and participants.) There is confusion because of the lack of structure. The staff is criticized for not having made plans—the participants are reluctant to own their own power. There are sometimes violent disagreements. There is a tendency to make "speeches" without listening to what has been said. Rivalry and power-seeking are evident, as members attempt to take control of the group, or to "give leadership." Squabbling arguments erupt over how to divide into small groups, a step desired by nearly everyone—but a dozen methods are proposed and then rejected. Similar tensions arise over such things as the scheduling of special-interest groups.

But in the presence of the facilitative attitude created by staff and by many participants, individuals gradually begin to *hear* one another, and then slowly to understand and to respect. The atmosphere becomes a *working* atmosphere, both in the large and the small groups, as people begin to delve into themselves and their relationships.

As this working process goes more deeply, it can bring great personal pain and distress. Nearly always, the pain has to do with insights into self, or with the fright caused by a change in the self-concept, or with distress over changing relationships. The same woman who, at the end of the workshop, was able to write poetically of her growth, wrote this while involved in the process:

Clutching, crawling, frightened
Crying deeply now,
My hurting, bleeding hands,
Are scaling down the walls
Of jagged, deadly fear,
Into some scary pit,
Descending steeper, down
In search of someone lost,
Whose life I value most,
And plunging, need to save . . .

Another passage, taken from a participant's diary, reflects the gradual, painful discovery of an understanding which relieves the tension.

I feel so torn. Part of me is proud for handling the situation this morning with Dorothy and Paul in what I think was a good way, yet I'm annoyed with myself for allowing it to tear me apart. I'm scared, too, because it all seems so unfinished. My whole body aches with unbearable tension as tears stream down my face. I rush down the hall to the room where our

group meeting is held. I barge in and tell the group why I am
late, of the emotional overload that I feel, of the exhaustion.
"I am not even recuperated from yesterday and already today
has been heavy. I can truly appreciate the toll it must take on
you who do counseling full time!"

Then George says, "You must learn to take care of your own
needs, Patty." A sense of peace floods over me as I hear his
words. How gentle and healing. That is all I really need to
hear at this time.

So there are, in the group, experiences of frustration,
distrust, anger, envy, and despair. In the individual
there are the personal experiences of suffering through
change, of being unable to cope with ambiguity, of fear,
of loneliness, of self-depreciation. But both the group
and the individual experience these sufferings as part
of a process in which they are involved and in which
they somehow trust—even if they could, at the
moment, give no rational reason for doing so.

The Basis of Value Choices

As the workshop proceeds, there is a shift in the basis
of value choices made by participants. Values that are
based on authority, that derive from sources external to
the person, tend to be diminished. Values that are
experienced tend to be enhanced. What the person has
been *told* is good and valuable, whether by parents,
church, state, or political party, tends to be questioned.
Those behaviors or ways of being that are *experienced*
as satisfying and meaningful tend to be reinforced. The
criteria for making value judgments come more and
more to lie in the person, not in a book, a teacher, or a
set of dogmas. The locus of evaluation is in the person,
not outside.

Thus, the individual comes to live increasingly by a set of standards that have an internal, personal basis. Because he or she is aware that these standards are based on ever changing experience, they are held more tentatively, less rigidly. They are not carved in stone, but written by a human heart.

The Process of Decision-Making

One of the astonishing learnings in such large group experiences is the incredibly complex ramifications of any decision. In ordinary life, a course of action is ordered by authority, and unless it outrages us, we tend to obey the order, follow the rule. Although people may mutter, it appears that, in general, everyone accepts the regulation. All the complex reactions are hidden.

But in a workshop community, where persons feel a sense of their own worth and a freedom to express themselves, the complexities become evident. Someone in the workshop proposes a way of dividing into small groups: "Let's draw numbered lots. Then, all the 'ones' will constitute a group, all the 'twos' another, and so on." It is hard to imagine the variety of responses. Reasons are given for this idea. Points are raised against it. Slight variations are offered. Exceptions are suggested. One discovers that there are not one or two, but dozens of personal reactions to this seemingly simple plan. Often the group seems on the verge of consensus, when one more member speaks up, "But I don't like this because it doesn't fit *me*."

Such a process can be seen as—and often is—a cumbersome, complicated, irritating, frustrating way of arriving at a decision. After all, does the wish of *everyone* have to be considered? And the silent answer of the group is that, yes, every person is of worth, every person's views and feelings have a right to be considered. When one observes this process at work, its awesome nature becomes increasingly apparent. The desires of every participant are taken into account, so that no one feels left out. Slowly, beautifully, painstakingly, a decision is crafted to take care of each person. A solution is reached by a process that considers each individual's contribution—respecting it, weighing it, and incorporating it into the final plan. The sagacity of the group is extraordinary.

The process seems slow, and participants complain about "the time we are wasting." But the larger wisdom of the group recognizes the value of the process, since it is continually knitting together a community in which every soft voice, every subtle feeling has its respected place.

The Transcendent Aspect

Another important characteristic of the community-forming process, as I have observed it, is its transcendence, or spirituality. These are words that, in earlier years, I would never have used. But the overarching wisdom of the group, the presence of an almost telepathic communication, the sense of the existence of "something greater," seem to call for such terms.

As in other instances, a participant expresses, eloquently, these thoughts. She writes, some time after the completion of a workshop:

I found it to be a profound spiritual experience. I felt the oneness of spirit in the community. We breathed together, felt together, even spoke for one another. I felt the power of the "life force" that infuses each of us—whatever that is. I felt its presence without the usual barricades of "me-ness" or "you-

*ness"—it was like a meditative experience when I feel myself
as a center of consciousness, very much a part of the broader,
universal consciousness. And yet with that extraordinary
sense of oneness, the separateness of each person present has
never been more clearly preserved.*

A PARADOX—AND ITS POSSIBLE
RESOLUTION

I have endeavored to sketch some of what we have
learned in our work regarding the formation of community. I have tried to point to some aspects of the complex process. I would like now to call attention to the
bearing that our experience may have on one of the
strange aspects of our Western culture.

We are a part of an incredible paradox. On the one
hand, we want self-sufficiency, independence, privacy.
Each person, even each family member, wants and
"needs" a car, so that one person never has to adjust to
the schedule or the wants of another. The family
acquires a dishwasher, so that family members need
not cooperate in washing the dishes. A separate room
for each member of the family is always the goal, if not
an absolute "must." When we commute by train or
bus, we bury our respective noses in our own newspa-
pers or books so that we can avoid communicating with
the person next to us. It is very clear that the utmost in
privacy is none too private. Our slogan could well be
that of Greta Garbo: "I vant to be *alone.*" As Phil
Slater (1970) has shown so clearly, we *pursue* privacy
and self-sufficiency in almost every possible way.

Yet in our workshop communities, there is an opposite tendency. Strangers room together without complaint. Sometimes a dozen people share an uncomfortable dormitory, and simply joke about it. Communal

and coeducational bathrooms are usually regarded as welcome places for more communication. In particularly intensive workshops, it is not at all unusual for persons to be in constant interpersonal and communicative contact with others for 18 or 20 hours in a day— and to be excited and positive about the experience. As the workshop concludes, there is a great sense of sadness at leaving. Plans are made for the continuing closeness of support groups originating in the workshop. We do everything possible to continue this depth of intimacy, which in daily life we so assiduously avoid. We wish to continue the very personal sharing, the honest feedback, the open confrontation, which we work so hard in our everyday situations to escape.

How is it possible to account for this paradox? One aspect of it can be easily understood. Many of us abhor superficial communication—chitchat, long conversations on trivial topics, cocktail-party burbling, lengthy arguments over everything from politics to baseball. So, to avoid such "a waste of time," we remove ourselves from situations in which such superficiality is the expected level of communication.

But there is more to the explanation than this. We in the West seem to have made a fetish out of complete individual self-sufficiency, of not needing help, of being completely private except in a very few selected relationships. This way of living would have been completely impossible during most of history, but modern technology makes this goal achievable. With my private room, private car, private office, private (and preferably unlisted) telephone, with food and clothing purchased in large impersonal stores, with my own stove, refrigerator, dishwasher, washer-dryer, I can be practically immune from intimate contact with any other person. What with massage parlors and call girls for men, "escort services" for women, and "singles bars" for both, even sexual needs can be satisfied without any personal intimacy. The utmost in privacy of personal life can be—and often is—achieved. We have reached our goal.

But we pay a price. From our alienated young people come our criminals, capable of senseless violence. From our private middle years, we "progress" to a very lonely "senior citizen" status. Both the young and the old are almost completely useless in our modern society, and are made keenly aware of that uselessness. They have no place. They are private, isolated—and hopeless.

It seems as though in our workshops, with participants from the ages of eighteen to seventy-five, we are, without being fully aware of it, acknowledging that the pendulum has swung too far in the direction of separateness. We discover that we prize deep intimacy, that it helps us to grow, that it empowers us to act in our society. We are sad with one another, and we rejoice with one another. We are quite willing to put up with discomfort in order to *be* together. We enjoy nourishing one another. We find our private selves lost in the larger endeavor of forming a community, and yet, we discover that this gives us a deeper and more solid sense of self.

SOME UNRESOLVED PROBLEMS

Though I believe our experience contains significant implications for the future, there are still problems we have not satisfactorily resolved. I will list them briefly.

1. Our experience is limited almost entirely to the formation of temporary communities. We need more experience with permanent communities, such as our Center itself.

2. We have been only partially successful with groups in which the members are bound by their constituency to voice a "party line," and do not feel free to enter the process as persons. This situation, however, is sometimes possible to overcome, as is shown by the astonishing effect of the Camp David experience (from September 6 to 17, 1978) on Egyptian President Sadat and Israeli Prime Minister Begin, who were able to drop their assigned roles temporarily, and converse and embrace as persons.

3. We do not yet feel sure of our ability to deal with violent revolutionaries and terrorists, though we moved in that direction in a group containing militant Catholics and Protestants from Belfast. (See McGaw, Rice, & Rogers, 1973.)

4. We have not resolved the "re-entry problem"—the person who seems to lose the gains he or she has made in the workshop upon return home. We are making progress in this, however, by discussing the potential problems before the workshop has ended and forming support networks which continue after the workshop.

IMPLICATIONS FOR THE FUTURE

A New Paradigm for Power

Perhaps the most dramatic and far-reaching future significance of our work is simply our way of being and acting as a staff. To create a climate where power is shared, where individuals are empowered, where groups are dealt with as being trustworthy and competent to face problems—this is unheard of in ordinary life. Our schools, our government, our businesses and corporations are permeated with the view that neither the individual nor the group is trustworthy. There must be power *over*, power to control. The hierarchical system is inherent in our whole culture. Even in many of our religions, persons are regarded as basically sinful, and hence, in need of discipline and guidance. In the psychological sphere, psychoanalysis takes a similar view—that at the core, individuals are full of unconscious impulses which, if uncontrolled, would wreak havoc upon society.

The paradigm of Western culture is that the essence of persons is dangerous; thus, they must be taught, guided, and controlled by those with superior authority.

Yet our experience, and that of an increasing number of humanistic psychologists, has shown that another paradigm is far more effective and constructive for the individual and for society. It is that, given a suitable psychological climate, humankind is trustworthy, creative, self-motivated, powerful, and constructive— capable of releasing undreamed-of potentialities.

The first paradigm of controlling the evil in human nature has brought civilization to the brink of disaster. Can society come to see the effectiveness of the second paradigm? It appears to be the only hope for survival.

Opportunities for Resolving International Frictions

As I read that the nine European Common Market nations have elected a European Parliament of some four hundred members, I grow excited by the possibilities. It is reported that its function will be more symbolic than legislative. This fact opens still more opportunities, since members will not be rigidly bound to "party lines" and can express their own selves. I have little doubt that a competent international facilitative staff could initiate in this diverse congress of nations the same sort of process I have been describing—a process that was strikingly illustrated in the intercultural workshop in Spain, creating a harmonious unity out of citizens of twenty-two countries. Imagine the members of such an international parliament reaching the point where they could truly hear and understand and respect one another, where a cooperative sense of community developed, where humanness had a higher priority than power. The results could have the most profound significance. I do not mean that all problems would be resolved. Not at all. But even the most difficult tensions and demands become more soluble in a human climate of understanding and mutual respect.

This is only one example of the way in which our know-how in forming community might be used to resolve and dissolve intercultural and international tensions. A plan is ready for working with Arab-Israeli relationships. Whether it will be tried is problematical. What is important is that such a plan is within the realm of possibility. If a group of individuals, no matter how antagonistic or hostile its members, are willing to gather in the same room together, we know the attitudes and skills that can move it in the direction of a communicative mutual respect, and eventually toward becoming a community.

The Significance for Education

Many experiments in a more person-centered mode of education are under way. I would like to paint, in broad strokes, the picture of what education in the future might be like if we utilize the knowledge we have today.

It could build a climate of trust in which curiosity, the natural desire to learn, could be nourished and enhanced.

It could free students, faculty, and administrators alike to engage in a participatory mode of decision-making about all aspects of learning.

It could develop a sense of community in which the destructive competition of today would be replaced by cooperation, respect for others, and mutual helpfulness.

It could be a place where students would come to prize themselves, would develop self-confidence and self-esteem.

It could be a situation in which both students and faculty would increasingly discover the source of values in themselves, coming to an awareness that the good life is within, not dependent on outside sources.

In such an educational community, students could find an excitement in intellectual and emotional discovery which would lead them to become lifelong learners.

These are not "pie-in-the-sky" statements. We have the know-how for achieving every one of these goals. Whether we, as a culture, will choose to bring them about is the uncertain element.

A New Level of Consciousness

I have mentioned the transcendent spirit of oneness which often occurs in our workshops. What does this signify for the future? I feel others are more competent than I to answer this question.

As historian of ideas Lancelot Whyte (1974) has pointed out, there is usually, in any new development, a subterranean current in the popular mind and feeling, which grows stronger and stronger until, with a seeming suddenness, it breaks forth into clearly articulated form in various places and countries. In this sense I believe there is, alongside the obviously destructive forces on our planet, a growing current that will lead to a new level of human awareness. There is the strong interest in holistic healing; the recognition of undeveloped psychic powers within each individual; the mysterious, unspoken communication that is so evident in our groups; a dimly sensed recognition that the strongest force in our universe is not overriding power, but love. When, or whether, this cluster of new ways of seeing human beings in relation to the universe will emerge fully into the open, I cannot predict. I simply point to the fact that the harmonious sense of community that occurs in our workshops enhances all the separate springs of this flowing subterranean current. Our workshop experiences, along with the many other manifestations of this current, mean to me that humankind may be moving into a far different type of consciousness than exists today.

Pilot Models

I do not deceive myself that our workshop communities, or similar efforts growing out of a humanistic, person-centered philosophy, have any chance of directly affecting the mainstream of world events or the lives of the multitudes that inhabit our planet.

What I do believe is that we are developing pilot models which are available to be utilized on a larger scale, when and if society so wishes. Our Belfast group had, even in the long run, only an infinitesimal impact on the troubled Irish situation. But, as a Belfast observer remarked, "If there could only have been a group like this in every block in Belfast, *that* would have made a difference!"

My point is that we all must wait upon the social will. If the time comes when our culture tires of the endless homicidal feuds, despairs of the use of force and war as a means of bringing peace, becomes discontent with the half-lives that its members are living—only then will our culture seriously look for alternatives. When this time comes, people will not find a void. They will discover that there are means for facilitating the resolution of feuds. They will find that there are ways of building community without sacrificing the potential and creativity of the person. They will realize that there *are* ways, already tried out on a small scale, of enhancing learning, of moving toward new values, of raising consciousness to unexpected levels. They will find that there are ways of being that do not involve power over persons or groups. They will discover that harmonious community can be built on a basis of mutual respect and enhanced personal growth. That, to my mind, is our basic contribution as humanistic psychologists with a person-centered philosophy—we have created working models on a small scale which our culture can use when it is ready.

REFERENCES

BOWEN, M., JUSTYN, J., KASS, J., MILLER, M., ROGERS, C. R., ROGERS, N., & WOOD, J. K. Evolving aspects of person-centered workshops. *Self and Society* (London), February 1978, *6*, 43–49.

MCGAW, W. H., RICE, C. P., & ROGERS, C. R. *The Steel Shutter.* Film. Center for Studies of the Person, La Jolla, California, 1973.

ROGERS, C. R. *Carl Rogers on encounter groups.* New York: Harper & Row, 1970.

ROGERS, C. R. *Carl Rogers on personal power.* New York: Delacorte Press, 1977.

SLATER, P. *The pursuit of loneliness.* Boston: Beacon Press, 1970.

WHYTE, L. *The universe of experience.* New York: Harper & Row, 1974.

Six Vignettes

I tend to learn the most from small, intense experiences which illuminate for me different aspects of what I am doing. They also illustrate in a vivid fashion some of the more abstract concepts of a person-centered approach. Frequently I write them down in order to store them as memories or to provide them for the use of the people involved. I have assembled six of these experiences here, each very different, but each illustrating some point or points. They are all true stories, yet they also have something of the quality of fables. Each one has been, and is, quite precious for my own growth or for my confidence in what I am doing.

The first, "I Began to Lose Me," contains a young woman's letter describing her experience in therapy. I do not know the woman, nor do I know the therapist. But her experience crams into one letter a whole gold mine of learnings about individual therapy.

"The Cavern" is an intensely personal account, again by letter, of how the experiencing of the emptiness of a person—the inner void—can become a rich and fulfilling event, when it is accepted. It, too, is an account of a one-to-one therapy relationship.

"Nancy Mourns" tells of an incident which will always remain fresh in my memory, involving my daughter and Nancy and several others in a large person-centered workshop, aimed both at facilitating personal growth and the building of community.

"*Being* Together" is a particularly well-documented story of the long-range effects of an encounter group experience. I was discussing recently with colleagues the rich data we have, in personal letters and contacts, of the frequently far-reaching effects of even a weekend group. Here is a case in which those effects can be shown in a series of "snapshots," starting with the original experience of one of the workshop participants, and ending with a letter I received from her nine years later.

"The Security Guard" is one of several fascinating examples of the kind of energy that emanates from a community-building experience. We influence, in unknown ways, people who have no direct contact at all with the workshop. Here is a clear instance of that influence.

"A Kids' Workshop" brings us back to hard reality. In addition to a rewarding account of how young children respond to a person-centered climate, it clearly pictures the frightening resistance to any way of being that threatens conventional ways and, especially, conventional power structures.

To me, this chapter is a refreshing bouquet of blossoms of different hues and fragrances. It has been plucked from all the different areas in which we have journeyed in this book— the qualities in a relationship, the inner experience of change, the impact of an intensive group experience, the community as a therapist, the rays of light that issue from a workshop, illuminating in unexpected ways. In picking it, I have wandered all over the garden. I offer it to you, now, as a bouquet gathered over the years, which has given me much pleasure.

1. "I BEGAN TO LOSE ME"

Dear Dr. Rogers,

I don't know how to explain who I am or why I am writing to you except to say that I have just read your book, *On Becoming a Person*, and it left a great impression on me. I just happened to find it one day and started reading. It's kind of a coincidence because right now I need something to help me find *me*. I do not feel that I can do much for others until I find me.

I think that I began to lose me when I was in high school. I always wanted to go into work that would be of help to people but my family resisted, and I thought they must be right. Things went along smoothly for everyone else for four or five years until about two years ago. I met a guy that I thought was ideal. Then nearly a year ago I took a good look at us, and realized that I was everything that *he* wanted me to be and nothing that *I* was. I have always been emotional and I have had many feelings. I could never sort them out and identify them. My fiancé would tell me that I was just mad or just happy and I would say okay and leave it at that. Then when I took this good look at us I realized that I was angry because I wasn't following my true emotions.

I backed out of the relationship gracefully and tried to find out where all the pieces were that I had lost. After a few months of searching had gone by I found that there were many more than I knew what to do with and I couldn't seem to separate them. I began seeing a psychologist and am presently seeing him. He has helped me to find parts of me that I was not aware of. Some parts are bad by our society's standards but I have found them to be very good for me. I have felt more threatened and confused since going to him but I have also felt more relief and more sure of myself.

I remember one night in particular. I had been in for my regular appointment with the psychologist that day and I had come home feeling angry. I was angry because I wanted to talk about something but I couldn't identify what it was. By eight o'clock that night I was so upset I was frightened. I called him and he told me to come to his office as soon as I could. I got there and cried for at least an hour and then the words came. I still don't know all of what I was saying. All I know is that *so much hurt* and *anger* came out of me that I *never really knew existed.* I went home and it seemed that an *alien* had taken over and I was hallucinating like some of the patients I have seen in a state hospital. I continued to feel this way until one night I was sitting and thinking and I realized that this alien was the *me* that I had been trying to find.

I have noticed since that night that people no longer seem so strange to me. Now it is beginning to seem that life is just starting for me. I am alone right now but I am not frightened and I don't have to be doing something. I like meeting me and making friends with my thoughts and feelings. Because of this I have learned to enjoy other people. One older man in particular—who is very ill—makes me feel very much alive. He accepts everyone. He told me the other day that I have changed very much. According to him, I have begun to open up and love. I think that I have always loved people and I told him so. He said, "Were they aware of it?" I don't suppose I have expressed my love any more than I did my anger and hurt.

Among other things, I am finding out that I never had too much self-respect. And now that I am learning to really like me I am finally finding peace within myself. Thanks for your part in this.

Let me paraphrase a number of crucial statements that summarize the feelings and attitudes expressed in the letter. By discussing these statements, I will try to provide a general explanation of personality growth and change.

I was losing me. Her own experiences and their meanings were being denied, and she was developing a self that was different from her real experienced self, which was becoming increasingly unknown to her.

My experience told me the work I wanted to go into, but my family showed me that I couldn't trust my own feelings to be right. This phrase shows how a false concept of self is built up. Because she accepted her parents' meanings as her own experience, she came to distrust her own organismic experience. She could hardly have introjected her parents' values on this subject had she not had a long previous experience of introjecting their values. As she distrusted more and more of her own experience, her sense of self-worth steadily declined until she had very little use for her own experience or herself.

Things went along smoothly for everyone else. What a revealing statement! Of course things were fine for those whom she was trying to please. This pseudoself was just what they wanted. It was only within herself, at some deep and unknown level, that there was a vague uneasiness.

I was everything he wanted me to be. Here again she was denying to awareness all her own experiencing—to the point where she no longer really had a self and was trying to be a self wanted by someone else.

Finally my organism rebelled and I tried to find me again but I couldn't, without help. Why did she finally rebel and take a good look at her relationship with her fiancé? One can only attribute this rebellion to the actualizing tendency that had been suppressed for so long but that finally asserted itself. However, because she had distrusted her own experience for such a long

period and because the self by which she was living was
so sharply different from the experiences of her organism, she could not reconstruct her true self without
help. The need for help often exists when there is such
a great discrepancy.

*Now I am discovering my experiences—some bad
according to society, parents, and boyfriend, but all
good as far as I am concerned.* The locus of evaluation
that formerly had resided in her parents, in her boyfriend, and others, she is now reclaiming as her own.
She is the one who decides the value of her experience.
She is the center of the valuing process, and the evidence is provided by her own senses. Society may call a
given experience bad, but when she trusts her own
valuing of it, she finds that it is worthwhile and significant to her.

*An important turning point came when a flood of the
experiences that I had been denying to awareness came
close to the surface. I was frightened and upset.* When
denied experience comes close to awareness, anxiety
always results because these previously unadmitted
experiences will have meanings that will change the
structure of the self by which one has been living. Any
drastic change in the self-concept is always a threatening and frightening experience. She was dimly aware of
this threat even though she did not yet know what
would emerge.

*When the denied experiences broke through the dam,
they turned out to be hurts and angers that I had been
completely unaware of.* It is impossible for most people
to realize how completely an experience can be shut out
of awareness until it does break through into awareness. Every individual is able to shut out and deny
those experiences that would endanger his or her self-
concept.

I thought I was insane because some foreign person had taken over in me. When the self-concept is so sharply changed that parts of it are completely shattered, it is a very frightening experience, and her description of the feeling that an alien had taken over is a very accurate one.

Only gradually did I realize that this alien was the real me. What she was discovering was that the submissive, malleable self by which she had been living, the self that had been guided by the statements, attitudes, and expectations of others, was no longer hers. This new self that had seemed so alien was a self that had experienced hurt and anger and feelings that society regards as bad, as well as wild hallucinatory thoughts—and love. As she goes further into self-discovery, it is likely that she will find out that some of her anger is directed against her parents. The hurts will have come from various sources; some of the feelings and experiences that society regards as bad but that she finds good and satisfying are experiences and feelings that probably have to do with sexuality. In any event, her self is becoming much more firmly rooted in her own gut-level experiences. Another person put something of this in the phrase "I am beginning to let my experience *tell me* what it means instead of *my* trying to *impose* a meaning on it." The more the individual's self-concept is rooted in the spontaneously felt meanings of his or her experiencing, the more he or she is an integrated person.

I like meeting me and making friends with my thoughts and feelings. Here is the dawning of the self-respect and self-acceptance of which she has been deprived for so long. She is even feeling affection for herself. One of the curious but common side effects of this change is that now she will be able to give herself more freely to others, to enjoy others more, to be more genuinely interested in them.

I have begun to open up and love. She will find that as she is more expressive of her love she can also be more expressive of her anger and hurt, her likes and dislikes, and her "wild" thoughts and feelings (which will turn out to be creative impulses). She is in the process of changing from psychological maladjustment to a much healthier relationship to others and to reality.

I am finally finding peace within myself. There is a peaceful harmony in being a whole person, but she will be mistaken if she thinks this reaction is permanent. Instead, if she is really open to her experience, she will find other hidden aspects of herself that she has denied to awareness, and each such discovery will give her uneasy and anxious moments or days until it is assimilated into a revised and changing picture of herself. She will discover that growing toward a congruence between her experiencing organism and her concept of herself is an exciting, sometimes disturbing, but never-ending adventure.

2. THE CAVERN:
AN EXPERIENCE IN THERAPY

Dear Dr. Rogers,

Reading this over preparatory to typing it up, I realized that I have launched into a monograph whose tone suggests it is addressed to a friend. First amazed at my temerity, on reflection I can see that it makes perfect sense. What has happened to me over the past three years, and most particularly in the past month, is in many ways attributable to you. No wonder I feel that you are a friend—and that no matter how many times you have heard my story you will know that for me it is unique. I realize too that I haven't really told you much about myself—my exterior self, perhaps I should say. That can wait. What is important is the event.

About a month ago, in the midst of a period of pretty deep hostility toward my therapist (Joe M————, your student at Chicago), I sought out some of your writing. My purpose was to gather ammunition for a broadside at Joe—something like, "Aha! Look here what your Rogers says—how can you explain *this* in light of my condition, Doctor! You people in your almighty normalcy should try life on this side for awhile." It was pretty much a last gasp in a losing fight—I felt if I couldn't trip or sting Joe with you, where it all started for him, I might as well give up— no other form of attack had bothered him.

This, then, was my purpose. But, Dr. Rogers, I have never in a generally confused life had anything go so completely contrary to expectations. What I felt then, and continue to feel as I read more and more of your philosophy, must have been close to the experience known loosely as revelation. Instead of ammunition to fire at Joe, I found in the first brief reading I encountered (a reprint of Chapter 3 of *On Becoming a Person*, "The Characteristics of a Helping Relationship") the feeling that here were explanations of, and answers to, everything we had been struggling toward during three long, difficult years of therapy. And as I have read more—three books and many articles—I find a philosophy so totally understandable and acceptable to me that as I said above, it has been almost a revelation.

Before I get into the things I want to share with you, I'll say a word about Joe. Because, although the immediate dramatic breakthrough I seem to have accomplished was triggered by your writing, without what Joe has done for me—no, with me—the static I had

lived with all my life would have been so distracting I
never could have even heard you, much less understood. In spite of the fact that he sprinkles his Roger-
ianism with an occasional Ellisian* onslaught (strange
juxtaposition but apparently successful with me), this
man is a concrete representation of every concept you
deem necessary for a successful therapeutic relationship. He *is* congruent; he *is* empathic; he *has* given
me unconditional positive regard; and some of the
most beneficial times in therapy for me have been during five- or ten-minute silences, when—even though I
didn't know it—the almost tangible peace was because
we were experiencing together. Finally, he has been
consistent—stable and unchanging through what must
have been, for him, some miserable, discouraging
times.

But my appreciation of Joe is really of secondary
importance here. The point at hand is that through
your words I have been able for the first time to actually see and understand what has happened to me.
This, I think, is what made me figuratively catch my
breath, and what I feel so pressed to communicate to
you: the sudden recognition of what I was really doing,
the identification of a goal I only hazily apprehended
even as I was almost upon it. I have repeatedly used,
in my therapeutic writing and in sessions, the phrase
"be a person," or rather, "be a PERSON." I had only
a very hazy knowledge of your work—I knew Joe was
basically a Rogerian—I knew that he listened a lot,
and many times has been able to clarify ideas, concepts, feelings that I, in my inarticulate intellectualiz-
ing, was groping for. But about becoming a person, I
knew only that I wanted to be one. I didn't know that

*Reference is to Albert Ellis, the originator of rational-emotive therapy.

you had spent your whole life finding the direction for me.

The most valuable thing you have led me to, of course, something I know we have been working toward these three hard years, is the ability—or maybe just my own permission (I've always had Joe's)—to have feelings. I have discovered, all at once, that I can feel—happy, depressed, touched, sad, exuberant—there is no need to deny or negate a feeling. If it's a good one, I won't scare it away by acknowledging it; if it's bad, recognizing it won't make it stay around forever. There really isn't anything static about life—it *is* fluid and changing—dynamic, and I can be dynamic and changing with it.

This new ability to feel has led to some pretty important insights. For example: as I first read excerpts from interviews in your books, I found myself troubled because people, as they began to experience rather than to intellectualize, could so clearly describe the sensation, feeling, image of what they were inside. But when I looked into myself there was emptiness. No crumbling of walls, no unleashing of floods, no peeling off of layers. There was just a cavern. Then, with this sudden gift of feeling, I stopped trying to intellectualize the cavern—trying to put something there that just didn't exist. And I *felt*, "So, inside me is a cavern—it's empty and clean of all the trash and waiting to be filled with experience and feeling—it's waiting for ME." And as I acknowledged the cavern, it started to fill. The insights, the experiences and feelings are continuous. Everywhere I turn I take another giant step forward. I want to tell you about two of them—the first, and another that I think was the best.

The first step was the most dramatic—because it was first, maybe. Close on the time I found you in

books I went to a convention. It was an event I hadn't
looked forward to with any great enthusiasm; having
an official part to play I had to attend. But you came
before the trip, and the complete reversal my outlook
was undergoing became immediately and almost
shockingly evident. I went alone—a condition that has
been synonymous with lonely in my intellectual lex-
icon. But suddenly, with my new-found me-ness, there
was no apprehension. I did anticipate a good experience, and it was. I was not lonely; not only were
there old friends who were as anxious for my company
as I for theirs, but there were interesting new contacts. I conducted two successful workshops, and had
in general such a strong positive reaction to the whole
experience that I woke in the middle of the night in
my hotel room thinking, "How fine this is . . . how
happy I am . . . how much at peace . . . how much a
PERSON."

That was the first giant step—truly gargantuan.
There have been many more. One of the finest, I
think, came last week with a pretty severe period of
depression, when I discovered that the eternal
squirrel-cage effect was totally missing. I felt very
down. I allowed myself to feel that way. That's all
there was to it. In a few days the depression passed,
without any frantic, despairing attempts on my part to
make it pass and without any trauma or fears about it
returning.

I am increasingly at peace with myself and my
world, and more sure every day that this is no fluke.
It's real: I am in a very dynamic process of becoming.
I'm not on top of the world yet (maybe, as Joe suggests, I'm somewhere around five on the process
scale), but now I know I will be. The cavern is filling
with experiencing, and feeling—and I'm in there—
ME—A PERSON.

I want to say thank you. But I don't know with you, any more than with Joe, what I'm thanking you for. I would like to write to you again.

> *Sincerely,*
> *Jennifer K.*

Do you know these lines—from Gerard Manley Hopkins' "Carrion Comfort":

> *I can;*
> *can something, hope,*
> *wish day come,*
> *not choose not to be.*

even if you want to want to pray

3. NANCY MOURNS

While it is fresh in my feelings, I want to write about an incident that occurred recently in a large workshop. It was a seventeen-day workshop consisting of seventy very diverse people, focused on cognitive and experiential learning. All had been in encounter groups for six sessions in the first six days. There had been special-interest topical groups and almost daily meetings of all seventy people. These community meetings had become deeper and more trusting. This episode occurred on the eighth day in a morning community meeting.

The Episode

(This portion is written in the third person because it is the product of several people. I prepared a first draft, then showed it to the major participants, each of whom corrected or rewrote the portion describing his or her own feelings and behavior to make it conform to his or her perception of reality. Consequently, I believe the account is as accurate a picture as can be obtained. All names are disguised except those of my daughter Natalie and my own.)

The group had been discussing, with great sensitivity and listening to all points of view, the issue raised by the fact that some people had brought visitors to the community sessions. Nancy had been one of these people, having brought her husband to the previous meeting, but she was not present this morning. A consensus was finally reached that in the future (without criticizing any person up to this point), anyone thinking of bringing a visitor should first raise the question with the community. The group passed on to another issue.

At this point Nancy arrived, very late. Ralph, trying to be helpful, quickly described to her the conclusion we had reached. None of us gave Nancy the opportunity to respond, though evidently she tried. The group went on in its discussion. After a few moments, someone sitting close to Nancy called attention to the fact that she was shaking and crying, and the community immediately gave her space for her feelings. At first it seemed that she felt criticized, but Maria gave her a more complete description of what had gone on, and she seemed to accept that she was not being blamed or criticized. But still she was trembling, and was very upset because she felt she had been cut off. It was not the first time, she said; she had felt cut off before. Encouraged to say more, she turned to Natalie, Carl's daughter, and said, "I've felt you as very cold, and you've cut me off twice. I keep calling you Betty [another participant]—I don't know why—and when I came to you to tell you how sorry I felt about that, you just said that was my problem, and turned away."

Natalie replied that her perception was very different: "I realized you were quite upset because you called me by the wrong name, but I said that though I could see it troubled *you*, it didn't bother me at all. I realize I haven't reached out to you, and I think you do want contact with me, but I don't feel I have rebuffed you."

It seemed that Nancy felt more and more strongly about all this, and that she had not heard, or certainly had not accepted, Natalie's response. She said that she had observed the close relationship Natalie had with Teresa, a Chicana, and that perhaps Natalie could relate only with minority persons, rather than with persons like her—tall, blonde, and middle-class. This led to an angry outburst from Teresa about being stereotyped, and about five minutes was spent rebuilding the relationship between Nancy and Teresa.

The group brought Nancy back to the issue between herself and Natalie. It seemed quite obvious that her feelings were so strong that they could not come simply from the incident she mentioned. Joyce said she had noticed that she, Nancy, and Natalie were all similar— tall, slim, blonde—and that perhaps Nancy was feeling that Natalie should at least relate to someone so like her, rather than to Teresa who was short and dark. Nancy considered this, wondered if there might be something to it, but clearly was not deeply touched by the idea.

At least two other possible bases for her strong feelings were caringly and tentatively suggested to her. To the first she said, "I'm trying on that hat, but it doesn't seem to fit." To the second she said, "That doesn't seem to fit either."

Carl sat there ". . . feeling completely mystified. I wanted to understand just what it was she was troubled about, but I couldn't get *any* clue to follow. I believe many others were feeling the same way. Here she was with tears in her eyes, feeling something far beyond some possible imaginary rebuff, but what *was* it?"

Then Ann said, "This may be inappropriate, but I'm going to say it anyway. When you arrived, Nancy, I thought you *were* Natalie, you looked so much alike. I feel envious when I watch the beautiful open relationship between Natalie and her father. I had that kind of relationship with my father. I wonder if there is any connection between you and your father and Carl?" "That's it!" Nancy sobbed, acting as though she had been struck by a bolt of lightning. She collapsed into herself, weeping her heart out. Between sobs she said, "I didn't really cry at all at my father's death. . . . He really died for me long before his death. . . . What can I *do*?" People responded that he was still part of her, and she could still mourn for him. Ann, who was near her, embraced and comforted her. After a long time she quieted down, and then in an almost inaudible voice, asked Carl if she could hold his hand. He reached out and she came across the circle and fell into his arms and her whole body shook with sobs as he held her close. Slowly she felt better and sat between Carl and Natalie, saying to Carl, "And you look like him too, but I never realized *that* was what I was feeling."

As the three sat there with their arms around each other, someone remarked on how much alike Nancy and Natalie looked. They could be sisters. Carl said, "Here we are, sitting for a family portrait." Nancy said, "But they'll ask, 'Why is that girl in the middle sitting there with such a big smile on her face?' " and the incident was rounded off as the whole group joined in her sparkling laughter of release and relief.

Carl's Comments, Later

I was very much involved personally and emotionally in this incident, which has, I believe, been quite accurately described. I have also thought about it much since. It is temptingly easy to diagnose the causes of the incident: Nancy, repressing her pain at losing her father, and seeing a good daughter-father relationship, projects her pain onto Natalie. First, she distorts an incident so she can be angry at Natalie; then she distortedly expresses her pain through anger at Natalie's close relationship with another woman, and on and on. To me, such "explanations" are irrelevant. However, when I try to view the incident from another perspective, it exemplifies many aspects of the existential dynamics of change in personality and behavior.

1. It shows clearly the depth to which feelings can be buried, so that they are totally unknown to the owner. Here, it is particularly interesting because it was obvious to Nancy and to the group that she was feeling *something* very deeply. Yet she was clearly labeling this feeling in ways that were not truly meaningful. The organism closes itself to the pain of recognizing a feeling clearly, if doing so would involve reorganizing the concept of self in some significant way.

2. It is a splendid example of how the flow of experiencing (Gendlin's concept) is used as a referent for discovering the felt meaning. Nancy tried on the various descriptions and labels that were given to her, and they didn't "fit." Didn't fit what? Clearly it is some ongoing organismic event against which she is checking. But when Ann told of her own feelings, thereby pointing at another possibility, Nancy realized *immediately* and with complete certainty that *this* was what she was experiencing. It *matched* what was going on in her. As is so often true when a person is acceptantly understood, she was able first to experience the feeling fully and clearly in her sobs. Then she was able to

follow her experiencing further and to realize that, in addition to the envy, she felt much pain, and that she had never mourned for her father, because for her he had died years before his death.

3. It is a very precise example of a moment of irreversible change, the minute unit of change which, taken with other such units, constitutes the whole basis for alteration of personality and behavior. I have defined these moments of change in this way: when a previously denied feeling is experienced in a full and complete way, in expression and in awareness, and is experienced acceptantly, not as something wrong or bad, a fundamental and irreversible change occurs. Nancy might, under certain circumstances, later deny the validity of this moment, and believe that she was not envious or not in mourning. However, her whole organism has *experienced* those feelings *completely* and, at most, she could only temporarily deny them in her awareness.

4. We see here an instance of a change in the way Nancy perceives herself. She has been, in her own eyes, a person with no close relationship to her father, unmoved by his death, a person who did not care. Possibly, she has also believed she was guilty because of those elements. Now, that facet of her concept of self is clearly changed—she can see herself as a person wanting very much a close relationship with her father, and mourning the lack of that as well as his death. The almost inevitable result of this alteration in her self-concept will be a change in some of her behaviors. I can only speculate at this point what those changes will be—possibly, her behavior toward older men will change, or perhaps, she will be able to feel and express

more sorrow over other tragedies. We cannot as yet be sure.

5. This is an example of the kind of therapeutic climate in which change can occur. The group is a caring one—one whose members respect her worth enough to listen to her intently even when such listening breaks into the "task" on which they were working. They are trying very hard to convey as much understanding as they can. Ann's realness in exposing her own feelings is an example of the openness and "transparency" of the group members. All the ingredients for growth and change are there, and Nancy makes use of them.

6. It is exciting evidence that this growth-promoting climate can evolve, even in such a large group. Sixty-nine people can be therapists, perhaps even more effectively than one, if the group is trustworthy and if the individual can come to *realize* that fact—and to trust that the others care, they understand, and they are being genuine.

This incident is a small gem—it has been both personally meaningful in my experience and rich in theoretical implications.

4. *BEING* TOGETHER:
A NINE-YEAR FOLLOW-UP REPORT

In the late 1960s, the staff of the Center for Studies of the Person was invited to work with the Immaculate Heart College and its High School in Montecito, California, in a program of self-directed educational change. In a few months we were deeply involved in all kinds of intensive groups in both institutions. One of the small groups which I facilitated was composed of high school girls who had been elected to some responsible office, along with some of their high school faculty members. I learned a great deal from that group, because I had not worked much with adolescents of high school age.

Almost exactly nine years later I received a letter from one of these girls. My recollection of her and our time together was very clear. It was so clear, in fact, that I wondered if I had written about it. I discovered that I had (Rogers, 1970). Here is my account of the experience that Ann and I had nine years ago:

"WHAT I REALLY AM IS UNLOVABLE"

One important element which keeps people locked in their loneliness is the conviction that their real self—the inner self, the self that is hidden from others—is one which no one could love. It is easy enough to trace the origin of this feeling. The spontaneous feelings of a child, his real attitudes, have so often been disapproved of by parents and others that he has come to introject this same attitude himself, and to feel that his spontaneous reactions and the self he truly is constitute a person whom no one could love.

Perhaps an incident which occurred recently in a group of high school girls and some of their faculty members will illustrate the way in which loneliness gradually comes to light and is discovered, by both the individual and the group, and the deep fear, even in a person outwardly decidedly lovable, that inwardly she would not be accepted. Ann was a rather quiet girl in this group, but obviously a sincere and serious one. She was a good student, an effective leader in the organization which had elected her as an officer. Rather early in the weekend encounter she had expressed some of the difficult times she was going through. She had found herself questioning her religious faith, questioning some of her values, feeling very uncertain as to the answers to these questions, and experiencing a certain element of despair. She knew that the answers must come from within herself, but they did not seem to be coming, and that frightened her. Some members of the group attempted to reassure her, but this had little effect. At another point she mentioned how frequently other students came to her with their problems. She felt that she was quite available to them and that she found satisfaction when she could be of help to another person.

The next day some very moving feelings were expressed, and the group paused for quite a time in silence. Ann finally broke into it with some highly intellectual questions— perfectly reasonable, but somehow not at all appropriate to what was going on. I felt, at some intuitive level, that she was not saying what she wanted to say, but she gave no clue as to what her real message might be. I found myself wanting to go over and sit next to her, but it seemed a crazy impulse, since she was not in any obvious way asking for help. The impulse was so strong, however, that I took the risk, crossed the room, and asked if I could sit by her on the couch, feeling that there was a large chance I would be rebuffed. She made room for me, and as soon as I sat down she leaped into my lap, threw her head over my shoulder, and burst into sobs.

"How long have you been crying?" I asked her.

"I haven't been crying," she responded.

"No, I mean how long have you been crying inside?"

"Eight months."

I simply held her like a child until the sobbing gradually subsided. Little by little she was able to tell what was troubling her. She felt that she could be of help to others but that no one could love her, and therefore no one could help her. I suggested that she turn around and look at the group and she would see a great deal of caring on the faces of those around her. Then one of the members, a nun, told how she had lived through the same kind of period in her own life—doubt, despair, and feeling unloved. Other members of the group also helped. Then Ann revealed that her parents had separated. She had greatly missed her father, and to have a man show a caring interest in her meant a great deal. Evidently by intuition I had acted wisely, but I have no idea of how this came about. Here, however, was a girl whom almost everyone would consider a charming and lovable person, yet within, she had seen herself as completely unlovable. My own caring and that of the members of the group did a great deal to change this perception. (pp. 111–113)

Following this weekend group, I had several letters from Ann telling how much the experience had meant to her. She said she still had many doubts and questions, but the hopelessness and the feelings of being alone and unloved had disappeared.

About six months later, I was in the parking lot of the Immaculate Heart campus. A car with several girls in it stopped. Ann jumped out of the car and came over, and we embraced warmly. It was clear that she felt secure and cared for in her relationship with me.

Now, nine years later, comes this letter:

Dear Carl,

Years ago in high school (Immaculate Heart) I was fortunate enough to have been a part of your sensitivity training for a weekend in Montecito. Just this summer I was attending San Jose State Grad Program for my teaching credentials, and lo and behold, in my sociology class we were to read *Freedom to Learn* by you. My thoughts turned to you time and again, over and over, and I just had to send you this message of how powerful an experience my *being* with you years ago has been. It was as clear nine years ago as it is to me today how real, how honest, genuine, valid, and true your human approach is. Little did I know then, however, how valuable this experience would be to me later as an adult in a society that I took for granted as all being, thinking, acting and feeling free. You inspired in me years ago the freedom to feel, to touch,

to reach out and be honest. I thank you for that courage and for the freedom it has been able to bring out
in others that I meet as well. The challenge is great
each day—in fact, I long for some encounter experience with you again—are you ever in this area? My
love I send to you and my hope that you are well.

>   *Peace be with you,*
>   *Ann*

If evidence is needed of the importance of even a brief
relationship that is real, caring, and understanding,
this is the kind of experience that provides such evidence.

5. THE SECURITY GUARD

The security guard at the side door of the Dental Building, where we held our workshop all day Saturday and
Sunday, was a friendly and helpful chap. We inquired
his name; it was Herman. Herman was required to sit
at the door all the time, except when relieved briefly by
a friend. He was in sight of the registration desk, where
Bernice, with her unusual memory for names, sat and
greeted the participants, checked off their names, and
engaged in a brief conversation with every one, some of
whom she knew from last summer's workshop, while
others she knew slightly from phone conversations. He
saw the people as they came in on Saturday morning,
left to and returned from meals, left at night; then, he
saw them repeat the same process on Sunday. He
doubtless saw our brochure, posted near the elevator,
which described our purpose and gave Bernice's phone
number. But our workshop was two floors above, and
he never so much as saw the whole group of more than
one hundred people together in the room.

So it was more than a bit of a surprise when, on the following Friday at 6:00 p.m., Bernice's phone rang. This is an approximation of the dialogue that followed:

BERNICE *Hello. (Usual friendly voice.)*

HERMAN *Uh, this is Herman, the security guard at the Dental Building.*

BERNICE *Oh Herman! I'm so glad to hear from you.*

HERMAN *You remember me? (A bit incredulously.)*

BERNICE *Of course! I was* so *sorry I didn't see you Sunday night to thank you for all your helpfulness. The staff didn't leave until much later, and another guard had already taken your place.*

HERMAN *Well, uh, I've talked this over with my wife, and we'd both like to attend one of your workshops. Is it really true that you only pay what you can afford?*

BERNICE *That's right. (He needed to be reassured on this point twice more in the conversation, seeming to find it unbelievable.) . . . Give me your name and address, and I'll put you on the mailing list, so you will get any information about what's going on.*

HERMAN *When will the next one be?*

BERNICE *I don't know.* Possibly *next fall.*

HERMAN *Not until then? (He seemed very disappointed. Then, after a pause:) Can I call you Bernice?*

BERNICE *Yes, surely.*

How could Herman—with so little direct contact with the workshop or its participants—*possibly* have picked up so much information that he went home, described it to his wife in such terms that it intrigued her, that they both decided to attend, and that he took the risk of phoning? It seems uncanny. But as I think it over, he had quite a bit of evidence, without once having actually seen the group in operation.

He saw Bernice's warmth and her interest in persons, which obviously impressed him.

He saw people going out, arm in arm, for meals, talking deeply with one another.

He saw the final farewells as people left the building Sunday night, embracing, exchanging phone numbers, eager to see one another again.

But most of all, he must have seen the change in the people. He saw one hundred people enter this formidable-looking building Saturday morning, a bit tense and anxious, greeting each other guardedly, if at all. He saw these same people leaving Sunday night, clearly having become close, warm, loving, communicative friends, oozing the "high" they had reached. The change must have seemed a bit miraculous to a man who has, I am sure, seen plenty of dental conferences come and go.

In other workshops, I have observed similar evidence that we have affected the kitchen staff, or the maintenance men, or the maids. I think that a workshop gives off such vital emanations, such good "vibes," that they are picked up by many people who have nothing to do with the group sessions.

But Herman's story seems to me pretty special and unusually convincing.

6. A KIDS' WORKSHOP

Barbara Williams is a very quiet woman who outwardly shows few signs of the determination and purpose that have shaped her life and her controversial activities. She, singlehandedly, started a very innovative school in a Colorado community not noted for its forward-looking views. The school is now, in every material and psychological sense, "owned" by the students, the parents, and the teachers. It is person-centered in its underlying philosophy.

Perhaps one incident will express the unconventional nature of the venture. Once the school was underway, the students were asked to choose a name. The name that came out at the top of the list was "De Silly Ol' School," a mark of the creative quality of the enterprise and of the students' affection for it. Then, to give it a prestigious note, the name was revised to "De Sillio School," and this title has remained!

Now Barbara has written to me, telling of her newest idea and its initial rejection by the community.

Dear Carl,

I have read only the foreword in your book on Personal Power and was immediately struck with the statement about "walking softly through life." I feel that is what I have done and am still doing. With De Sillio I was excited and talked about it and the student-centered idea and everyone told me it couldn't be done (I wasn't realistic but too idealistic). I said nothing more and now after seven years of extremely hard work it is a beautiful student-centered school. It is all and even more than I ever thought it could be and I feel very good about it—the theory does work.

Now I fear that it is happening again. I had the idea of doing a kids' workshop. I believe that children are closer to being able to be real, to give unconditional positive regard, to communicate directly, to have empathy, and to use fantasy and spontaneity for self-growth. The group would be like a support group for children to become even more aware of these abilities they already have and to increase them and to keep them for their self-growth as they grow into an adult world and culture that tends to erase these qualities.

I was all excited about this idea and decided to do a kids' workshop and spent a lot of time going around and telling everyone about it like the Mental Health Clinic and everyone I could think of. I put up signs everywhere too and got *zero* calls even asking about it. I never think my ideas are so strange and am always surprised by how strange others think they are.

Last fall I decided to approach the De Sillio kids about the idea of a workshop and to my amazement parents and kids were excited about it and parents willing to pay so I did one series of workshops, they talked me into doing another and every time I see the kids they beg me for another.

These are children (a group of ten) from six to thirteen who knew they did not have to go or do anything they did not want to do and could walk out at any time. I am still staggering from the results and what it all means. In one sentence the kids seemed to understand immediately what I meant by believing they had the ability to be real and communicate directly and how that is different from much of our culture and the adult world but that I believed that it is possible to increase these qualities, become more aware of them and keep them as they grow.

Two of these children are kind of hyperactive and I'll never forget the picture of them as I told them— they suddenly stood still, their eyes grew big and they started nodding and they became deeply involved in the workshop. All of them reacted in that way, even those who usually don't get involved in anything, have problems at home, etc. I still can't believe it. Behavior and problems changed at home and in school and people commented on it. It was like watching something magic happen that I had very little to do with. I feel that it struck something very deep in the children that they could immediately recognize and use and I feel it would be that way with all children. Needless to say I am very excited and intrigued with all of this. I am not sure as to where to go with it.

I thought of the possibility of working out of other growth centers such as doing groups for them or perhaps doing a workshop for children at the same time some of their parents might be involved in a workshop for themselves. These thoughts are all very new to me and I have no idea if something like that would be possible or even how to go about finding out.

To me, this is a revealing account of the struggle that any truly innovative idea goes through in its formative stages. At first, it is seen as ridiculous and impossible. When evidence is offered that in a climate ready to accept the new, the idea is *not* ridiculous and it *is* possible, it is still unacceptable to the community at large. We all profess a great interest in the welfare of children and in the improvement of children's adjustment. Yet a project that promotes both is completely unacceptable to most people, because it threatens conventional ways of thinking, conventional power relationships, and conventional institutions.

I see a long, tough road ahead for this very promising project.

REFERENCE

ROGERS, C. R. *Carl Rogers on encounter groups*. New York: Harper & Row, 1970.

Some New Challenges to the Helping Professions

This is a passionate paper, addressed to psychologists but applying almost equally, I believe, to members of other helping professions and to educators.

It is an outpouring of pent-up criticism. As I read it now, I find some of the language intemperate and extreme. Yet I do not apologize. The feelings were, and are, very real. Although written in 1972 (and first presented to the American Psychological Association meeting in September of that year), the issues raised are still valid and controversial. So I simply present it for what it is—an emotional statement that attacks a number of the "sacred cows" of the professional world.

I appreciate being invited to address psychologists. It has been a long time indeed since I have attended an APA convention. I have a temptation to reminisce, to think and talk about the forty-five years I have been engaged in clinical psychology or work that is related to it—helping troubled individuals, conducting research in this field, promoting personal growth and development in individuals and groups, endeavoring to work with organizations such as our educational systems, even voicing my concerns about our very sick society and the near fatal illnesses of our culture.

235

Such reminiscences would cover such things as the strenuous effort that was necessary to make a place for that small infant, clinical psychology, in the APA—a struggle that seems ludicrous now; the struggle to prove that psychologists could actually and legally carry on psychotherapy, involving various professional struggles with psychiatry; the attempt to open up therapy to detailed scrutiny and empirical research; the effort to build a theoretical formulation that would release clinical work from the dying orthodoxy of psychoanalytic dogma, and promote diversified and creative thinking; the efforts to broaden the scope and the vision of clinical and other psychologists; and perhaps finally the effort to help psychologists become true change agents, not simply remedial appliers of psychic Band-Aids. Each one of those phrases could be a long story in itself.

But I do not wish to yield to this temptation. I prefer to look ahead, to try to describe some of the challenges that are currently facing us, or will, in my judgment, face us in the near future.

I am afraid that these challenges have little or no logical sequence. They are the dilemmas that I perceive as most significant. For this reason, what follows may seem disjointed, just as I think life rather ruthlessly presents us with many divergent issues, some of which we would sweep under the rug if we conveniently could. Here are some that I think cannot be wished away.

DARE WE DEVELOP A HUMAN SCIENCE?

The first challenge I wish to mention is not particularly new, but it is definitely unmet. It is this: Does our profession dare to develop the new conception of science which is so necessary if we are to have a true *psychological* science? Or will we continue as a pseudoscience? Let me explain my meaning, in terms which are full of personal meaning to me.

Psychology, for all its thousands of experiments, its multitude of white rats, its vast enterprises involving laboratories, computers, electronic equipment, highly sophisticated statistical measures, and the like, is in my estimation slipping backward as a significant science. We have failed dismally to heed Robert Oppenheimer's (1956) warning, addressed to the APA, when he pointed out that the worst thing psychology might do would be "to model itself after a physics which is not there anymore, which has been outdated (p. 134). But we have determinedly tied ourselves to this old Newtonian conception of science, seemingly unaware of the changes in the views of science that have been taking place in theoretical physics and in various other "hard" as well as "soft" sciences. I and others have endeavored to spell out some of these changes (Koch, 1959; Rogers, 1955, 1964; Schultz, 1970) and I do not wish to repeat those formulations here. For me the heart of the change is best summed up in a paragraph by my friend, Michael Polanyi (1958). It is a complex thought:

> To say that the discovery of objective truth in science consists in the apprehension of a rationality which commands our respect and arouses our contemplative admiration; that such discovery, while using the experience of our senses as clues, transcends this experience by embracing the vision of a reality beyond the impressions of our senses, a vision which speaks for itself in guiding us to an ever deeper understanding of reality—such an account of scientific procedure would be generally shrugged aside as out-dated Platonism: a piece of

mystery-mongering unworthy of an enlightened age. Yet it is precisely on this conception of objectivity that I wish to insist. . . . (p. 5)

A beautiful example of Polanyi's view of a man being pulled, by his subjective vision, into a deeper and more significant view of reality is contained in the account of how he became a scientist by none other than B. F. Skinner (1959). It is a human, private, inner view. It is full of the use of such subjective clues as "when you run onto something interesting, drop everything else and study it" (p. 363). It is unfortunate that Skinner now regards this beautiful personal account as no more than an epiphenomenon, insignificant in itself. Yet I have had the same kind of story from prominent scientists at Caltech—the dream, the vision, the hunch as to the structure of the nucleus of the atom or some other mystery, and the valuable work which has been guided by that informed but vaguely transcending dream. Hans Reichenbach (Schilpp, 1959) reports a conversation with Albert Einstein: "When I, on a certain occasion, asked Professor Einstein how he found his theory of relativity, he answered that he found it because he was so strongly convinced of the harmony of the universe" (p. 292). He had, in other words, a subjectively formed guiding vision.

I myself (Coulson & Rogers, 1968) have tried to sum up this newer view:

All of this which we [psychologists] have known as science becomes but one modest part of science. It can be seen as imbedded in an impressive personal context in which personal and group judgment of plausibility becomes as important as statistical significance. The model of a precise, beautifully built, and unassailable science (which most of us hold, consciously or unconsciously) becomes, then, a limited and distinctly human construction, incapable of precise perfection. Openness to experiences can be seen as being fully as

*important a characteristic of the scientist as the understand-
ing of research design. And the whole enterprise of science
can be seen as but one portion of a larger field of knowledge
in which truth is pursued in many equally meaningful ways,
science being one of those ways. (p. 8)*

These quotations indicate the kind of challenge that
faces psychologists if they are to develop a science of
man. (See also Dagenais, 1972, and Schultz, 1970.) It
will become a science based on careful observation of
inner cognitive processes, such as we find in Piaget. It
will involve the exploration of inner, personal, emotionalized meanings, such as I and my colleagues have
pioneered. It will be based upon understanding the
phenomenological world of man, as well as his external
behavior and reactions. This trend toward convergent
lines of confirmation has been evident in research in
psychotherapy. It also shows up dramatically in the
increasingly sophisticated work on dreams by numerous investigators, tying together the completely subjective irrational dream world of the individual with his
responses on various electronic measuring devices.
Here, indeed, one of the most ancient subjective
realities—the dream—is linked to the most modern
technology. It is to be noted that in all of these trends
toward a newer science, we do not push the individual
into some contrived situation to investigate some
hypothesis we have imposed on him. We are instead
opening our minds and our whole selves to learning
from him.

Why is this important? Because, otherwise, man
becomes but an object to us. Hanna (1971) states it
well:

*Man uses that which he perceives to be unlike himself, but
he searches for a common understanding and common harmony with that which he perceives to be like himself. The*

former perception leads to manipulation and authentic tech-
nology; the latter perception leads to understanding and
authentic science.

I believe that until we develop this authentic human science, we are but developing a technology for the use of planners and dictators, not a true understanding of the human condition. Perhaps our graduate departments, those bastions of traditionalism, have kept us from bringing about this change. The Ph.D. thesis has, in most universities, become a travesty of its true purpose. To follow one's informed curiosity into the mysteries of some aspect of human nature, and out of that rigorous, personal, independent search to come up with a significant contribution to knowledge—this is the true picture of the Ph.D.; but this is *not* an accurate description of most doctoral dissertations today. We have settled for safe mediocrity, and frowned on creativity. If our concept of science is to change, our departments must change. If that change does not come about, psychology will become more and more irrelevant to the search for the truth of man.

DO WE DARE TO BE DESIGNERS?

Another great challenge of our times to the psychologist is to develop an approach that is focused on constructing the new, not repairing the old; that is, designing a society in which problems will be less frequent, rather than putting poultices on those who have been crippled by social factors. The question is whether our group can develop a future-oriented preventive approach, or whether it will forever be identified with a past-oriented remedial function.

Let me give a few examples. Will the school psychologist be content with the attempt to diagnose and rem-

new view for school psych

edy the individual ills created by an obsolete educational system with an irrelevant curriculum; or will he insist on having a part in designing an opportunity for learning in which the student's curiosity can be unleashed and in which the joy of learning replaces the assigned tasks of the prisons we now know as schools?

To work in such a way demands that the psychologist be a radical in the true sense of that word. It means that he leaves his secure little office and works—often at great risk, I know—with school administrators, teachers, and community leaders to plan and design a learning environment. His task will no longer be to try to assuage the pain of the victims of the old system, for whom failure has become a daily experience; he will, instead, have embarked on the broader task of building a flexible institution—if such is possible—with students as the core and all others as the servants of the learners. As clinicians, we have seen our task in such degrading ways that I do not know whether we can lift our view enough to see the function we might be serving.

Why are psychologists not at the heart of designing environments—cities, schools, homes, cultures—that enhance rather than degrade, that utilize technology rather than becoming its slaves? To their credit, let it be said that there are a few psychologists so employed, but they are *very* few.

Take one example of which I have some personal knowledge. A psychologist—I suppose he would be termed a consulting psychologist—is working with a large firm in its efforts to design an enormous new plant. He is working to plan for the satisfactoriness of human relationships in that plant, so he deals with the architects, with the technicians designing the automation, with the labor-union leaders, with the production-line specialists, with teams of all of these. His effort is not simply to modify or soften the deadening human effects of such a plant. He sees his job as putting the person at the heart of the whole enterprise, trying to discover whether a large modern unit of production can be so constructed, so organized, as to enhance the human spirit, to enrich the lives of the persons involved. I believe he is engaged in an attempt to build a system that is, first of all, human. To the extent that the whole team can be successful, we will not need to speak of the dehumanizing effects of modern industry, of the enormous damage done to the human psyche. To be sure, he may lose, or he may win. But he is engaged in the preventive effort to *construct* a human enterprise. Would that more psychologists were similarly engaged!

The same comment applies if we are thinking of developing whole new communities from the start. The one with which I have some familiarity is Columbia, Maryland. To build a community for persons—without regard to their race, cultural background, or economic level—is an exciting experiment. I know they have already made mistakes, and will undoubtedly make more, but it is an attempt to build for persons, not simply to make profits for the developer. How many social scientists were involved I do not know, but not enough. How much attention is being given to building continuing relationships within the community? Far too little. But this is the kind of area in which, in my judgment, there lies an important place for psychologists, if they can be creative as well as down-to-earth, if they can free themselves from their traditionalism as well as their professionalism, and work imaginatively with others from all pertinent fields—physicians and architects and plumbers and educators—to build a new unit of a new society.

In another area, can we be of significant help in improving relationships between minority groups—blacks, Chicanos, Indians, women—and the so-called Establishment? Here is the kind of relevant, risky field that offers great opportunities. I know, and I am sure you do too, of individual psychologists, black, white, Chicano, and female, who have been highly influential in bringing about improved communication in crucial interface situations. Some have worked with ghetto members and police; some with the health-consuming poor and the medical establishment; some with the drug culture and the community. We, as psychologists, have available many of the skills for facilitating communication and problem-solving procedures between these often bitter and alienated groups and the culture which has mistreated them. We can help both sides to find solutions that constitute a quiet revolution without violence. Will we do so? Will we receive any backing whatsoever from our university roots, our professional societies, and our governmental agencies set up to serve the public, when we do engage in such activities? It is too soon to know, but it is not too soon to make a concerted gamble.

DARE WE DO AWAY WITH PROFESSIONALISM?

The third challenge I wish to raise, especially for clinical and social psychologists, is the radical possibility of sweeping away our procedures for professionalization. I know what heresy that idea is, what terror it strikes in the heart of the person who has struggled to become a "professional." But I have seen the moves toward certification and licensure, the attempts to exclude charlatans, from a vantage point of many years, and it is my

considered judgment that they fail in their aims. I
helped the APA to form the ABEPP* (as it was then
known) in 1947 when I was president of the APA. I was
ambivalent about the move then. I wish now that I had
taken a stand against it.

I am not in any way impugning the motives, the
integrity, and the efforts of those who aim toward certification and all that follows from it. I sympathize
deeply. I wish there were a way to separate the qualified from the unqualified, the competent worker from
the opportunist, the exploiter, and the charlatan. But
let's look at a few facts.

As soon as we set up criteria for certification—
whether for clinical psychologists, for NTL group
trainers, for marriage counselors, for psychiatrists, for
psychoanalysts, or, as I heard the other day, for psychic
healers—the first and greatest effect is to freeze the
profession in a past image. This is an *inevitable* result.
What can you use for examinations? Obviously, the
questions and tests that have been used in the past
decade or two. Who is wise enough to be an examiner?
Obviously, the person who has ten or twenty years of
experience and who therefore started his training fifteen to twenty-five years previously. I know how hard
such groups try to update their criteria, but they are
always several laps behind. So the certification procedure is always rooted in the rather distant past and
defines the profession in those terms.

The second drawback I state sorrowfully: there are
as many *certified* charlatans and exploiters of people as
there are uncertified. If you had a good friend badly in
need of therapeutic help, and I gave you the name of a

*American Board of Examiners in Professional Psychology, now named the
American Board of Professional Psychology.

therapist who was a Diplomate in Clinical Psychology, with no other information, would you send your friend to him? Of course not. You would want to know what he is like as a person and a therapist, recognizing that there are many with diplomas on their walls who are not fit to do therapy, lead a group, or help a marriage. Certification is *not* equivalent to competence.

The third drawback is that the urge toward professionalism builds up a rigid bureaucracy. I am not personally aware of such bureaucracy at the national level, but it certainly occurs frequently at the state level. Bureaucratic rules become a substitute for sound judgment. A person is disqualified because he has 150 hours of supervised therapy, while another is approved because he has the required 200. No attention is given to the *effectiveness* of either therapist, or the quality of his work, or even the quality of the supervision he received. Another person might be disqualified because his excellent psychological thesis was done in a graduate department that is not labeled "psychology." I won't multiply the examples. The bureaucrat is beginning to dominate the scene in ways that are all too familiar, setting the profession back enormously.

Then there is the other side of the coin. I think of the "hot-line" workers whom I have been privileged to know in recent years. Over the phone, they handle bad drug trips, incipient suicides, tangled love affairs, family discord, all kinds of personal problems. Most of these workers are college students or those just beyond this level, with minimal intensive "on-the-job" training. And I know that in many of these crisis situations they use a skill and judgment that would make a professional green with envy. They are completely "unqualified," if we use conventional standards. But they *are*, by and large, both dedicated and *competent*.

I think also of my experience in groups, where the so-called naive member often has an inner wisdom in dealing with difficult individuals and situations which far outclasses that of myself or of any other professional facilitator. It is a sobering experience to observe this. Or, when I think of the best leaders I know for dealing with groups of married couples, I think of a man and a woman, neither of whom has even the beginning of satisfactory paper credentials. Very well qualified people exist outside the fence of credentials.

But you may protest, "How are you going to stop the charlatans who exploit persons psychologically, often for great financial gain?" I respect this question, but I would point out that the person whose purpose is to exploit others can do so without calling himself a psychologist. Scientology (from which we might have learned some things, had we been less concerned about credentials) now goes its merry and profitable way as a religion! It is my considered judgment that tight professional standards do not, to more than a minimal degree, shut out the exploiters and the charlatans. If we concentrated on developing and giving outstanding personal help, individuals would come to us, rather than to con artists.

We must face the fact that in dealing with human beings, a certificate does not give much assurance of real qualification. If we were less arrogant, we might also learn much from the "uncertified" individual, who is sometimes unusually adept in the area of human relationships.

I am quite aware that the position I am taking has disadvantages and involves risks. But so does the path to certification and licensure. And I have slowly come to the conclusion that if we did away with "the expert," "the certified professional," "the licensed psychologist," we might open our profession to a breeze of fresh air, a surge of creativity, such as it has not known for years.

In every area—medicine, nursing, teaching, brick-laying, or carpentry—certification has tended to freeze and narrow the profession, has tied it to the past, has discouraged innovation. If we ask ourselves how the American physician acquired the image of being a dollar-seeking reactionary, a member of the tightest union in the country, opposed to all progress and change, and especially opposed to giving health care where it is most needed, there is little doubt that the American Medical Association has slowly, even though unintentionally, built that image in the public mind. Yet the primary initial purpose of the AMA was to certify and license qualified physicians and to protect the public against the quack. It hurts me to see psychology beginning to follow that same path.

The question I am humbly raising, in the face of what I am sure will be great shock and antagonism, is simply this: Can psychology find a new and better way? Is there some more creative method of bringing together those who need help and those who are truly excellent in offering helping relationships?

I do not have a final answer, but I would point to one suggestive principle, first enunciated for me by my colleague Richard Farson (personal communication, 1966): "The population which has the problem possesses the best resources for dealing with the problem." This has been shown to be true in many areas. Drug addicts, or former drug addicts, are most successful in dealing with individuals who have drug problems; similarly, ex-alcoholics help alcoholics, ex-convicts help prisoners—all of them probably more effectively than professionals. But if we certify or otherwise give these individuals superior status as helpers, their help-fulness declines. They then become "professionals," with all the exclusiveness and territoriality that mark the professional.

So, though I know it must sound horrendous, I would like to see all the energy we put into certification rules, qualifications, licensure legislation, and written and oral examinations rechanneled into assisting clinical psychologists, social psychologists, and group leaders to become so effective, so devoted to human welfare, that they would be chosen over those who are *actually* unqualified, whether or not they possess paper creden-tials.

As a supplement to guide the public, we might set up the equivalent of a Consumer Protective Service. If one complaint comes in about ineffective or unethical behavior, it might well be explained away. But if many complaints come in about an individual's services to the public, then his name should be made available to the public, with the suggestion "Let the buyer beware."

Meanwhile, let us develop our learning processes in psychology in such new ways that we are of signifi-cantly more service to the public than the "instant gurus," the developers of new and untried fads, the exploiters who feed on a public obviously hungry to be dependent on someone who claims to have *the* answer to all human problems. When our own lasting helpful-ness is clearly evident, then we will have no need for our elaborate machinery for certifying and licensing.

CAN WE PERMIT OURSELVES TO BE
WHOLE MEN AND WOMEN?

Now I wish to move on to a quite different, yet perhaps not unrelated, challenge. Most of us spent twenty or more years in educational institutions where the intellect was *all*. Anything that counted, anything of any importance, occurred above the neck—in absorbing and memorizing, in thought and expression. Yet in life, in therapy, in marriage, in parent-child and other intimate relationships, in encounter groups, in university faculty meetings, we were forced to learn that feelings were an equally important part of living. But, due largely to our education, we still tend to dichotomize these two aspects. I have observed this so strongly in groups: if the group is assembled for an intellectual task, feelings are denied, though they are often painfully evident; if the group is assembled for personal encounter, ideas are often strongly rejected as having no place in such a group. It seems that we live on an either-or basis. We are aware of, and express, what we think; or we are aware of, and express, our emotional reactions. Almost never are the two sides of our life brought together.

The state of clinical psychology is an interesting indication of the depth of this division. Training is usually separated into courses—the straight intellectual effort—and practicum experience, in which one deals with the emotions of others, and occasionally with one's own. But the rift is most clearly indicated if I present a hypothetical example. One student states that for his dissertation he wishes to measure, with all sophisticated precaution, the differences between group A and group B. He believes he will find this intellectually stimulating and valuable. Another states that for his dissertation he wishes to present, in appropriate form and thoughtfully viewed, the most important learning in all his graduate years: the deeply insightful self-learning in his relationship with a difficult client with whom he discovered mutual growth, bringing about lasting changes in his own and his client's behavior. We all know that the first plan would be accepted without question. The second would not only be rejected, but probably angrily and summarily rejected. Who does the student think he is, trying to bring in his feelings, his understanding of his and his client's gut-level reactions, together with his thoughts about these? This would be regarded as a ridiculous subject for a dissertation.

Although this seems only normal educational procedure to the older generation, the younger generation is more and more frequently refusing to accede. I think of a weekend encounter between faculty and students at a strife-torn university. It ended inconclusively. I thought one student summed up the dilemma accurately when he finally told the faculty: "I don't know if our two worlds can *ever* meet—because our world has feelings in it." For me, this said it.

Why are so many of our best students leaving universities? Because they find no place for the whole person. Why are so many young people finding life perplexing, without meaning? Partly because they do not know that it is possible to live as a person of thought united with passion, of feeling suffused with intellect and curiosity. Thomas Hanna (1970), in his excellent book, *Bodies in Revolt*, puts up a strong plea for the soma, a beautiful unity of the pulsing human organism in all of its manifestations. About the feelings of many young people about our "absurd" world, he says: "The experience of 'meaninglessness' is a living accusation of that hypertrophy of one aspect of our somas: namely conscious attention and rational effort" (p. 227). I could not agree with him more. It is the overstress on the conscious and the rational and the underestimation of the wisdom of our total reacting organism that prevent us from living as unified, whole human beings.

Yet I can testify from personal experience that it is not easy for people whose lives have been dichotomized for decades to achieve this unity. I have conducted courses in which the whole group, including myself, have agreed that our feelings are as important a part of the curriculum as our ideas. Yet, if a member starts exploring some highly emotionalized experiences into which he is beginning to gain understanding, other members hesitate to bring up anything but feeling reactions. And if one person starts a class meeting excitedly propounding the ideas involved in a budding theory he is just beginning to develop, that session tends to be intellectual in focus. Only occasionally has a group been able to *be* whole persons in the experience. Yet, when they have achieved this, the results have been unforgettable. Some members turn in highly original and scholarly papers; others express their deepest learnings in poetry or creative writing; still another brings to the final meeting a painted wooden "construction" in which he has tried artistically to set forth what his learnings have been; and still another has written a sardonic and dramatic play, very pertinent to the course. For the traditional grade-bound instructor, this would be chaos. For one who is interested in expressions of learning by the total and unified person, this is heartwarming.

But in spite of such innovative efforts—and they are increasingly frequent—dichotomized persons are still an overwhelming majority. We still go to our universities for ideas, and to encounter groups or therapy to emit any "primal scream" of our pent-up emotions.

Yet if we are truly aware, we can hear the *silent* screams of denied feelings echoing off every classroom wall and university corridor. And if we are sensitive enough, we can hear the creative thoughts and ideas that often emerge during and from the open expression of our feelings. Most of us consist of two separated parts, trying desperately to bring themselves together into an integrated soma, where the distinctions between mind and body, feelings and intellect, would be obliterated.

Who can bring into being this whole person? From my experience I would say that the least likely are university faculty members. Their traditionalism and smugness approach the incredible. I remember with something approaching horror the statement of a Columbia University professor shortly after buildings were seized and campus turmoil erupted among the students, who could not be heard in any other way. This professor told me, "There's no problem of communication at Columbia. Why, I speak to students almost every day." He sounded like a southern slaveowner in the 1850s.

No, I think that if change is to come about in dealing with ourselves and others as complete somas with thought and feeling intertwined, it will be the younger generation who achieve it. They are throwing off the shackles of tradition. They have largely discarded the religious dogmas that proclaimed the body evil and only the mind and spirit capable of good. They are a strong hope against the dichotomized, dehumanized being who can drop bombs on Vietnamese civilians, and handle this quite comfortably at the intellectual level. (In his mind, he has not murdered people, or torn flesh from bone: he has only engaged in "a protective reaction strike.") Only the younger generation, I believe, can help us to see the awful dehumanization we have bred in our educational system by separating thoughts, which are to be approved, from feelings, which are somehow seen as animal in origin. Perhaps the young can make us whole again. God knows we need once more to be unified organisms, responsive to *all* of ourselves and *all* of our environment.

IS THIS THE ONLY REALITY?

Finally, I must mention a challenge that is, I believe, the most dreadfully threatening to psychologists. It is the very strong possibility that there is more than one "reality," that there may indeed be a number of realities. This is far from a new thought. William James (1928) said "that our normal waking consciousness is but one special type of consciousness. . . . Parted from it by the filmiest of screens there lie potential forms of consciousness entirely different." He concluded that the facts then available to him "forbid our premature closing of accounts with reality."

Now, with knowledge of many types of drug-induced states of expanded consciousness and changed reality, with all the years of careful study of ESP, with the international studies of psi phenomena, with serious theorists such as LeShan (1969) explicating such phenomena, we will have a harder and harder time closing our eyes to the possibility of another reality (or realities), operating on rules quite different from our well-known common-sense empirical reality, the only one known to most psychologists.

I would like to make this a bit more personal. I have never had a mystical experience, nor any type of experience of a paranormal reality, nor any drug-induced state that gave me a glimpse of a world different from our secure "real" world. Yet, the evidence grows more and more impressive. One could pass off as inadequate reporting such books as *Psychic Discoveries Behind the Iron Curtain* (Ostrander & Schroeder, 1971), yet there are some aspects of that which are hard to brush aside.

One could regard James's thinking as just an aberration of an otherwise great psychologist. One could try to dismiss the mystics of many ages and countries, were it not for remarkable similarities in their accounts, quite separate from the religious views they held. One would have a harder time with the closely reasoned arguments of Lawrence LeShan (1969), in which, starting out to destroy the myth of other realities, he gradually found himself building a theory that points in the opposite direction. He shows the astonishingly close relationship of the person "sensitive" to paranormal phenomena, the mystic of all periods, and surprisingly enough, the modern theoretical physicist. A reality in which time and space have vanished, a world in which we cannot live, but whose laws we can learn and perceive, a reality that is based not on our senses but on our inner perceptions, is common to all of these. The fact that he is continually devising ingenious ways to test his theory adds to his credibility.

I would have to say that the most vividly convincing documents I have read come from one man, Carlos Castaneda (1968, 1971). Beginning with a thorough-going skepticism worthy of a university-trained anthropologist, his excursion into a new way of knowing as practiced by a wise old Yaqui Indian becomes a truly exciting and hair-raising adventure. Then his attempt to reduce all of this to acceptable rational ways of thinking (probably to obtain his Ph.D.) is simply ludicrous (1968). Obviously, he was too frightened to admit, as he does in his second book, that there is "a separate reality" (1971).

Why is this idea of another reality so threatening to psychologists? I believe it is because we are one of the most insecure of the sciences. We do not *dare* to investigate the mysterious. Yet, I think of a notably prominent physicist, very well read in psychology, who was thinking of transferring his interest and changing his profession to the field of psychology because he felt he was too old to make further contributions to theoretical physics (he was thirty-two!). The major question he wished to consult me on concerned the areas of "greatest mystery" in psychology, since it was to those he would wish to devote his time. I could not help but think that I had never heard of a psychologist aiming his work toward areas of "greatest mystery." It is only the secure scientist who can do that.

I am not suggesting that we "know" there is a separate reality (or realities). What I am saying is that we would not be demeaning ourselves if we became open-minded to such a possibility and started investigating it, as the Russians and British are doing.

To be sure, much more study is needed. I would wish to see a replication of the experiment on the mother rabbit and her litter. The mother rabbit, her brain hooked up to electrodes, was kept on shore. Her infants, far off at sea in a submarine, were killed one at a time at varying periods by the investigators. At each synchronized instant of the death of one of her babies, the mother rabbit reportedly showed clearly registered electronic reactions (Ostrander & Schroeder, 1971, pp. 33–34). What do we make of this?

A clairvoyant woman picks up an envelope which she has never seen before (containing a fragment of an ancient cuneiform tablet) and begins to describe "a girl associated with this," giving completely the portrait and life history of a secretary who had assisted in packing the object. Her report was so detailed that not one other woman in a thousand would have matched it. Yet, she said not one word that could be construed as having anything to do with the tablet. Here is a double kind of mystery which LeShan (1969, pp. 53–54) thinks he begins to understand. Yet, similar studies and the testing of his theory are certainly necessary.

And what of the various instances of precognition or simultaneous cognition of the pain or death of a loved one far away? Or telepathic communication by which a hypnotist, out of sight and at a distance, can put to sleep a trained hypnotic subject simply by concentrating on the message he wishes to get across to her (Ostrander & Schroeder, 1971, p. 104)? And finally, what do we make of the strange and unearthly experiences of Carlos Castaneda (1968, 1971)?

Perhaps in the coming generations of younger psychologists, hopefully unencumbered by university prohibitions and resistances, there will be a few who will dare to investigate the possibility that there is a lawful reality which is not open to our five senses; a reality in which present, past, and future are intermingled, in which space is not a barrier, and time has disappeared; a reality which can be perceived and known only when we are passively receptive, rather than actively bent on knowing. This is one of the most exciting challenges posed to psychology.

CONCLUSIONS

When I began this discussion, I stated that the various issues I was raising had little logical connection, but were simply diverse challenges. As I have worked over the material, I do see—from my own bias, I am sure—a certain unity to the questions I have raised. I am far from sure that I have raised the most important issues. I may be greatly deceived in the way I perceive these challenges. But let me try to restate them in fresh ways and then indicate the thread that, for me, binds them together.

I have raised the question of whether psychology will remain a narrow technological fragment of a science, tied to an outdated philosophical conception of itself, clinging to a security blanket of observable behaviors only; or whether it can possibly become a truly broad and creative science, rooted in subjective vision, open to all aspects of the human condition, worthy of the name of a mature science.

I have raised the question of whether we dare to turn from being a past-oriented remedial technology to focusing on future-oriented planning, taking our part in a chaotic world to build environments where human beings can choose to learn, where minorities can choose to remake the establishment through relating to it, where people can learn to live cooperatively together. Will psychologists continue to be peripheral to our society, or will we risk the dangers of being a significant social factor?

I have pointed out that perhaps the safety, the prestige, the vestments of traditionalism that can be earned through certification and licensure may not be worth the cost. I have wondered aloud if we would dare to rest our confidence in the quality and competence we have as persons, rather than the certificates we can frame on our walls.

I have questioned—a bit despairingly, I fear— whether we could possibly see the day when faculty and students and psychologists in general could function as whole persons—not as minds walking around on stilts, or headless feelings muttering wild cries to one another. Could we accept ourselves as total organisms, with wisdom in every pore—if we would but hear and be aware of that wisdom?

I have hesitantly pointed out that the reality we are so sure of, the reality so plainly shown to us by our senses, may not be the only reality open to humankind.

I have raised the query as to whether we would ever be willing to take the frightening risk of investigating this possibility, without prejudgment.

As I mull over these issues, I believe that if psychology—as a science and a profession—gave a clear affirmative answer to each of these questions, gave a positive response to each of these challenges, it would be moving forward.

So the thread that I see in the issues I have raised is that each one represents a possible move toward the enhancement, the deepening, the enrichment of our profession. Each issue, in a word, represents for psychology a step toward self-actualization. If my perceptions have been even approximately correct, then the final question I would leave with you is, Do we dare?

REFERENCES

CASTANEDA, C. *The teachings of Don Juan: A Yaqui way of knowing*. New York: Ballantine Books, 1968.

CASTANEDA, C. *A separate reality: Further conversations with Don Juan*. New York: Simon & Schuster (A Touchstone Book), 1971.

COULSON, W. R., & ROGERS, C. R. (EDS.) *Man and the science of man*. Columbus, Ohio: Charles E. Merrill, 1968.

DAGENAIS, J. J. *Models of man*. The Hague, Netherlands: Martinus Nimhoff, 1972.

HANNA, T. *Bodies in revolt: A primer in somatic thinking*. New York: Holt, Rinehart, & Winston, 1970.

HANNA, T. The project of somatology. Paper presented at the annual meeting of the Association for Humanistic Psychology, Washington, D.C., September 1971.

JAMES. W, *The varieties of religious experience*. London: Longmans, Green, 1928.

KOCH, S. Epilogue. In S. Koch (Ed.), *Psychology: A study of a science* (Vol. 3). New York: McGraw-Hill, 1959.

LE SHAN, L. *Toward a general theory of the paranormal.* New York: Parapsychology Foundation, 29 W. 57th Street, New York, 1969.

OPPENHEIMER, R. Analogy in science. *American Psychologist,* 1956, *11*, 127–135.

OSTRANDER, S., & SCHROEDER, L. *Psychic discoveries behind the Iron Curtain.* New York: Bantam Books, 1971.

POLANYI, M. *Personal knowledge.* Chicago: University of Chicago Press, 1958.

ROGERS, C. R. Persons or science? A philosophical question. *American Psychologist,* 1955, *10*, 267–278.

ROGERS, C. R. Toward a science of the person. In T. W. Wann (Ed.), *Behaviorism and phenomenology: Contrasting bases for modern psychology.* Chicago: University of Chicago Press, 1964.

SCHILPP, P. A. (ED.) *Albert Einstein: Philosopher-scientist.* New York: Harper Torchbooks, 1959.

SCHULTZ, D. P. (ED.) *The science of psychology: Critical reflections.* New York: Appleton-Century-Crofts, 1970.

SKINNER, B. F. A case history in scientific method. In S. Koch (Ed.), *Psychology: A study of a science* (Vol. 2). New York: McGraw-Hill, 1959.

Part III

THE PROCESS
OF EDUCATION
AND ITS FUTURE

Can Learning Encompass
both Ideas and
Feelings?

This chapter ranges widely over the field of education, from a definition of whole-person learning, to a plan for a radical change in teacher education, to some of the research carried out on the effects of teachers' attitudes on students' learning. But I believe that underlying these different topics, there is a unified theme: the value of combining experiential with cognitive learning. This topic has long been of intense interest to me. I deplore the manner in which, from early years, the child's education splits him or her: the *mind* can come to school, and the body is permitted, peripherally, to tag along, but the feelings and emotions can live freely and expressively only outside of school.

I wrote this paper to show that it is not only feasible to permit the whole child to come to school, with feelings as well as intellect, but that learning is thereby enhanced.

This chapter mentions experiences with the Immaculate Heart high school and college system, in Los Angeles, and with the inner-city school system of Louisville, Kentucky. In an epilogue to the chapter, I give an updated report on each of these situations.

In classes and seminars I have tried to communicate ideas and intellectual concepts to others. In psychotherapy and in encounter groups I have facilitated personal learnings in the realm of feelings—the experiencing, often at a nonverbal gut level, of the important emotional events going on in the organism. But I cannot be satisfied with these two separate kinds of learning. There should be a place for learning by the *whole* person, with feelings and ideas merged. I have given much thought to this question of bringing together cognitive learning, which has always been needed, and affective-experiential learning, which is so underplayed in education today. Since I am using abstract terms, let me illustrate this merged kind of learning with a personal example.

For four years I have been trying to grow two beautiful golden-leaved shrubs at either side of the entrance to our driveway. Recently they have, at long last, been really thriving. Then the other day I was in a hurry. I backed quickly down the driveway, swung the wheel, hit something, and stopped the car. To my horror, the rear wheel had gone right over the center of one of the shrubs. My physiological reaction was extreme, as though my whole body tensed and shrank at what I had done. As I surveyed the crushed shrub, calling myself names I can't repeat (certainly damaging to my self-concept) and feeling a regret possible only to a gardener, I found myself repeating over and over the sentence, "Don't turn your wheel until you're out in the street! Don't turn your wheel until you're out in the street!" Now that was *learning*. It had its cognitive element, which a five-year-old could have grasped. It certainly had its feeling components—several of them. And it had the gut-level quality of experiential learning. All of me had learned a lesson that I will not soon forget. That's the sort of thing I wish to talk about.

Of course, an experiential learning need not be negative. It can be the warm physical glow of discovering that someone you have just met has all sorts of congenial interests, and realizing, in your mind and in your feelings, "I'm on the way to making a new friend!"

Let me try to give some additional dimensions of this kind of learning. I'm certainly not talking about a situation such as a professor lecturing, where all the affective and experiential meanings exist outside of what is ostensibly going on. The professor, in addition to the ideas he or she is expounding, is anxiously wondering, "Can I make this last for 50 minutes?" And the students, while partially grasping the professor's thoughts, are experiencing equal anxiety: "Do you suppose this junk will be a question on the final exam?" But all these affective-experiential aspects are completely divorced from the lecture itself.

Nor am I talking about a passionate intellectual argument between two professors. Here, both the affective and cognitive coexist in the same experience, but they run in totally different directions. The mind of each professor is saying coolly, "My abstractions are more rational and logical than your abstractions," while the feelings are saying, "I'll beat you down, if it's the last thing I do!" The speakers, unfortunately, are aware only of their cognitive processes.

We get closer to what I'm speaking of in a human-relations group, where a person may have a deeply moving experience of relating to another and then attend a general session where the process of the encounter group is discussed. "Oh," the person thinks, "that's what I've just been through." The affective-experiential and the cognitive have been brought close together in time, and each is well tied in with the other. People who have read my books frequently write letters to me, saying essentially, "Now I understand what I've been going through in therapy (or in a group)." The cognitive and the affective-experiential have been brought together in awareness.

So if I were to attempt a crude definition of what it means to learn as a whole person, I would say that it involves learning of a *unified* sort, at the cognitive, feeling, and gut levels, with a clear *awareness* of the different aspects of this unified learning. I suspect that in its purest form, this occurs rarely, but perhaps learning experiences can be judged by their closeness to or remoteness from this definition.

Let me give an example closer to the academic world. Roger Hudiburg (undated), a teacher in a Colorado junior high school, describes a number of the effects of his attempts to be open in his classroom. He says, "Openness scares the hell out of me—it also makes me feel good." In its effect on learning he speaks of the shared learning through inquiry and discovery:

> *Excited girl peering through microscope at snow crystals: "Wow, look at this, Teach!" Boy experimenting with electromagnetism inadvertently produces copper carbonate: "What's this weird blue stuff? Where'd it come from?" He follows this for weeks, happy and excited. Others are surprised when they put alcohol and salt in snow and frost forms on outside of container: someone says "ice cream!"—they learn much more than this, for they fool around for days; in fact they turn the whole class on to their "freezer."*
>
> *Students do learn in an open environment. They learn about the excitement and importance of discovery, about their capabilities, their limits, self-discipline, and responsibility. They also learn facts. How many? Who knows? I just know that they learn some facts. They know this, too. I don't think I every really knew this before, and I don't think that they did either. It makes me feel good to really know something and to know down deep that we are learning. Openness. . . . You've got to experience it, live it, do it!*

To me, this description sounds like learning by the whole person. It has plenty of cognitive elements—the intellect is working at top speed. It certainly has feeling elements—curiosity, excitement, passion. It has experiential elements—caution, self-discipline, self-confidence, the thrill of discovery. So it is another example of what I am endeavoring to speak about.

THE CURRENT SITUATION

I am deeply concerned with what is going on in American educational institutions. They have focused so intently on *ideas*, have limited themselves so completely to "education from the neck up" that the resulting narrowness is having serious social consequences. I think of a weekend attempt to close the communications gap at Columbia University—with trustees, administrators, students, and faculty participating. Some progress was made, but not much. It seemed as though the faculty could communicate only intellectual ideas, while the students were expressing deep feelings about their education and about the institution.

Following this weekend, one of the students, Greg Knox, wrote a letter (Lyon, 1971). He tells how, as a freshman, he had heard a talk saying that the goal of the student at Columbia was to become a "whole man," and this thought "blew" his mind. He continues:

I think I have succeeded, not just in becoming a whole man, but more importantly, in understanding what one is. What I discovered was that a whole man is comprised of mind, heart, soul, muscle, and balls. What I discovered about the faculty, for the most part, is that it is men comprised of mind. It was an unfortunate discovery, difficultly tolerated in an age in which so much understanding, strength and action are essential. (p. 26)

Archibald MacLeish stated the problem very well years ago: "We do not feel our knowledge. Nothing could better illustrate the flaw at the heart of our civilization. . . . Knowledge without feeling is not knowledge and can lead only to public irresponsibility and indifference, and conceivably to ruin" (as quoted by Reston, 1970). This "knowledge without feeling" has made it possible for our military men, and for us as a people, to commit incredible atrocities without any particular sense of guilt. We should not forget some of the events of the war in Southeast Asia. In the bombings of North and South Vietnam, and of Cambodia, we were frequently engaged in a slaughter of the innocents. But thanks in part to our successfully compartmentalized cognitive education, we simply know the intellectual facts and do not *feel* our knowledge. Yet, when we are forced to look at the bodies of men and women machine-gunned by our own boys, then the gut-level reaction breaks through, and we are horrified at what we have done. Only if we individually were to walk through the awful human aftermath of our bombing raids would the experiential horror be joined to the intellectual label, and we would *learn*, in a total way, the incredible things we have done.

But we have been schooled for years to stress only the cognitive, to avoid any feeling connected with learning. We have been denying a most important part of ourselves, and the awful split I have described is one result. Another result is that the excitement has, in large measure, gone out of education—even though no one can take the excitement out of real *learning*.

I have days when I think that educational institutions at all levels are doomed, and perhaps we would be well advised to bid them farewell—state-required curricula, compulsory attendance, tenured professors, hours of lectures, grades, degrees, and all that—and let true learning begin to blossom outside the stifling hallowed walls. Suppose every educational institution, from kindergarten through the most prestigious Ph.D. program, were to close tomorrow. What a delightful situation that would be! Parents and children and adolescents and young people—even a few faculty members, perhaps—would begin to devise situations in which they could *learn!* Can you imagine anything more uplifting to the spirit of all our people? It would be sad and it would be utterly marvelous at the same time. Millions of people would be asking the same question: "Is there anything I want to learn?" They would find that there are such things, and they would invent means by which they could learn them.

Closing all schools would forever kill the attitude best expressed by a student (unpublished paper) in a self-directed course (facilitated by Robert Menges) at the University of Illinois:

What is educational has been viewed by me as something to do before I can finally be left alone to do something I want to do. . . . When I came home from first grade my mother asked me, "How did you like it?" She says I answered with a question, "How long do I have to go?" Until this course I had never thought about how I learn, or why.

THE CONDITIONS FOR INTELLECTUAL, AFFECTIVE, GUT-LEVEL LEARNING

There are a few experiences in my professional life that I remember vividly. One is the beautiful, air-conditioned, plush-seated auditorium at the University of Michigan in 1956. Those elements only surprised me—they are not the reason I remember the occasion. I was talking to a highly sophisticated professional audience, and I was advancing a theoretical view—very new, very tentative—as to what conditions were necessary and sufficient to produce change in individuals in one-to-one psychotherapy. I was dimly aware— fortunately, only dimly—that I was challenging almost all of the "sacred cows" in the therapeutic world. I was saying in effect, although not very openly, that it wasn't a question of whether the therapist had been psychoanalyzed, or had a knowledge of personality theory, or possessed expertise in diagnosis, or had a thorough acquaintance with therapeutic techniques. Rather, I was saying that the therapist's effectiveness in therapy depended on his or her *attitudes*. I even had the nerve to define what I thought those attitudes were (Rogers, 1957).

It wasn't a very popular talk. Perhaps because I was frightened of the possible reaction, it was one of the most closely reasoned, carefully stated talks I have ever given. I am still proud of it. And, though not very popular, it has sparked more research than any other talk I've ever given. First, a number of studies showed that when these conditions existed in psychotherapy, the self-learning that occurred did promote change.

Then I became bolder and postulated that these same attitudinal conditions would promote any wholeperson learning—that they would hold for the classroom as well as the therapist's office. This hypothesis has also sparked research. Before I comment briefly on some of these studies, let me describe these attitudinal conditions as they relate to education, and as I have come to see them over the years. They are attitudes that, in my judgment, characterize a facilitator of learning. I have described them before (see Chapter 6), but I wish to repeat them here, since they relate to learning.

Realness in the Facilitator of Learning*

Perhaps the most basic of these essential attitudes is realness, or genuineness. When the facilitator is a real person, being what he or she is, entering into relationships with the learners without presenting a front or a façade, the facilitator is much more likely to be effective. This means that the feelings that the facilitator is experiencing are available to his or her awareness, that he or she is able to live these feelings, to be them, and able to communicate them if appropriate. It means that the facilitator comes into a direct, personal enounter with the learners, meeting each of them on a person-to-person basis. It means that the facilitator is *being*, not denying himself or herself. The facilitator is *present* to the students.

Prizing, Acceptance, Trust

There is another attitude that stands out in those who are successful in facilitating learning. I have observed this attitude; I have experienced it. Yet, it is hard to know what term to put to it, so I shall use several. I think of this attitude as a prizing of each learner, a prizing of his or her feelings, opinions, and person. It is a caring for the learner, but a nonpossessive caring. It is an acceptance of this other individual as a separate person, a respect for the other as having worth in his or her own right. It is a basic trust—a belief that this other person is somehow fundamentally trustworthy. Whether we call it "prizing," "acceptance," "trust," or

*The three descriptions that follow, under the headings "Realness in the Facilitator of Learning," "Prizing, Acceptance, Trust," and "Empathic Understanding," are adapted from Rogers, *Freedom to Learn*, 1969, pp. 107, 109, 111–112.

some other term, it shows up in a variety of observable ways. The facilitator who has a considerable degree of this attitude can be fully acceptant of the fear and hesitation of the students as they approach new problems as well as acceptant of the pupils' satisfaction in achievement. Such a teacher can accept the students' occasional apathy, their erratic desires to explore byroads of knowledge, as well as their disciplined efforts to achieve major goals. He or she can accept personal feelings that both disturb and promote learning— rivalry with a sibling, hatred of authority, concern about personal adequacy. What I am describing is a prizing of the learners as imperfect human beings with many feelings, many potentialities. The facilitator's prizing or acceptance of the learners is an operational expression of his or her essential confidence and trust in the capacity of the human organism.

Empathic Understanding

A further element that establishes a climate for self-initiated, experiential learning is empathic understanding. When the teacher has the ability to understand each student's reactions from the inside, has a sensitive awareness of how the process of education and learning seems *to the student,* then, again, the likelihood that significant learning will take place is increased.

This kind of understanding is sharply different from the usual evaluative understanding, which follows the pattern of, "I understand what is wrong with you." When there is a sensitive empathy, however, the reaction in the learner follows something of this pattern: "At last someone understands how it feels and seems to be *me,* without wanting to analyze or judge me. Now I can blossom and grow and learn."

This attitude of standing in the students' shoes, of viewing the world through their eyes, is almost unheard of in the classroom. But when the teacher responds in a way that makes the students feel *understood*—not judged or evaluated—this has a tremendous impact.

Perception of These Attitudes

There is still a further condition for learning by the whole person, which is especially important in education: the students must, to some extent, perceive that these attitudinal elements exist in the teacher. Students are even more suspicious than clients in therapy. Students have been "conned" for so long that a teacher who is real with them is usually seen for a time as simply exhibiting a new brand of phoniness. To have a teacher prize students in a nonjudgmental way arouses the deepest disbelief. To have a teacher truly and warmly understand each student's private world is so unbelievable that the students are certain they must not have heard correctly. Yet, the empathic response is probably the first element to get through, the first reaction that begins to convince the students that this *is* a new experience.

WHAT ARE THE PERSONAL RESULTS?

What are the results? I would like first to give some living pictures of what happens when these attitudes exist, and then turn to the research findings.

Dr. Anderson is a high school teacher whom I have come to know well. She teaches in a school that is a cross section of an urban community. She seems to be without pretense or façade or defensiveness. You can't talk with her for five minutes without realizing that she thinks high school students are "the greatest." I have a suspicion that she likes the troublemakers best of all. And the way she can move sensitively and empathically (in her blunt, direct manner) into the feelings and reactions of her students is uncanny.

Her courses have been titled Psychology, Human Relations, and the like, but they would be better labeled Learning Experiences. The students discuss anything that concerns them—drugs, family problems, sex, contraception, pregnancy, abortion, dropping out, getting a job, the grading system—literally any topic. They have learned to trust her and one another, and the level of honesty and self-disclosure is amazing.

At this point, some of you may be thinking, "O.K., O.K., perhaps they get help in their personal adjustment, but do they actually *learn* anything?" They do indeed. Miss Anderson is a tremendous reader, and her enthusiasm for books is contagious. Her students are literally "turned on" by the chance to read the books they want on the subjects that interest them. And what books they choose! Some of the students are classed as slow learners, but they are reading Martin Buber, Sören Kierkegaard, Erich Fromm, my books, Philip Slater, Wilhelm Reich, John Holt, A. S. Neil (*Summerhill*)—you name it, they have read it. People tell her that these books are far too advanced for high school students: she just laughs and says that they love to tackle difficult challenges. They also choose the films they want to see, and plan community trips. They are excited, personally involved *learners*.

Miss Anderson has received the oddest and most flattering compliment a teacher could receive. In her school, if a student is found to have any connection with drugs, he or she is suspended and not permitted to attend school. There are quite a number of these. But they have found that if they skirt the parking lot, go in a back door, and take a circuitous route, they can reach Miss Anderson's room without being observed. They know she won't throw them out, so they sneak into school to continue to attend her class. They are bootlegging their learning! And yet, people say that high school students "just aren't motivated."

Let me give one more example. A university teacher tried to believe in the students' capacity to act responsibly in preparing themselves for the teaching positions they would soon be filling. He dropped all tests. He encouraged personally oriented book reviews and personal-growth journals. He exemplified in himself, so far as he was able, the sort of attitudes I have been describing.

The results? The students read and reviewed an average of almost seven books apiece in a six-week course; they kept personal journals; they tried a mini-school; they did a variety of innovative things. Here are three brief examples* of what students learned, the first from a personal journal:

> *If anybody asks what the hell did you get out of that psych course? I'll say love. Love, man. Dig? I got a glimpse of the unity of all things. A moment of truth. How does it look on a transcript? Lovely. It's empty. I realized that which I have always tried to realize. I became motivated, and forever will allow the truth to soar through me.*

Or, if you wish less emotional examples, this is one student's reaction to the whole course:

> *I was honored to be given the responsibility for my own education, and in a more general sense, my own life.*

*Personal account of a class from Professor John E. Merryman.

Here is what another student—with the help of his pupils—learned from conducting a two-week summer mini-school:

They taught me something. Children have a need to love people and they readily give it away and all they need is someone to be receptive to this love. And this should be one of the functions of the teacher, that is, he should be able to receive love and give it back to them. They showed me that a teacher cannot stand aloof from his students but rather must participate and share with them.

Never has a class helped me as much as this one. I really feel like I'm growing.

I believe that these examples indicate the way in which two educators have put together the cognitive and the affective-experiential to involve learning by the whole student. I could describe others—a teacher of poetry (Moon, 1966), a French teacher (Swenson, 1974), a professor of higher mathematics (White, 1974), a teacher of "incorrigible nonreaders" in the fifth grade, an English instructor (Carr, 1964)—but this would take too much space. Let us turn instead to the empirical studies that have been made, to see what they show us.

WHAT ARE THE RESEARCH RESULTS?

It has been truly fascinating to see research evidence pile up over the years indicating that there is some validity to the hypotheses that I so tentatively presented years ago. I wish to dwell on the evidence from education, but first, one small finding from the field of therapy.

In a study of therapist-client relationships, Barrett-Lennard (1962) found that those clients who eventually showed more therapeutic change perceived more of these therapist qualities at the time of the fifth interview than did those who eventually showed less change. This finding has been corroborated in a larger group of cases by Reinhard Tausch (1978), who found that prediction could be made after only the second interview. I feel certain that this finding would hold in the classroom world as well. If we measured the teacher's attitudes during the first five days of the school year—the attitudes as they exist in the teacher and as they are perceived by the students—we could predict which classrooms would contain learners, and which would contain prisoners. To the degree that these attitudes were held and perceived, we could predict the classrooms in which learning would be by the whole person, with its accompanying involvement and excitement. We could also predict the classrooms in which students would be passive, restless, or rebellious, in which mostly rote learning would be going on.

The research that has endeavored to discover specific relationships between these attitudinal conditions and various elements of the learning process has come about largely through the efforts of Dr. David Aspy and his colleagues, although others have also contributed. There is not the space here to describe the details of the researches, but I will discuss very briefly some of the findings.

To give some samples: The levels of these interpersonal conditions can be measured with reasonable objectivity. It has been shown that they are significantly and positively related to a greater gain in reading achievement in third-graders (Aspy, 1965). They are positively related to grade point average (Pierce, 1966); similarly, to cognitive growth (Aspy, 1967; Aspy, 1969; Aspy & Hadlock, 1967); to an increase in creative interest and productivity (Moon, 1966); to levels of cognitive thinking and to the amount of student-initiated talk (Aspy & Roebuck, 1970). They are related to a diffusion of liking and trust in the classroom, which in turn is related to the students' better utilization of their abilities and greater confidence in themselves (Schmuck, 1966).

One exciting aspect of this research was uncovered by Aspy (1971). He has shown that it is possible to select, quite accurately, teaching personnel who possess those interpersonal qualities that have been shown to be specifically facilitative of whole-person learning. This has many implications.

Adding to his earlier research, Aspy (1972) has not only presented in convincing form these and other investigations, but has shown that the attitudinal qualities we have discussed can be assessed by the teacher for himself or herself, or by others. He also has demonstrated that a school can use such measures to increase the effectiveness of the learning climate in its classrooms.

The conclusion to be drawn from these many studies is that it pays to be personal and human in the classroom. A humane atmosphere is not only more pleasant for all concerned; it also promotes more—and more significant—learning. When attitudes of realness, respect for the individual, understanding of the student's private world are present, exciting things happen. The payoff is not only in such things as grades and reading achievement, but also in more elusive qualities such as greater self-confidence, increased creativity, and more liking for others. In short, such a classroom leads to a positive, unified learning by the whole person.

IMPLICATIONS FOR TEACHER TRAINING

If, then, we can choose to have learning that combines the cognitive and the affective-experiential—the intellectual and the gut-level—and if we know, with a modest degree of accuracy, the interpersonal conditions that produce such learning, what is the next step? It seems obvious to me that we need a change, amounting almost to a revolution, in the training of our teachers. Unfortunately, most teacher-training institutions are highly traditional, stressing only cognitive learning and the methods by which it can be achieved. They are past masters at providing an atmosphere that says, "Don't do as I do. Do as I say." Is it possible to effect change in such institutions?

First, we must ask this question: Is it possible to help develop these interpersonal qualities in student teachers or others preparing for the teaching field? I believe the answer is definitely yes, on two counts. First, as I have mentioned, it would be entirely possible now to select candidates who showed a high potentiality for realness, prizing, and empathic understanding in their relationships. Thus, we could select teacher candidates on different bases from those now used. And second, there is increasingly ample evidence that such attitudes can be developed. I have seen them develop in counselors-in-training. Aspy (1972) has shown that teachers can improve through in-service training. I am sure that we do not yet know all the available means, but some variant of the intensive group experience seems to be of great assistance, providing there is a follow-up of such a task-oriented or encounter group. Another avenue would be to provide student teachers with ample opportunity for independent study. This would encourage teachers to rely on choice, rather than passivity, in their future teaching careers.

Let me give one example of how such changes can come about. A school principal, in his thirties, had been exposed during the course of a seminar to much independent study and also to two weekend encounter group experiences. For his final report he begins,

As I sit at my desk to begin this paper, I have a real feeling of inner excitement. This is an experience that I have never had. For as I write I have no format to follow and I will put my thoughts down as they occur. It's almost a feeling of floating, for to me it doesn't seem to really matter how you, or anyone for that matter, will react to my thoughts. Nevertheless, at the same time I feel that you will accept them as mine regardless of the lack of style, format, or academic expression. . . . My real concern is to try to communicate with myself so that I might better understand myself.

I guess what I am really saying is that I am writing not for you, nor for a grade, nor for a class, but for me. And I feel especially good about that, for this is something that I wouldn't have dared to do or even consider in the past. . . . (Rogers, 1969, p. 84)

It seems clear that he had learned a great deal at the affective and experiential level, for the first time in twenty years of education. He has grown as a person. However, one might well question whether this change would really make him a different kind of administrator or teacher. Here is another small portion of his report:

My staff meeting Tuesday was truly significant as I was able to relate to the staff how I really felt. Many told me afterwards that they were very surprised and impressed and wanted to applaud, not because I had said anything different, but it was the way I said it. I have had various teachers in my office daily who have wanted to relate to me and state they now find me more accepting than ever. . . . I feel that life has so much more meaning. (p. 89)

This has been my experience: when inner changes take place in the attitudes and self-concept of the person, then changes begin to show up in his or her interpersonal behavior.

A Program of Change in Teacher Training

I should like to turn now to the more difficult question of whether it would be possible to change the teacher-training institutions. I am bold and brash enough to say that if I were given a free hand, and if I had the energy and ample funding (say the equivalent of the cost of a half dozen B-52 bombers), I think that in one year I could introduce such a ferment into schools of education that it would initiate a revolution. Since I am sure that must sound like an arrogant statement, I would like to state as precisely as I can what I would do. Much of the plan would change, of course, as obstacles were encountered and as the participants desired to move in somewhat different directions.

First, I would enlist the aid of a large number of skilled facilitators, who are familiar with small-group process. This would be entirely feasible. Then, since it is necessary to begin somewhere, I would in each institution indicate that task-oriented groups would be formed around the topic, "How can this school help the whole person to learn?" Students and faculty would be invited to join on a voluntary basis.

In a general meeting, I would explain that the purpose of these groups would be not only to learn *about* the topics, but that the participants themselves would learn as whole persons; it would not be a purely cognitive experience. This would turn away a great many. People are fearful of getting personally and experientially involved in learning. Suppose only a very small percentage volunteered? That would not concern me.

I would aim to have three weeks of the intensive group experience with cognitive and experiential elements, probably during the summer; a follow-up session with each small group every week; and perhaps a weekend three months later for the same group to discuss the problems that they have met, to evaluate the changes that have come about, and to plan the future steps that they want to take in the direction of change.

The choice of the facilitators would be extremely important, but, again, there are both objective measures and subjective guidelines for selecting facilitators who rank high in the qualities I have described. Aspy (1972) has shown the way to do this, and unintentionally, I believe, he has also shown how important such a choice is. He found that when the facilitator's rankings on these qualities were high, the teachers and supervisors in his or her group showed positive changes in "interpersonal functioning, self-concept, and ability to obtain student-initiated behavior in their classrooms." But when the facilitator rated low, there were no significant changes in the group participants. In other words, to train teachers to provide the attitudinal conditions for whole-person learning, the facilitators must already possess those attitudes. Then, the personal and behavioral changes which I have described in *Freedom to Learn* (1969) occur.

Many educators might be fearful that personal damage would result from these intensive group experiences. Yet, the research by Lieberman, Yalom, and Miles (1973) indicates that damage results primarily when the leader is confronting, challenging, attacking, or intrusive. When the facilitator possesses the attitudes I have described, the potential for psychological damage is minimal, and is certainly outweighed by the potential for positive change. I have discussed this and many other problems related to the leadership and process of the intensive group in *Carl Rogers on Encounter Groups* (1970).

One precondition, if this whole program were to be initiated in teacher-training institutions, would have to be absolutely clear. It could either be laid down by the dean or, preferably, by the funding agency. This condition would be that no one could be discharged because of dissent from the ongoing practices in the institution, or because of introducing innovative ideas and practices in the classroom. In recent years, there have been all too many well-documented instances of teachers and teachers-in-training who have been dismissed from their institutions for nonconformity. The student teacher who believes pupils should have a voice in the curriculum; the instructor—elementary, high school, or college—who attempts to create a freer atmosphere in the classroom, to encourage independent thought, or to experiment with a new approach to grading, is simply dismissed. (See Brownfield, 1973, for one instance.) Administrators are not happy with individuals who rock the boat. Hence, in our teacher-training experiment, protection from such arbitrary action must be provided.

Change and Turbulence

There is one institutional result that I would like to stress. I feel quite certain, on the basis of my experience, that the process I have described would tend to polarize both the faculty and the students and create turbulence within the institution. I happen to believe that such turbulence would be constructive. Traditionalists would be angry at these new innovators, and vice versa. Sacred cows would be questioned. Student teachers, and even their faculty, would tend to think and learn and grow.

One very probable outcome of this kind of ferment would take the form of a "free university" type of teacher-training institution, in which the students would form their own curricula, participate in the facilitation of learning, and find other means of evaluation than grades. The persons who emerged from such a training program could be channeled into one of a limited number of schools that would welcome them. And here again, some polarization would be likely to occur in these schools.

What would such new teachers *do* in their classrooms? Most importantly, they would simply *be* the attitudes that I have described, and new participatory methods would emerge. But if they felt somewhat at a loss, Harold Lyon's book *Learning to Feel— Feeling to Learn* (1971) is full of very practical means of implementing these attitudes. The teachers would be developing classrooms so new in their approaches that they would have little or no resemblance to the old form.

The Ferment of Continuing Change

These, then, would be some of the steps necessary to initiate changes in teacher training. Taken together, what is the essence of their meaning? By the end of one year, there would be many people in the teacher-training institutions who would themselves have learned in a total way, and who would be enthusiastic and eager to have their students learn in the same fashion. This is like an infusion of yeast into a lump of dough. The numbers of people initially involved might be small, but the pervasive effect would be enormous. You may well ask, "How can you be so sure of all this?" I feel assurance because I have, with my own eyes, seen it happen twice. The first was in the Immaculate Heart school system in Los Angeles, where self-directed change is going on apace years after our brief interventive efforts ceased. The second case concerns such a program with better financing and better planning, which introduced an incredible ferment into the inner-city school system of Louisville, Kentucky (Dickenson, et al., 1970; Department of Research and Evaluation, 1973). Can you imagine intensive communication work-shops and human-relations labs for 1600 school person-nel coming into being within only six months? Taking part in these programs were the Board of Education, central-office staff, principals, and teachers. In both school systems the polarization seemed most unfortu-nate for a time, but out of it grew a new and confident sense of direction, with new and more vital individuals in charge of those new directions. The change in teacher education at Immaculate Heart College was unbelievable. A professor of education in the college wrote:

We are working on a self-initiated and self-directed pro-gram in teacher education. We had a fantastically exciting weekend workshop here recently. Students, faculty, and administration, seventy-five in all, brainstormed in a most creative and productive way. The outcome is that students will immerse themselves in schools all over the city observing classes, sitting in on faculty meetings, interviewing teachers, students and adminstrators. Our students will then describe what they need to know, to experience, to do, in order to teach. They will then gather faculty and other students around them to assist in accomplishing their own goals. (Per-sonal communication, 1969)

The lessons from this experience are several. The professor was very deeply affected by the encounter group experience, which led her to take further training in group leadership and group dynamics, and to facili-tate groups on her own. She became not only much more open to her students, but also a much more confi-dent person, able to initiate and implement new ideas. She had learned as a whole person. She became so much more influential in the college that she was placed in charge of a teacher-training program. Her letter gives evidence of the way in which she is encouraging these young teachers-to-be to incorporate both the cognitive and the affective-experiential into learning how to teach. As usual, when given the chance to be self-directing, when trusted to learn, students work harder than anyone would have a right to demand of them. There can be little doubt that they, in turn, will provide a similar opportunity to *their* students, and conditions whereby these students can also learn to feel as well as to think. This is the exciting, pervasive ferment occasioned when an individual has a chance to learn as a whole person.

CONCLUSIONS

I cannot help but conclude by saying that we have the theoretical knowledge, the practical methods, and the day-to-day skills with which to radically change our whole educational system. We know how to bring together, in one experience, the intellectual learning, the range of personal emotions, and the basic physiological impact that constitute significant learning by the whole person. We know how to develop student teachers into agents for this sort of change. Do we have the will, the determination, to utilize this know-how to humanize our educational institutions? That is the question we all must answer.

EPILOGUE

Since I have already given examples from our experience with the Immaculate Heart school system in Los Angeles, I will present an extremely abbreviated account of the project, and then some excerpts from a follow-up study at the end of three years and another personal follow-up report after seven years.

In 1967, I wrote a paper entitled "A Plan for Self-Directed Change in an Educational System." (This can be found in Rogers, 1969, pp. 303–323.) Some of the administrators and faculty of Immaculate Heart wished their system to be the target system for the experiment, and so the project was started as a joint enterprise with the Center for Studies of the Person.

The heart of the program consisted of a series of encounter groups offered to all of the faculty and administrators, and later to a number of student groups, with faculty included. Participation was voluntary, and a number of people did not wish to join.

Although many mistakes were made in the planning and implementation of the project, the response of the participants was almost entirely enthusiastic. Faculty began to change their methods of teaching, and some important administrative policy changes were made. The nonparticipants were often shocked by the degree of chaos involved in the changes, and they became, in some instances, violently critical. But there is no doubt that some of the changes were significant and far-reaching. The statement by the professor of education about the totally innovative program of teacher education (see page 285) is evidence of one of these changes.

Three years later, two outside evaluators who had been observing the program from the beginning made their final study. In summary, the assessment team observed a number of positive changes that had been predicted, some that had not been predicted, and a number of turbulent and polarizing attitudes that definitely exceeded expectations. The positive changes were greatest among the students and younger faculty.

The least amount of change was in the administrative staff and structure and in older members of the faculty and administration.

Seven years after the eighteen-month experiment, the faculty member who headed the teacher-training program that had been started as a result of the experiment wrote me a lengthy letter of her personal perceptions. I will quote only three statements.

I know beyond a shadow of a doubt that I wouldn't have volunteered for the faculty seminar [which led to the new program of teacher education] if I had not had the opportunity in the encounter groups to go a bit beyond my paralyzing fears of inadequacy. . . .

The new self-initiated and self-directed teacher-education program is now in its fourth successful year. . . .

My guess is that there are any number of system changes on campus that wouldn't have happened without the project.

The Louisville program was initiated by Dr. Newman Walker, the superintendent, who was employed by a desperate Board of Education to try to renovate a rapidly deteriorating inner-city school system.

In addition to human-relations labs for the Board of Education and all of the faculty and administration, Walker introduced all kinds of innovations: open classrooms, neighborhood school boards composed of parents and teachers, and other new ideas. He *trusted* students, teachers, parents, school-board members, and even the violent critics from the John Birch Society. There was a period, as in the Immaculate Heart project, of a high degree of turbulence and chaos. Gradually this diminished, and by the end of three years, a highly innovative school system was running with as much smoothness as could be expected in a large organization. Morale was excellent. (A more complete account is contained in Foster & Back, 1974.)

Then, a tragic set of circumstances, having nothing to do with the innovative policies in the system, brought an end to the whole experiment. Walker had brought a full quota of blacks into the faculty and administration, but the pupils were predominantly black. So a court order merged the inner-city system with the very conservative county system, composed of the white suburban population. The two philosophies of education were antithetical, and Walker was forced to resign. There were violent antibusing riots—an "unholy mess" of antagonistic events. They were sufficient to bury the growingly successful enterprise. Many of the innovative teachers left. Only one neighborhood school board managed to survive—its powers greatly curtailed. Thus was brought to an end a most promising adventure in a large educational system.

REFERENCES

ASPY, D. N. A study of three facilitative conditions and their relationship to the achievement of third grade students. Unpublished doctoral dissertation, University of Kentucky, 1965.

ASPY, D. N. Counseling and education. In R. R. Carkhuff (Ed.), *The counselor's contribution to facilitative processes*. Urbana, Illinois: Parkinson, 1967.

ASPY, D. N. The effect of teacher-offered conditions of empathy, positive regard, and congruence upon student achievement. *Florida Journal of Educational Research*, 1969, *11*(1), 39–48.

ASPY, D. N. Supervisors, your levels of humanness may make a difference. Unpublished.

ASPY, D. N. *Toward a technology of humanizing education*. Champaign, Illinois: Research Press, 1972.

ASPY, D. N., & HADLOCK, W. The effect of empathy, warmth, and genuineness on elementary students' reading achievement.

Reviewed in Truax, C. B., and Carkhuff, R. R. *Toward effective counseling and psychotherapy.* Chicago: Aldine, 1967.

ASPY, D. N., & ROEBUCK, F. N. An investigation of the relationship between student levels of cognitive functioning and the teacher's classroom behavior. Unpublished manuscript, University of Florida, Gainesville, 1970.

ASPY, D. N., & ROEBUCK, F. N. The necessity for facilitative interpersonal conditions in teaching. Unpublished manuscript, University of Florida, Gainsville.

BARRETT-LENNARD, G. T. Dimensions of therapist response as causal factors in therapeutic change. *Psychological Monographs,* 1962, *76*(Whole No. 562).

BROWNFIELD, C. A. *Humanizing college learning: A taste of hemlock.* New York: Exposition Press, 1973.

CARR, J. B. Project freedom. *The English Journal,* March 1964, pp. 202–204.

DEPARTMENT OF RESEARCH AND EVALUATION, Louisville Independent School District, 1972–73 Final Evaluation Report, Louisville, Kentucky, 1973 (mimeographed).

DICKENSON, W. A., ET AL. A humanistic program for change in a large inner-city school system. *Journal of Humanistic Psychology,* Autumn 1970, *10*(2), 111–120.

FOSTER, C., & BACK, J. A neighborhood school board: Its infancy, its crises, its growth. *Education,* Winter 1974, *95*(2), 145–162.

HUDIBURG, R. Some frank comments on openness. *ES/ESTPP Newsletter* No. 3. Burbank Junior High School, Boulder, Colorado.

LIEBERMAN, M., YALOM, I., & MILES, M. *Encounter groups: First facts.* New York: Basic Books, 1973.

LYON, H. C., JR. *Learning to feel—feeling to learn.* Columbus, Ohio: Charles E. Merrill, 1971.

MOON, S. F. Teaching the self. *Improving College and University Teaching.* Autumn 1966, *14*, 213–229.

PIERCE, R. An investigation of grade-point average and therapeutic process variables. Unpublished dissertation, University of Massachusetts, Amherst, 1966. Reviewed in

Carkhuff, R. R., & Berenson, B. G., *Beyond counseling and therapy.* New York: Holt, Rinehart & Winston, 1967.

RESTON, J. *The New York Times,* November 29, 1970.

ROGERS, C. R. The necessary and sufficient conditions of therapeutic personality change. *Journal of Consulting Psychology,* 1957, *21,* 95–103.

ROGERS, C. R. *Freedom to learn.* Columbus, Ohio: Charles E. Merrill, 1969.

ROGERS, C. R. *Carl Rogers on encounter groups.* New York: Harper & Row, 1970.

SCHMUCK, R. Some aspects of classroom social climate. *Psychology in the Schools,* 1966, *3,* 59–65.

SWENSON, G. Grammar and growth: A "French connection." *Education,* Winter 1974, *95*(2), 115–127.

TAUSCH, R. Facilitative dimensions in interpersonal relations: Verifying the theoretical assumptions of Carl Rogers in school, family education, client-centered therapy, and encounter groups. *College Student Journal,* Spring 1978, *12*(1), 2–11.

WHITE, A. M. Humanistic mathematics. *Education,* Winter 1974, *95*(2), 128–133.

Beyond the Watershed:
And Where Now?

In this chapter I have focused on several topics relating to a humanistic education. The material is drawn from talks that I presented to educational groups between 1972 and 1979. While I stress the innovative progress being made, I in no way overlook the present trend toward the conservative and the traditional.

One of the elements that I bring in is the power aspect of education. I have been slow to recognize this. It was many years before I realized why my writings and my way of counseling and teaching were so controversial. Only in recent years have I recognized how threatening were my views. If accepted, they effectively reduced the political power of therapists or teachers: they no longer had "power over" other individuals. In this chapter I endeavor to make more clear the threat posed by a person-centered approach in education—to the administrator, the teacher, and even the student.

I also bring in the exciting new research evidence supporting the efficacy of the humanistic way in education. I have been puzzled by the fact that the massive research efforts of David Aspy, Flora Roebuck, and their colleagues seem to have gone relatively unnoticed in educational circles. I wonder if this is because they are doing a new type of research, or whether the findings are, again, too threatening. I do not know.

At the end of the chapter, I let my imagination wander into possible future frontiers of learning, especially frontiers of investigation. Here my thoughts are rather "far out" and may surprise some readers. But I will let the chapter speak for itself.

CROSSING THE WATERSHED

I firmly believe that innovative, humanistic, experiential learning, whether taking place in or out of the classroom, is here to stay and has a future. So I am not only going to complain about what *is* in education. I am also going to look forward. We are beyond the watershed. Let me explain what I mean.

When the early explorers and pioneers struck out for the West, they followed the rivers and watercourses. For a long time they were traveling upstream, always going against the current, which became increasingly swift as they climbed through the foothills and into the mountains. Then came the moment when they passed the divide. The going was still very rough, the streams no more than trickles. But now they were moving *with* the current, which was flowing into stronger, larger rivers. There were now important forces working *for* them, not always against them.

I believe that is where we are today in education. We have passed the watershed. Now, instead of a few lonely pioneers, we find an increasing flow of movement into an education more fit for humans. Every city has its alternative schools, free schools, and open classrooms. At the college level, I get letters from teachers of astronomy, mathematics, mechanical engineering, French, chemistry, biology, psychology, English—all telling of the tentative steps they have taken toward providing for their students a freedom to learn, and the exciting rewards of such steps. Academic credit is even being granted for learnings outside of school. There are other signs, too. I am part of a program in which nine hundred medical educators have attended workshops on the humanizing of medical education; they now are calling in consultants to help them achieve that aim in their separate medical schools. Universities without walls, programs of independent study, graduate schools that grant students more autonomy—all are burgeoning. We are a current to be reckoned with in American education.

THE POLITICS OF POWER

But although a human type of education is here to stay, it is most certainly not the prevailing type of education. So I would like to take a look at the two polar extremes of our modes of education and at the politics that is implicit in each approach.

Before I go any further, I should say what I mean by the word "politics." I am not at all thinking of political parties or government organizations. I am using the term in its modern sense. We hear talk of the "politics of the family," or the "politics of psychotherapy," or "sexual politics." In this present-day sense, I believe that the word "politics" has to do with power or control in interpersonal relationships, and the extent to which persons strive to gain such power—or to relinquish it. It has to do with the way decisions are made. Who makes them? Where is the locus, or center, of decision-making power? "Politics" concerns the effects of such power-oriented actions on individuals or on systems. So when I use the word "politics," it is with such meanings in mind.

THE TRADITIONAL MODE

If we think of the political characteristics of education, the traditional mode is at one end of a continuum, and a person-centered approach at the other. I think every educational effort and every educator can be located somewhere on this scale. You may want to be thinking about where you, or your department, or your institution, would place on this continuum.

First, let's take a look at conventional education as we have known it for a long time in the United States. I will describe what I believe are its major characteristics as experienced by students and faculty.

1. *The teachers are the possessors of knowledge, the students the expected recipients.* The teachers are the experts; they know their fields. The students sit with poised pencil and notebook, waiting for the words of wisdom. There is a great difference in the status level between the instructors and the students.

2. *The lecture, or some means of verbal instruction, is the major means of getting knowledge into the recipients. The examination measures the extent to which the students have received it. These are the central elements of this kind of education.* Why the lecture is regarded as the major means of instruction is a mystery to me. Lectures made sense before books were published, but their current rationale is almost never explained. The increasing stress on the examination is also mysterious. Certainly its importance in the United States has increased enormously in the last couple of decades.

3. *The teachers are the possessors of power, the students the ones who obey.* (Administrators are also possessors of power, and both teachers and students are the ones who obey.) Control is always exercised downward.

4. *Rule by authority is the accepted policy in the classroom.* New teachers are often advised, "Make sure you get control of your students on the very first day." The authority figure—the instructor—is very much the central figure in education. He or she may be

greatly admired as a fountain of knowledge, or may be despised, but the teacher is always the center.

5. *Trust is at a minimum.* Most notable is the teacher's distrust of the students. The students cannot be expected to work satisfactorily without the teacher constantly supervising and checking on them. The students' distrust of the teacher is more diffuse—a lack of trust in the teacher's motives, honesty, fairness, competence. There may be a real rapport between an entertaining lecturer and those who are being entertained; there may be admiration for the instructor, but mutual trust is not a noticeable ingredient.

6. *The subjects (the students) are best governed by being kept in an intermittent or constant state of fear.* Today, there is not much physical punishment, but public criticism and ridicule and the students' constant fear of failure are even more potent. In my experience this state of fear appears to increase as we go up the educational ladder, because the student has more to lose. In elementary school, the individual may be an object of scorn or be regarded as a dolt. In high school, there is added to this the fear of failure to graduate, with its vocational, economic, and educational disadvantages. In college, all these consequences are magnified and intensified. In graduate school, sponsorship by one professor offers even greater opportunities for extreme punishment due to some autocratic whim. Many graduate students have failed to receive their degrees because they have refused to obey, or to conform to every wish of, their major professor. Their position is analogous to that of a slave, subject to the life-and-death power of the master.

7. *Democracy and its values are ignored and scorned in practice.* Students do not participate in choosing their

individual goals, curricula, or manner of working. They are chosen for them. Students have no part in the choice of teaching personnel nor any voice in educational policy. Likewise, the teachers often have no choice in choosing their administrative officers. Teachers, too, often have no participation in forming educational policy. All this is in striking contrast to all the teaching *about* the virtues of democracy, the importance of the "free world," and the like. The political practices of the school are in the most striking contrast to what is taught. While being taught that freedom and responsibility are the glorious features of "our democracy," the students are experiencing themselves as powerless, as having little freedom, and as having almost no opportunity to exercise choice or carry responsibility.

8. *There is no place for whole persons in the educational system, only for their intellects.* In elementary school, the bursting curiosity and the excess of physical energy characteristic of the normal child are curbed and, if possible, stifled. In junior high and high school, the one overriding interest of all the students—sex and the emotional and physical relationships it involves—is almost totally ignored, and certainly not regarded as a major area for learning. There is very little place for emotions in the secondary school. In college, the situation is even more extreme—it is *only* the *mind* that is welcomed.

If you think that such views have vanished or that I am exaggerating in this respect, we have only to turn to the *Los Angeles Times* of December 13, 1974. Here we find that the University of California (embracing all of the state universities—Berkeley, University of California at Los Angeles, and others) is lobbying to keep John

Vasconcellos, a state legislator, off any committees having to do with university policy. Vasconcellos for the previous three years had headed, with distinction, a legislative study of higher education. And why is the university trying to keep him from having anything to do with university policy? Because of two changes he favors: First, he favors setting aside a percentage of the budget for innovative educational programs. This is strongly opposed by university officials. But the most important reason for opposing him, according to Dr. Jay Michael, a vice president of the university, is that he favors the inclusion of *both* "affective and cognitive" learning. Says Michael, "We believe . . . there is knowledge that exists separate and apart from how a person feels . . . and that accumulated knowledge of mankind is cognitive. It can be transmitted, it can be taught and learned, and the pursuit of that kind of knowledge is academic research." He continues, "It appears to us that he [Vasconcellos] would like to abandon cognitive learning, or at least reduce its importance to a level unacceptable to scholars."

In reply, Vasconcellos says he values cognitive skills, "but I also believe that the affective, the emotional component . . . is terribly important." He believes that cognitive skills should be combined with better knowledge of self and of interpersonal behavior.

The politics of this difference is quite fascinating. The vice president clearly holds to the "jug and mug" theory of education, where the faculty possess the purely intellectual and factual knowledge and transfer it to the passive recipients. So threatened is Dr. Michael by any possibility of change that he opposes *any* innovation in educational procedure. But most threatening of all is the idea that faculty and students alike are *human* in their experiencing of a feeling component in all knowledge. If this were even partially admitted, students and faculty would be on a more equal level, and the politics of domination would be weakened. This is the position of a leading official of one of the "great" university systems in 1975! He is opposed to innovation; he is opposed to learning by the whole person!

This traditional picture of education is exceedingly common. I am sure that we have all seen it and experienced it. Now, however, it is no longer viewed as the one and only way by which education may proceed. The humanistic, person-centered, process-oriented way of learning has made much progress. This makes it worthwhile to try to describe the characteristic features of such learning in operation. Here is an attempt, with an eye to the politics of the enterprise.

THE FUNDAMENTALS OF A CENTER FOR PERSON-CENTERED LEARNING

The first fundamental is essentially a precondition. The others listed are features that may be experienced or observed in such a school, college, or graduate school where humanistic education has taken root.

1. *Precondition.* The leaders, or persons who are perceived as authority figures in the situation, are sufficiently secure within themselves and in their relationship to others that they experience an essential trust in the capacity of others to think for themselves, to learn for themselves. If this precondition exists, then the following aspects become possible and tend to be implemented.

2. *The facilitative persons share with the others— students, and possibly also parents or community*

members—the responsibility for the learning process.
Curricular planning, the mode of administration and
operation, the funding, and the policy-making are all
the responsibility of the particular group involved.
Thus, a class may be responsible for its own curriculum, but the total group may be responsible for overall
policy. In any case, responsibility is shared.

3. *The facilitators provide learning resources—from
within themselves and their own experience, from books
or other materials, or from community experiences.* The
learners are encouraged to add resources of which they
have knowledge or in which they have experience. The
facilitators open doors to resources outside the experience of the group.

4. *The students develop their own programs of learning, individually or in cooperation with others.*
Exploring their own interests, facing this wealth of
resources, they each make choices as to their own
learning directions, and they carry the responsibility
for the consequences of those choices.

5. *A facilitative learning climate is provided.* In meetings of the class or of the school as a whole, an atmosphere of realness, of caring, and of understanding listening is evident. This climate may spring initially from
the person who is the perceived leader. As the learning
process continues, it is more and more often provided
by the learners for one another. Learning from one
another becomes as important as learning from books
or films or community experiences.

6. *The focus of the learning center is primarily on fostering the continuing process of learning.* The content
of the learning, while significant, falls into a secondary
place. Thus, a course is successfully ended not when
the students have "learned all they need to know," but

when they have made significant progress in learning *how to learn* what they want to know.

7. *The discipline necessary to reach the students' goals is a self-discipline,* and is recognized and accepted by the learners as being their individual responsibilities. Self-discipline replaces external discipline.

8. *The evaluation of the extent and significance of each student's learning is made primarily by the learner himself or herself,* although the self-evaluations may be influenced and enriched by caring feedback from other members of the group and from the facilitator.

9. *In this growth-promoting climate, the learning tends to be deeper, proceeds at a more rapid rate, and is more pervasive in the life and behavior of the students than learning acquired in the traditional classroom.* This comes about because the direction is self-chosen, the learning is self-initiated, and whole persons, with feelings and passions as well as intellect, are invested in the process. (Later in this chapter, I will describe some research to support this statement.)

THE POLITICS OF A
PERSON-CENTERED EDUCATION

Perhaps we can best consider the political implications of such an approach by thinking back to the definition given early in this chapter and endeavoring to apply it here.

Who has the essential power and control? It is clear that it is the learner, or the learners as a group, including the facilitator-learner.

Who is attempting to gain control over whom? The students are in the process of gaining control over the course of their own learnings and their own lives.

The facilitator relinquishes control over others, retaining control only over himself or herself.

What are the strategies used in relation to power? I see two. The facilitator provides a psychological climate in which the learner is able to take responsible control. The facilitator also helps to de-emphasize static or content goals, and thus encourages a focus on the process, on *experiencing* the way in which learning takes place.

Where is the decision-making power? Such power is in the hands of the individual or individuals who will be affected by the decision. Depending on the issue, the choice may be up to the individual student, or to the students and facilitators as a group, or it may involve administrators, parents, members of the local government, or community members. Deciding on what to learn in a particular course may be entirely in the hands of each student and the facilitator. Whether to build a new building affects a much larger group, and would be so dealt with.

Who regulates the modes of feeling, thought, behavior, values? Clearly, each person does.

It is obvious that the growing, learning person is the politically powerful force in such education. The *learner* is the center. This process of learning represents a revolutionary about-face from the politics of traditional education.

WHY EDUCATORS SHIFT
THEIR POLITICS

What is it that causes educators to move in the direction of becoming facilitative, to move away from conventional education and toward a person-centered type of learning? I would like, first, to cite my own experience.

In doing individual counseling and psychotherapy, I found it more and more rewarding to trust the client's capacity for moving toward self-understanding, for taking constructive steps to resolve his or her problems. These things happened if I could create a facilitative climate in which I was empathic, caring, and real.

If clients were trustworthy, why couldn't I create this same kind of climate with students and foster a self-guided process of learning? This question nagged at me more and more. So, at the University of Chicago I decided to try. I ran into a great deal of resistance and hostility in students, more than I had found in clients. Typical comments were, "I paid good money for this course and I want you to teach me," or "I don't know what to learn—you're the expert." Part of this resistance grew out of the fact that for years, these students had been dependent. Part of it, I think, was due to the fact that I probably put all responsibility on the class, instead of on all of us together. I certainly made many mistakes. Sometimes I doubted the wisdom of what I was attempting to do, but in spite of my clumsiness, the results were astonishing. Students worked harder, read more deeply, expressed themselves more responsibly, learned more, did more creative thinking than in any previous classes. So I persevered, and gradually I improved as a facilitator of learning. I found I couldn't go back.

In this new approach, I was much encouraged by the experience of others. More and more teachers wrote me that they were taking the plunge of changing their approach, of moving along the continuum in a person-centered direction. The experience was very threatening to those teachers who had taught in a conventional way or were working under a restrictive school administration. Yet, they were finding it so rewarding when they trusted students that the satisfactions more than balanced the frightening relinquishment of status and control.

As I, and an increasing number of others, have come to experience the satisfactions of a person-centered education, this small trickle of pioneering educators has grown into a highly significant trend in present-day learning enterprises. I would like to mention some of my personal learnings regarding this kind of development.

THE THREAT

I have gradually recognized the terrific *political* threat posed by a person-centered approach. The teacher has to face up to the fearful aspects of the shift of power and control from the teacher to the whole group of learners, including the former teacher, now a learner-facilitator. Giving away power seems terrifying to some. One person-centered teacher in a school constitutes a threat to every other teacher.

I know a teacher, a fine facilitator of learning, who was selected by the students as one of the two or three best teachers in the college. She was finally dropped from the faculty because she repeatedly and resolutely refused to agree to grade on a curve; in other words, she refused to promise in advance that she would fail a certain percentage of her students no matter what the quality of their work. This was taken as evidence that she did not believe in standards, since in the circuitous logic of the conventional school "standards" means, in practice, failing students. She was also saying in effect, "I refuse to use grades as an instrument of punishment." So she was not only undermining "standards," but she was undermining the punitive power of the faculty. It was such an uncomfortable threat that they *had* to get rid of her, although they were embarrassed to do so. This is far from being an isolated incident. It shows how even one individual can threaten a whole faculty.

One thing I have learned, both from my experience and that of others, is that I had better be fully willing to take the risk before I take any step toward relinquishing my control. Better to move very gradually, by comfortable degrees, than to relinquish power, become frightened, and then try to take it back: that is the worst thing that can happen.

A second recognition is that it is as frightening for many students to take responsible control of themselves as it is for the instructor to give them that opportunity. Many students who loudly demand more freedom come to a complete and confused stop when they are allowed responsible freedom. Nothing in their background has prepared them to make choices, to make mistakes and live with the consequences, to endure the chaos of uncertainty as they try to select directions in which they wish to move. They need understanding companionship from the facilitator as they all search for new ways. They need a supporting atmosphere so that they can fail and still accept themselves, and can succeed without feeling competitive.

Administrators, too, need our understanding. In a culture that understands nothing but control from the top down, they are fearful that they will be considered weak if they put trust and decision-making power in the hands of teachers and students and parents. Yet, this can be excitingly and satisfyingly done, as shown by the experiences of some schools and school systems.

In summary, then, we should recognize that the transformation to a truly humanistic, person-centered education constitutes a full-scale revolution. It is not a way of tinkering with conventional education. Rather, it entails turning the politics of education upside down. We need to recognize that fact. I like to think of myself as a quiet revolutionary. Many other teachers are in the same category. We need to face the sobering responsibility of this new politics while we move with courage and hard work toward the fulfillment of our revolutionary vision. We are working toward a democracy in education that goes clear to the grass roots. It is worth our best effort.

PERSONAL ISSUES

The fact that we have crossed the watershed, that it is no longer sufficient to be simply *against*, brings with it new personal perplexities for the educator. It raises new problems of interpersonal politics in education. Teachers or administrators who are moving in the direction of innovative humanistic education are asking themselves a number of tough questions:

To what extent do I, in my deepest feelings, trust students, in a facilitative climate, to be self-directing? What do I do with the ambivalence I often feel in this respect?

Where do I find my rewards? Do I need a great deal of direct satisfaction for my hungry ego? Or can I find equally great ego rewards in being facilitative of the development of others?

How do I prevent myself from becoming a rigid, dogmatic "true believer" in humanistic education? The intolerant "true believer" is a menace to any field, yet I suspect each one of us finds traces of that person in ourself. Do I believe I have the final, best way in education? If so, how can I move beyond that?

How can I maintain my integrity and yet hold a position in a system that is philosophically opposed to what

I am doing? This is a terribly difficult problem, often faced, I suspect, by many of us.

I cannot answer these questions. Each educator must find his or her own answer in an individual, personal way.

IS THERE ANY EVIDENCE?

I have spoken of the superiority of a person-centered approach to education, and it is surely clear to the reader that this is my bias. Is there any evidence to back up this claim and this attitude? The answer is yes; there is indeed a solid body of evidence.

The research studies of David Aspy and his colleagues in the National Consortium for Humanizing Education are only beginning to be known, but I regard them as highly important. For a number of years, Aspy has been the leader in a series of research studies aimed at finding out whether human, person-centered characteristics in a classroom have any measurable effects, and if so, what these effects are. He and his major colleague, Flora Roebuck, have written a general report of their findings (1974a); with other colleagues, they have also written a series of technical reports of their studies (1974b).

As a starting point, Aspy took the basic hypothesis that we had formulated in client-centered therapy, redefining the terms slightly to make them more appropriate to the school setting. Empathy (E) was redefined as a teacher's attempt to understand the personal meaning of the school experience for each student. Positive regard (PR) was defined as the various ways in which the teacher shows respect for the students as persons. Congruence (C) needed no redefinition; it was the extent to which the teacher was genuine in relationship to the students.

The method was first to obtain tape-recorded hours of classroom instruction. Rating scales, ranging from low to high, were developed to assess various degrees of these three primary attitudes, as shown in teachers' behavior. Basing their measurements on these three scales, unbiased raters measured the "facilitative conditions" as exhibited by each teacher. These ratings were then correlated with students' achievement-test scores, problem-solving ability, number of absences from class, and a large number of other variables.

Having established a methodology, the researchers applied it on a previously unheard-of scale. Their final report indicates that they recorded and assessed nearly 3,700 hours of classroom instruction from 550 elementary and secondary school teachers! These studies were done in various parts of the United States and in several other countries. They involved black, white, and Mexican-American teachers and students. No other study of comparable magnitude has ever been made.

Here is my summary of the findings of Aspy and his colleagues:

1. There was a clear correlation between the facilitative conditions provided by the teacher and the academic achievement of students. This finding has been repeatedly confirmed. Students of "high-level" teachers (those high in the facilitative conditions) tended to show the greatest gains in learning. A sobering finding was that students of "low-level" teachers may actually be retarded in their learning by their teachers' deficiencies.

2. The situation most conducive to learning was one in which teachers who exhibited high levels of the facilita-

tive attitudes were backed up and supervised by principals with similarly high levels. Under these conditions, students showed greater gains not only in school subjects but also in other important areas.

They became more adept at using their higher cognitive processes such as problem-solving. (This was especially noteworthy when the teacher showed a high degree of positive regard and respect. Creative problem-solving evidently requires a nurturant climate.)

They had more positive self-concepts than students in the other groups.

They initiated more behavior in the classroom.

They exhibited fewer discipline problems.

They had a lower rate of absence from school.

In one exciting study, they even showed an increase in IQ. In this study, twenty-five black first-graders with "high-level" teachers and twenty-five with "low-level" teachers were given individual intelligence tests nine months apart. The first group showed an average IQ increase from 85 to 94. The figures for the second group were 84 and 84—no change whatsoever.

3. Teachers can improve in their levels of facilitative conditions with as little as 15 hours of carefully planned intensive training, involving both cognitive and experiential learning. Considering the demonstrated influence of these attitudinal conditions, it is highly important to know that they can be increased.

4. Of significance for all areas of education is the finding that teachers improve in these attitudes only when their trainers exhibit a high level of these facilitative conditions. In other words, this means that such attitudes are "caught," experientially, from another person. They are not simply intellectual learnings.

5. Teachers exhibiting high levels of facilitative conditions tend to have other characteristics:

They have more positive self-concepts than low-level teachers.

They are more self-disclosing to their students.

They respond more to students' feelings.

They give more praise.

They are more responsive to students' ideas.

They lecture less often.

6. Neither the geographical location of the classes nor the race of the teacher or racial composition of the students altered these findings. Whether we are speaking of black, white, or Chicano teachers; black, white, or Chicano students; or classes in the North, the South, the Virgin Islands, England, Canada, or Israel, the findings are essentially the same.

Aspy and Roebuck (1974a) conclude as follows after analyzing their mountains of data:

The results are by and large supporting our original findings though we have been able to sharpen them greatly. That is, the measures of the conditions (E, C, PR) continue to relate positively and significantly to positive student growth. Additionally, they relate negatively and significantly to student deterioration such as discipline problems and negative attitudes about school.

For me, these studies offer adequate evidence that the more the psychological climate of the classroom is person-centered, the more are vital and creative learnings fostered. This statement holds for both elementary and secondary classes. It has yet to be investigated at the college level, but there is no reason to suppose the findings would be sharply different. So I trust it is clear from what I have said that I believe person-centered education can be defined, and that it is effective.

A POSSIBLE EMPHASIS IN RESEARCH

I am not so bold as to try to predict the future of this new mode of promoting learning, except to say that its future is likely to be multifaceted, exciting, controversial, and revolutionary in its implications. I would, however, like to express two hopes in regard to that future.

The first has to do with the research that is necessary to learn more about the meaning of this changed way of learning. I believe that it will be a great mistake if the primary emphasis is on the assessment of the *outcomes* of a self-directed experiential learning. Here I would like to draw upon my own experience in research in psychotherapy.

Person-centered therapists were under pressure—just as innovative educators are today—to prove that our approach to therapy was effective. We gradually carried on more and more sophisticated studies to assess the outcomes. But when this was the sole purpose of the research, the results, even though the evidence of effectiveness was positive, were always disappointing. We found, as could have been predicted, that some clients were more successful than others, some therapists more effective than others. But assessment studies are not heuristic, do not lead forward. They offer almost no clues to the elements we need to know to improve therapy or to understand its process. Only when we developed hypotheses of the "if-then" variety could we begin to discern that *if* certain elements were present in the relationship, *then* certain constructive changes occurred. If other elements were present, the changes might lead to a deterioration or a disintegration in behavior.

This is one reason that I described Aspy's research at such length. I personally hope that research will go in this general direction. Starting from a well-developed if-then theory, Aspy investigated relationships between antecedent attitudinal elements and a wide variety of outcome variables. So, in his findings, he was able to point to those elements that had a positive effect on learning and those that had a negative influence. Consequently, the end result was not only an assessment of the learning, but a pinpointing of specifics that should be stressed in the training of teachers. Then he went ahead to show that teachers could, with training, improve in these specifics.

So I hope that research in innovative education will place secondary emphasis on assessment and primary stress on theory-based hypotheses that may give us deeper understanding of the antecedent conditions associated with effectiveness or ineffectiveness in such education.

THE EXPLORATION OF INNER SPACE?

Up to this point I have, whether right or wrong, felt quite secure in what I have been saying. Now it is with some trepidation that I wish to express a second hope, not very clearly formulated in my mind and indefinite in its outline.

I believe that the next great frontier of learning, the area in which we will be exploring exciting new possibilities, is a region scarcely mentioned by hard-headed researchers. It is the area of the intuitive, the psychic, the vast inner space that looms before us. I hope that innovative education moves forward the learnings in this primarily noncognitive realm, the area that currently seems illogical and irrational.

There is a growing body of evidence, which is hard to ignore, that shows capacities and potentials within the psyche that seem almost limitless, and that fall almost entirely outside the field of science as we have known it. It would seem obvious, for example, that an individual floating weightless in a tank of warm water, with almost zero input of stimulation from sight, sound, touch, taste, or smell, would be experiencing nothing. But what is the fact? Such an individual is bombarded by rich visual imagery, hallucinations, imagined sounds, all kinds of bizarre and often frightening experiences coming from unknown sources of inner stimulation. What is the meaning of this? It appears that our inner world is continually up to something we know nothing about, unless we shut off the outer stimuli.

Or another question, another possible aspect for exploration: Is it possible for the whole body, the whole organism, to learn something that the mind does not know, or only learns later? What about the well-substantiated reports of telepathic communication between members of the Masai tribe in Africa, as well as other so-called primitive tribes? Could it be that our Western culture has forgotten something they know? Can we know, as they seem to have known, when we are in tune with the pulse beat of the world? A compelling fictional but true-to-life account of such abilities is contained in Water's (1942) classic book, "The Man Who Killed the Deer." We need, I believe, to learn more about our intuitive abilities, our capacity for sensing with our whole organism.

A friend of mine is working on a book of psychic dreams, of which he has collected and studied a large number. A "psychic dream" is defined as a dream about an actual event that occurs at a distance from the dreamer, and about which the dreamer has not been previously informed, or a dream that is precognitive, predicting an event that actually occurs. For example, a woman I know had a dream (or a vision) of a relative of hers being near death in a hospital bed in a foreign country. A phone call confirmed that this was true—the dream matched the fact. Another person I know received a message through the Ouija board that predicted "death soon." The message was ambiguous as to the person concerned but gave the date when death was to be expected. Within two days of the date given, her brother was killed in an auto accident.

I believe that many people have such dreams or precognitions, but we have quite systematically ruled them out of our general consciousness. But if we, or even some of us, have little-understood abilities and capacities, they should be a prime field for learning.

I will not press my point further. I would only say that this whole intuitive and psychic world is being opened to thoughtful, serious investigation. Two examples are the scholarly review of intuition by Frances Clark (1973) and the careful research of Dr. Grof (1975) on the puzzling and challenging inner experiences of individuals under LSD. There is ample reason to think that the inner experiences of individuals constitute as vast and mysterious an area for exploration as the incredible galaxies and "black holes" of outer space. I am simply expressing the hope that innovative educators and learners may have the courage, the creativity, and the skill to enter and learn this world of inner space.

CONCLUSION

I have endeavored to make a quick survey of the new issues that are being and will be faced by a human, innovative education as it increasingly comes into its own as a major social force. I have defined this new person-centered approach to learning as I perceive it, and contrasted it with the traditional approach. I have sketched some of the ways in which the educator is and will be challenged as innovative education grows.

The political threat to institutions posed by these new developments is not often discussed. Here, I have emphasized the enormous threat that innovative educators pose to establishment power.

From the field of research, I have presented some recent findings that are all too little known, and have also expressed the hope that continuing research will not limit itself to assessment, but will diligently search for relationships of an if-then nature.

Finally, I have speculated that the next great frontier of learning may have to do with some of the least appreciated capabilities in Western culture—our intuitive and psychic powers.

REFERENCES

ASPY, D. N., & ROEBUCK, F. N. From humane ideas to humane technology and back again many times. *Education*, Winter 1974a, *95*(2), 163–171.

ASPY, D. N., ROEBUCK, F. N., ET AL. *Interim reports 1, 2, 3, 4.* Monroe, Louisiana: National Consortium for Humanizing Education, 1974b.

CLARK, F. V. Exploring intuition: Prospects and possibilities. *Journal of Transpersonal Psychology,* 1973, *5*(2), 156–170.

GROF, S. *Realms of the human unconscious: Observations from LSD research.* New York: Viking Press, 1975.

WATERS, F. *The man who killed the deer.* Chicago: Sage Books, The Swallow Press, 1942.

Learnings in Large Groups:
Their Implications for
the Future*

The experiences recounted in this chapter are ones I will never forget. A team composed of five members of the Center for Studies of the Person traveled to Brazil in January 1977 to do a series of large-group workshops. We were a support group for one another in taking what often seemed like foolhardy risks with audiences of up to eight hundred.

The account of our exciting adventure was written by four of us shortly after the events themselves. The concluding portion of the chapter, from "Implications for the Education of the Future," was written by me in August 1977 after a period alone, during which I had had time to read some of the troubling recent material about the general directions being taken by Western culture.

I only hope that the chapter conveys to the reader the sort of tightrope excitement that we experienced as we risked our professional reputations by putting our trust in very large groups, and in their wisdom.

A DESCRIPTION OF THE *CICLOS*

Our team facilitated three large-group workshops, called *ciclos*, in Recife, São Paulo, and Rio de Janeiro. The impact of those very large groups was deep. We

*Written by Maria Bowen, Ph.D., Maureen Miller, Ph.D., Carl R. Rogers, Ph.D., and John K. Wood, Ph.D.

felt they were profoundly important, not only in their short-term effects, but also in their long-range possibilities. The learnings from these groups could have great significance for the future; they could help us formulate a long-range aim of what education might become.

These two-day *ciclos*, or institutes, were not our major purpose in going to Brazil, but they provided our most exciting new learnings. In each case, they were organized by a local committee of dedicated individuals, mostly professionals, representing different organizations or interests. The aim was to recruit large numbers of people who, for a fee (often waived), signed up for the twelve hours of the two-day *ciclo*—two afternoon and two evening sessions. The response was excellent, and the audiences were about equal in each city. During one afternoon session there were only five hundred people, but the evening sessions were attended by six hundred to eight hundred. The meeting places varied in the number of rooms available for smaller groupings and in the formality or informality of the auditorium itself.

The audiences displayed much diversity. There were many educators, from elementary school teachers to college professors. There were counselors, psychologists, psychiatrists, students, housewives, and a miscellany of other occupations. Ages ranged from twenty-five to seventy. Judging from appearances, however, participants were largely middle-class. And about three-fourths were women: in Brazil, interest in the social sciences and in human problems seems still to be regarded as largely a feminine concern.

THE CONTENT OF THE *CICLOS*

We had a variety of resources at our disposal. One of the most impactful was a documentary film, *Ô Gente*, of a group of very low-income peasants in northeastern Brazil. To meet the havoc created by a drought, they began forming what must be called a person-centered community. They were a self-directed group in which power was shared by all: "No one commands, no one rules. We all command, all rule." They made decisions by "always discussing, discussing until we reach an agreement." They developed listening skills for helping those with problems. They knew the value of a support group: "When you have companions, you have more courage, don't you? . . . We know we are no longer alone . . . but many together." The parallels with our thinking were astonishing. To have this example of home-grown Brazilian person-centeredness was very valuable. It took away the "foreign" flavor of what we were doing.

Although many in the audiences came "just to hear Carl Rogers," his only really successful talk was a short and somewhat poetic commentary on this film, showing how many person-centered principles it exemplified and illuminated. John also gave a meditative commentary on the film. In addition, Carl gave two short talks in Recife, and one in Rio. These were generally disappointing to the audience because they were in such contrast to the vividness of the spontaneous interchange in the large group, although the questioning after these talks was lively and sophisticated.

Twice, Maria (who speaks Portuguese) led demonstration encounter groups "on stage," and these were of great value and interest, undoubtedly modeling to some extent the self-expression, the empathic listening, the facilitation which eventually came to be a part of the large group.

Several times the staff offered groups with a special topical focus. The following suggest the range of issues explored: a women's group; a men's group; groups on education, psychotherapy, community development, homosexuality, sexual therapy, group process, and the evolution of consciousness.

The largest blocks of time were spent in great circles, involving the whole audience, with no agenda except that which emerged from all of us collectively. This was where we learned the most.

THE LARGE-GROUP PROCESS

The Chaotic Beginning

The most difficult period for everyone was the groping, confused, highly emotional beginning of the process— the initial large-group session. Imagine, if you can, an enormous circle of eight hundred people, ten to fifteen deep, sitting in chairs or on the floor. Place yourself randomly in this crowd, as did the five of us from the United States. Three of us have interpreters by our side to help understand the gushing flow of Portuguese. Four persons with microphones on long wires stand in the open space, passing one to each person desiring to speak. Perhaps some of the chaotic, disconnected aspect of these beginning meetings can be suggested by quoting statements from a reporter who published an almost verbatim account of one of these sessions. Here is some of his account:

> The tension starts to increase. The atmosphere heats up. Rogers appears to collect himself in silence. Many who take the microphone ask him to lecture. He does not respond.
>
> A woman speaks. "I came to listen to Rogers, not to listen to questions without answers. Let's all leave."
>
> Another woman: "Listen. I came here to give, not just to receive. I want to give something here."

A young man: "This is not a lecture, folks, this is an experience, and I think we should do something together."

A man, far back in the audience: "It's always like this. Everybody is expecting someone to come and tell us what to do. We are always eager to receive packaged knowledge. I think we should go back to ourselves and look within ourselves for the answer as to what we want to do."

A woman: "We have to do something. We have to take the initiative. We have to overcome our anxiety instead of letting it overcome and guide us. We don't need answers, but to do something."

The audience is nervous, excited, tense, silent and expectant.

A woman: "I know! Let's sing songs that everybody knows."
Laughter and protests.

Others speak up, again asking Rogers to lecture "because we all paid."

A man proposes organizing into working groups. Others talk about a schedule.

Then a woman tells of a sharing community experience she is having with a group of other women in the city. This group has been meeting once a week. "We discuss life and our anxieties. It is not idle chatter about maids and children."
Appreciative laughter.

Rogers says: "I'm not certain what is happening, but I do know that groups, when they realize they are free and autonomous, have enormous strength and force. Someone spoke of chaos. I'm accustomed to this kind of chaos. I believe, though, that when a group is autonomous this power emerges, coming from all of us here."

There is complete silence in the room. Much expectancy.

Some suggest small groups. Others want a clear structure. Others insist that groups be organized with a staff member in each group. The audience is divided, some shouting for Rogers, others for more structure.

Then a calm young woman stands up and speaks to everyone: "I believe it is possible to learn from what is going on

*here right now. We don't seem to be aware of what's happen-
ing here. Some of you show that you want a leader, a com-
mander. I think those people would function better with what
Rogers calls a facilitator. But we can learn a lot from what is
going on right now. Some of you call yourselves Rogerians,
but you seem to be upset with learning through experiencing."*

*Toward the end of the meeting, Rogers rises and says: "I
have no idea of what will happen as a result of this session,
but I would like you to know that I'm open to whatever will
happen. I feel very close to the woman who said that we could
learn much from what is happening here."*

The Pattern of Group Development

Since for us, and for others, this confused beginning is
the hardest to understand and endure, perhaps we
could point out some of the elements that were common
to each of the initial large-group meetings of the *ciclos*.
These seem to occur when a group is beginning to learn
how to use its own strength.

There is a demand for leadership, for someone to
take charge.

There is a desire for "packaged knowledge," help,
advice, answers, something to take back home.

There is a demand for structure, schedule, imposed
order.

Frustration, anger, and disappointment because of
the unmet expectations are both experienced and—in
the freedom of the climate—expressed. The gurus have
not provided the answers!

There is the extreme discontinuity of the statements.
Each person functions separately, without paying attention to others' statements or hearing what has been
said.

There is the desire to do something, *anything*, rather than stay with the unknown and the anxiety it creates.

There is the desire for quick solutions that would take care of everything.

The large group becomes paralyzed when it tries consciously to make specific choices, such as whether to break into groups. Only later does it recognize that it oozes along, organically, making few clear, conscious choices.

There is the excitement of being part of a fluid process whose outcome is unknown. (This is why the best of presentations seems pale by comparison.)

There is the desire to participate, to give, to initiate.

There is a beginning sharing of significant experience.

There is the recognition that the resolution of the situation lies within the power of the group, exhibiting itself through the spontaneous functioning of each person.

The middle portion of the process might be called the working portion. During this portion, which, of course, is not clearly demarcated, individuals begin to use the sessions for expression of more feelings about themselves and the group, their personal problems and concerns. There is a beginning willingness on the part of the group to listen and to hear. The speakers, though talking of highly personal things, are unwittingly speaking for many others in the audience. Thus, even though only a small minority are able to obtain "air time," many persons find comfort and help in discovering that their own problems are being voiced by the speaker. This recognition of so many common feelings and experiences lays the foundation for the sense of community that is building.

In the final portion of the process, the whole group is able to give its undivided attention to one person, if necessary. There is a sense that "we are together." Individuals begin to talk about how they will deal with their new learnings in the "back-home" situation—in marriage, on the job, with colleagues, with students. A majority of the crowd of eight hundred has jelled into a cooperative community, although some are skeptical, and others are openly opposed to what is going on. But the individuals experience their own strength. They have struggled through to a successful process of decision-making. They feel together.

STAFF FUNCTION AND THE DYNAMICS
OF THE LARGE GROUP

The Staff as Participants

At the outset, there was a tremendous dissonance between the expectations of the audience and the reality they experienced. There was the expectation and anticipation that this "noted psychologist" and his "staff" from the United States would give them authoritative new knowledge, new theory, and the answers to their dilemmas. The reality of the situation was that here were five very human people who, instead of providing answers, seemed to create more questions, who gave only brief talks, generating something less than enthusiasm, and whose expertise was offered in the form of facilitating a strange and seemingly formless *process*. The rug of expectations was pulled out from under the participants, and we were in a complicated process together. A newspaper headline summed it up: "Psychologists Create Turmoil—Say Little."

But during the course of giving vent to emotions, a kind of "energy concentrate" was generated, and the whole group moved from a passive attitude of hanging on the word of a guru to experiencing their own creative energy and their own power. From a chaotic beginning, an order was developing; the energy of emotional expression and acceptance was finding its direction.

Although the staff was not exercising authoritarian control over the process, we were nonetheless contributing to it in consistent and precise ways. During periods of questioning, antagonism, even chaos, it was clear that staff members were listening intently, focusing on each person as he or she spoke, and making a point of responding to a person if someone else had not.

For example, in one initial session, a woman voiced a torrent of criticism of the staff, speaking very bitterly. Others criticized her. But in a moment John got hold of a microphone and said, "Sonia, I have no excuses or answers to offer, but I am *not* ignoring you. I *do* hear your disappointment, and it matters to me. And I hear your anger and it reached me." Sonia's belligerence visibly softened. She felt heard and respected as a person.

What the staff does by such behavior is to help focus the attention of the whole community on what is actually happening, as it happens. Simple observations have a powerful organizing effect. In the middle of chaos, a statement such as "In the last few minutes I've noticed that several people have spoken, yet none have been responded to," or "Right now I feel irritated; I sense it in others too, but I don't know what to do about it," all help to bring attention to the present. We pay attention to details, the obvious. It is as though we hold a multifaceted mirror up to the group and say,

"Look, this is how we are at this moment." It is not necessary to suggest solutions. The group wisdom will handle that aspect.

We also hear the small voices, the differing opinions, the hesitant feelings, thus conveying to eight hundred people that each person present is worth listening to. Each person is validated in his or her own worth, an exciting new realization for many. When the whole community focuses its attention on the totality of its present situation—both personal and group—no matter how seemingly disorganized the group is, it somehow invents the next step, based on the information of which it is now aware.

Another attitude we have which has influenced our work is that *outcome*, personal or group, does not have a high priority for us. We are focused—"creatively invested" is a better term—in facilitating a certain process over which we have no fundamental control. We know from experience that in this process, certain classes of outcomes may in general be expected, but we also know there will be outcomes we could never have predicted. These may result in changes in individual participants, in the whole group, and in ourselves as well. Another way of saying all this is that for the staff, the evolution of a life-affirming process *is* the outcome.

Our philosophy was part of everything we did. In a facilitative climate, persons can be trusted. Initiate a process in which they are trusted as they are, and worthwhile results will emerge. This philosophy was expressed in the trusting attitudes that staff members took toward themselves and toward one another. It was also clear in their relationships with the audience. It was not preached, but it was experienced at a deep level. We have faith that the process will become life-affirming, but this does not lead us to take a passive stance in the proceedings. As individuals and as a team, we are aware of our own power and choose to use it by becoming involved in the process each in our own way. We participate not by attempting to control the outcome but by actively responding as whole beings with thoughts, feelings, hunches, and values as each moment unfolds. We are very much present as persons.

There were some very uncomfortable moments for us at the beginning of the sessions. We sometimes found ourselves the target of a confused, disappointed, and angry group of about eight hundred people. A vivid picture of the difficulties and rewards of facilitating the group process is contained in the following journal account, written by one of the staff after more than ten hours with the *ciclo:*

Even now in this last session my feelings take the familiar up and down roller-coaster ride. My mind returns to the time we have spent in community meetings, and the ebb and flow: chaos, humor, intellectual debate, preaching, emotional explosions, delicate reaching out, tears, boredom, fear, a bubbling cauldron of human experience.

But now, there is deep inside a feeling of calm connectedness and assurance. We are breathing together and there is an order here. Not the order of rules and rigidity, but an order more like the dynamic organization in a living system. The community has discovered not only its own organization but also its own strength and tenderness, and I no longer feel afraid. People are listening to each other, responding and taking time to be silent together.

Reflecting, I realize how glad I am that I had not acted on my earlier fear-induced impulse to control the process. I had been so unsure at one time that I had really wanted to stop what was happening and to impose some structure of my own. I had wanted to turn the whole thing into a few well-organized talks! I had felt guilty when charges of staff irre-

sponsibility had come blistering out of the mass, but always, just as I was about to give up, someone would say something that would bring me back in touch with the wisdom of the group and its own process.

And now it is time to separate. Isabel is speaking: "I haven't said anything until now, but I just have to express my joy. I cannot go to the longer workshop you are holding, but now I don't mind. You see I got more than I dreamed of already. I came here feeling so lost, like I was all alone in my pain and my struggle. It's all just too big for me, the poverty of my people, the political realities of the world in which I live, the pain in my marriage, my family, my job. I couldn't do it alone . . . and now I realize that I am not facing it alone. Everyone here in some way or another is part of my support, from Carl Rogers in the books he has written, to those of you who disagree with much that I say but are still struggling with the same issues. I feel strong, I feel nourished, and now I can go on. Maybe this won't last, but in a way that doesn't really matter. What matters to me is that I feel it today." She continues, but now I am aware of my own tears, I am breathing deeply and I look around for my friends. Maybe we are not crazy after all, to trust that a group of eight hundred can initiate its own constructive process. I smile as I think of the incredible flow of these twelve hours together. It has been a confirming experience.

SHORT-TERM EFFECTS OF THE *CICLOS*

There have been a number of promising results from the three *ciclos*.

John led an interest group at Rio for those who wanted to continue to share personal experiences with one another. Five months later, the group continues to meet, spending all day together each Sunday. Membership varies, but a core of twelve to fifteen persons say it grows more and more useful to them.

The women's group led by Maureen in Rio was the first such group for most of the women. Maureen was informed that a dozen or so of those women now meet regularly in a consciousness-raising group.

The Brazilian organizing group in Recife talked out their bitter feelings toward one another, with some facilitation from our staff. This was the first time in their lives that they had ever dealt with one another, or with any professional colleagues, in this frank and open way. This group—representing various local organizations—has continued as a support group for its members. They are organizing their professional and personal lives in new ways, attributing the beginning of change to the *ciclo* experience.

The wife of a wealthy professional, who had been struggling to live the life of the dutiful (and helpless) Brazilian woman, has finally taken the courage to challenge the rigid constraints of her role expectations and go after her personhood. She has since applied for several workshops in the United States, and has decided to go against her husband's ultimatum—"It's either your career or our marriage"—and follow her own powerful need to find her own independent self. And the marriage appears to be mending.

A successful psychoanalyst decided to get training as a humanistic psychologist because he felt his "power as a person" was as important as his professional orientation and, after the *ciclos*, he felt he had faith in himself.

Literally dozens of people reported that at night after they left the meetings, they found themselves relating to people they loved in new and more straightforward ways.

A Brazilian psychologist wrote to Carl four months after the *ciclos* with these reports:

A woman therapist in Rio thought the first day ridiculous

and on the second one, discovered something extremely important might be happening. She is changing her way of working.

One of my clients can't accept your ideas on education, and said it to you in public, which for her was a profound experience because she has always feared speaking even to a small group. The ciclo *showed her you (or any other "authority") were not threatening, and this is giving her a whole new way of being.*

A psychiatrist reports that the Rio ciclo *was decisive in changing many people's professional or personal directions, and helped others to take bolder steps or greater risks.*

On the other hand, many, it seems, were just disappointed and angry at the chaos and unproductivity, calling it anarchy. They gained little or nothing, they believe.

Thus, while many were untouched, or antagonized, the overall impact of these group experiences seems astonishing considering the enormous numbers and the brevity of the time. Clearly, large-group work is a powerful mode of approach.

IMPLICATIONS FOR THE EDUCATION
OF THE FUTURE

In order to consider the meaning of our experiences for education in the long-range future, I wish to step back and try to gain a perspective on the significant social trends in Western culture.

Many of the shrewdest thinkers of our time agree that we are approaching the end of a historical period. The postindustrial era has reached its limit, says William Thompson (1977). We are approaching a new but promising Dark Age, says Leften Stavrianos (1976). In a particularly profound analysis by the Stanford Research Institute, Willis Harman (1977) points to the insoluble problems of our civilization, and the necessary transfiguration of human beings, their motives, and their values, if we are to survive. Very compelling is the evidence that our most serious problems are not brought about by the failures of our society, but by its successes. Hence, our past and current paradigms cannot possibly deal with our present problems by extending the old principles. We cannot deal with the increasing maldistribution of wealth, the increasing alienation of millions, or the lack of a unified purpose and goal by increasing the efficiency of production, increasing the automation of industry, accelerating our technology, or increasing our reliance on the profit motive of multinational corporations—some of the major operational principles that have brought us to our present state. Science and manipulative rationality are not sufficient to meet these problems.

Our culture has deep and, by current means, irresolvable dissonances. Following are a very few of these dissonances, selected from a great many:

1. It is reported that at the American standard of living, the earth could currently support only 500 million people; but there are 3.5 *billion* people now alive* (Stavrianos, 1976, p. 138). The more our standard of living increases, the more our incredible greed and wasteful consumption become apparent.

2. The per capita income in developed countries in 1800 is estimated to have been three times the per capita income in underdeveloped countries. In 1914, it was seven times greater. Currently, the individual in a developed country has twelve times the income of a person in an underdeveloped country (Stavrianos,

*The 1980 *World Almanac* estimated world population to be 4.3 billion.

p. 169). It is hardly necessary to stress the growing anger aroused by such a discrepancy, especially since the all-pervasive media make crystal clear to the impoverished masses the wealth of the few.

3. In the United States, *real* unemployment—including that of nonworkers who desire jobs, such as the young, the elderly, those who despair of finding work, is estimated at 25 to 35 percent of the potential work force. This figure is more likely to increase with improved technology than to decrease. It means we have no productive use for perhaps one-third of our potential working population. We can hardly be surprised by the alienation that this causes.

What will be the result of these widening gaps—like earthquake faults—in our civilization? One possibility is the nuclear destruction of most of the life on this planet, in which case there is little more to say.

But barring nuclear or ecological apocalypse, what is most likely to happen is what Thompson (1977) calls the "destructuring of civilization" (p. 55), in which our institutions will gradually collapse of their own weight and complexity. Impossible? That is what the Romans thought. But the structure of their great empire fell apart, partly from barbarian attack, even more from the empire's own flaws and bureaucratic overcomplexity. In similar fashion, this may happen to us. Perhaps the blackouts in our great urban centers, the bankruptcy of our largest city, the feverish panic at the time of the gasoline embargo, and most of all our inability—even using all our might—to impose our culture on tiny Vietnam, are but the faintest whisperings of such a future collapse.

What is needed to help us meet this new Dark Age with its turbulences, its combinations of somber and exciting possibilities? What will aid in bringing about this "coming transfiguration," as Harman (1977) calls it? What characteristics will lead to survival? Here there is considerable agreement among those who have thought deeply about the subject. There are at least three points that may be stressed.

First, the basis for values will be recognized as discoverable within, rather than out in the material world. In short, the inner life, a higher awareness, a recognition that enormous resources for the creation of the good life lie within the person, is one of the characteristics needed for this coming age.

A second point of agreement is that another key to survival is "the participatory impulse," which is already an observable trend.* People will increasingly demand to take part in choices that affect their lives, in policy planning, in the operation of governmental and industrial organizations. These organizations are likely to become smaller as the great bureaucracies fall apart, thus making possible more and more participatory choice. An organization will tend to become "our organization," in which "we" make the decisions, rather than "their organization."

Finally, there is agreement that one of the most essential elements for survival is the development of a greater sense of cooperation, of community, of ability to work together for the common good, not simply for personal aggrandizement. The People's Republic of China has accomplished wonders in this direction by widespread education from birth, stressing such slogans as "Fight Self—Serve the People." Perhaps our Western culture can accomplish some of the same pur-

*There is also an increasing trend toward dependence, looking for answers from gurus, wishing life to be controlled by someone else. But the desire for participation seems the stronger of the two trends.

poses by changing that slogan to "Be Yourself—Build Community."

It seems clear that if we are to live through the coming turbulence in a constructive way, the situation demands *drastic* changes in the purposes, the values, the behavior, the guiding principles of our lives.

What is missing from these analyses and predictions is any procedure by which these drastic human changes are to come about. Granted, they are necessary if we are to survive, but by what process can they occur? The experts have no answer to this, simply stressing the fact that the social pressures make such basic human transformations imperative. Here is where we see our experience with the large groups in Brazil as a hopeful small model, a pilot project educating for this future.

Our experience showed us that we know how to facilitate much greater participation in making choices, determining directions. It demonstrated that eight hundred people can participate together, choosing ways of action that are aimed at satisfying all, not simply a majority or a few. A crowd can become participants in a unified way, given the right conditions.

In these *ciclos*, the basis for a cooperative community was laid within the short space of twelve hours. People were beginning to work toward the common good. The extent to which competitive status-seeking and self-seeking dropped away was remarkable. The foundation had been laid for an effort in which all could comfortably work together for all. Each person was empowered to be all that he or she could be.

Perhaps most important, there was an incredible shift away from looking for answers and values and standards outside of the self. Very perceptibly, persons began to seek within for what they were *experiencing* as valuable, instead of looking for what they were *told* was valuable. Without question, they were beginning to meet the first condition for living in the new age. They were discovering the sources of the good life within themselves, not in some outer dogma or dictum, or in some material form.

In another very important respect, they were preparing themselves for the life of the future. They were developing a "wisdom of the group," a self-correcting course of action. When a group is following a charismatic leader, a theoretical or theological dogma, or any human formulation, it is, in the long run, going to be misled. The direction pointed toward by any person or any formulation always contains some error. As time goes on, the direction becomes more and more erroneous, eventually becoming destructive of its own goal. But when a group struggles through to a choice, having heard this need and that demand, this proposal and another that contradicts it, gradually all the data become available and the decision reached is a hard-won harmony of all the ideas, needs, and desires of each and every one. Furthermore, since the decision has been their own, they are continuously open to feedback and can correct the direction as new data occur. This probably represents the most error-proof mode of decision-making that we know.

CONCLUSION

Our experience with the large *ciclos* contains important lessons in what the education of the future might be.

We learned that in a very short space of time, large groups of people could begin to live in ways more appropriate to our uncertain future.

They could develop a participatory mode of decision-making that is adaptable to almost any situation and contains its own self-correcting gyroscopic mechanism, as error-free as any decision-making process known.

They could develop a sense of community in which respect for others, and cooperation rather than competition, were the keynotes.

They could develop a new confidence in themselves, discovering the source of values within themselves, coming to an awareness that the good life is within, not dependent on outside sources.

We learned that these changes, so appropriate for living in a disintegrating culture, could be initiated in a short space of time and in a very large group of people, if we ourselves were able to *be,* in a fashion suitable to that changing world.

Not one of these learnings is entirely new, but taken together, they indicate that we have the educational strategy for making these human changes possible, and that this approach is feasible here and now. All in all, our experiences give a challenging hint of what an education for the next century might become.

REFERENCES

HARMAN, W. W. The coming transfiguration. *The Futurist*, February 1977, *11*(1), 4–12; and April 1977, *11*(2), 106+.

STAVRIANOS, L. S. *The promise of the coming Dark Age.* San Francisco: W. H. Freeman, 1976.

THOMPSON, W. I. Auguries of planetization. *Quest*, July/August 1977, *1*(3), p. 55–60, 94–95.

Part IV

LOOKING AHEAD:
A PERSON-CENTERED
SCENARIO

The World of Tomorrow,
and the Person
of Tomorrow

I have long had a keen interest in the future. This is a world of change, and I take pleasure in trying to discern the directions in which we are moving, or will move. I am convinced that at this point we are going through a transformational crisis, from which we and our world cannot emerge unchanged. But I like the analogy drawn from the Chinese language, in which the same character stands for two meanings: "crisis" and "opportunity." I take the same view—that the very difficult crises of tomorrow represent equally great opportunities. I speculate about these in this chapter.

In a very real sense, I regard this paper as a fragile one. I am exposing my thinking in process, as it is at the present time. It contains ideas I have not formulated before, and infant ideas always feel shaky. It tries to draw together many vague thoughts which have been cropping up in my mind during this past year, ignited by sparks from my reading. This is particularly true of the first part of the chapter.

Then I draw on both current and past experience as I endeavor to picture the person who will be able to live in this transformed world.

I have an uneasy feeling about this chapter, a feeling I have experienced before. In some vague way I believe that what I am saying here will someday be fleshed out much more fully, either by me or by someone else. It is a beginning, an outline, a suggestion. So in all its infant awkwardness and imperfection, I present it to you. It pictures where I am now, in relation to the future.

What does the future hold? There are many people who now make it their business to try to predict our future, but all of such work is, at best, informed speculation. Scientists can predict, with almost absolute accuracy, the date and hour of arrival of Halley's comet in 1985, but what the human world will be like on that date, no one knows. The reason can be given in a phrase: the existence of choice. Edward Cornish (1980), president of the World Future Society, puts it well:

> *The 1980s—more than any previous decade—will be a period in which human choice will operate more decisively than ever before. The rapid development of technology has freed man from slavery to environmental and biological circumstances. No longer is he a prisoner of a particular geographic locality, because he can travel easily to the other side of the world. He can converse with people around the globe via new electronic devices. New bio-medical advances are making it possible for him to have a longer life and better health. Improved economic systems have removed—at least in many nations—the once ever-present danger of starvation. . . . We now see the future not as a world that is forced upon us, but as a world that we ourselves create. (p. 7)*

THE WORLD OF TOMORROW

Three Scenarios

Thinking in these terms, we can visualize various scenarios for the years ahead. At one extreme is the possibility of nuclear war. Its utter horror is forcibly brought home to me by the calm, factual words of George Bush, who has been a high government official and who is, as of this writing, a Republican candidate for president. The following interview took place between George Bush and Robert Scheer, an interviewer from the *Los Angeles Times* (Scheer, 1980):

SCHEER *Don't we reach a point with these strategic weapons where we can wipe each other out so many times and no one wants to use them or is willing to use them, that it really doesn't matter whether we're 10 percent or 2 percent lower or higher?*
BUSH *Yes, if you believe there is no such thing as a winner in a nuclear exchange, that argument makes a little sense. I don't believe that.*
SCHEER *How do you win in a nuclear exchange?*
BUSH *You have a survivability of command in control, survivability of industrial potential, protection of a percentage of your citizens, and you have a capability that inflicts more damage on the opposition than it can inflict upon you. That's the way you can have a winner, and the Soviets' planning is based on the ugly concept of a winner in a nuclear exchange.*
SCHEER *Do you mean like 5 percent would survive? Two percent?*
BUSH *More than that—if everybody fired everything he had, you'd have more than that survive.*

Let us think for a moment exactly what those words mean. In the case of nuclear war, Bush is saying, the top military personnel and government officials would survive (deep in some mountain, no doubt), and some industrial leaders and manufacturing plants would survive. But what about the rest of us? Let us say that between 2 percent and 15 percent survive. That means that, almost certainly, you and I and over 200 *million* other Americans would be killed! And Mr. Bush calls that *winning!* And he takes satisfaction in the proposition that an even greater percentage of Russians would be destroyed.

When we add to that the deadly radioactivity of almost every surviving object in both countries, and the radioactive fallout that would encircle the globe, the picture becomes even more incredible. It seems that such a scenario could be conceived only in the mind of a raving lunatic. But we know that it is held by thoughtful persons in government and the military, in the United States and the Soviet Union. And at the moment of this writing, as we threaten to use military force, if necessary, to protect our oil interests in the Middle East, it appears terrifyingly possible. So that is one almost suicidal scenario that we cannot dismiss, although its horror is such that we don't like to think about it.

If we assume that world leaders will pull back from committing planetary suicide, other scenarios become possible. One would be that things will proceed throughout the 1980s pretty much as they have until now. Terrorism and crime will persist, but so will scientific and technological breakthroughs. Some aspects of the world's problems will grow worse, but others will improve, and our lives will not greatly change.

Another scenario would see us being carried away by the newest developments in technology. Incredible advances in computer intelligence and decision-making; "test-tube" babies implanted in a woman's uterus, or perhaps grown entirely outside the human body; new species of microscopic and macroscopic life being created through recombinant work with the genes; cities under domes, with the whole environment controlled by people; completely artificial environments permitting human beings to live in space: these are some of the new technologies that may affect our lives. They have in common the fact that each removes humankind further and further from nature, from the soil, the weather, the sun, the wind, and all natural processes. These developments would produce changes of unknown magnitude as we endeavor to manufacture decisions and lives and environments that are completely man-made. Whether we would be affected for good or ill one cannot say; the only certainty is that our separation from the natural world would be far greater than it is today.

A Basis for a Different Scenario

There is another type of scenario, based on changes, having to do with the person. It is on this picture that I wish to dwell. There are many new developments today that alter our whole conception of the potentialities of the individual; that change our perceptions of "reality"; that change our ways of being and behaving; that alter our belief systems. I want simply to list, without explication, a number of these new directions, many of which will be familiar to you, while some may be strange. For a vivid and much more complete description of these and other trends, one can turn to Marilyn Ferguson's provocative book, *The Aquarian Conspiracy* (1980), better explained by its subtitle, "Personal and Social Transformation in the 1980s."

First, some of the developments that enlarge our view of the potentialities of the person. (The categories I am using overlap to a considerable degree, but I am sorting them for convenience in thinking.)

There is a strong and growing interest in all forms of meditation—the recognition and use of inner energy resources.

There is an increased respect for and use of intuition as a powerful tool.

Multitudes of people have experienced altered states of consciousness—many through drugs, but an increasing number through psychological disciplines. Our capacities in this direction open new worlds.

Research in biofeedback shows that our nonconscious mind can learn in a few moments, without being taught, to control the activity of a *single cell*. With a visual display of the action of some of his or her muscle groups, the ordinary person can change the action of a muscle group controlled by *one cell* in the spinal cord (Brown, 1980). The implications of this potential are mind-boggling.

Paranormal phenomena such as telepathy, precognition, and clairvoyance have been sufficiently tested that they have received scientific acceptance. Furthermore, there is evidence that most people can discover or develop such abilities in themselves.

We are learning that we can often heal or alleviate many of our diseases through the intentional use of our conscious and nonconscious minds. Holistic health is broadening our understanding of the inner capacities of the person.

There is a rapidly growing interest in the spiritual and transcendent powers of the individual.

Leading scientific students of the brain concur in the opinion that there is a potent mind, with an enormous capacity for intelligent action, which exists quite apart from the structure of the brain (Brown, 1980).

It is possible that evolution will lead us to a supraconsciousness and supermind of vastly more power than mind and consciousness now possess (Brown, 1980).

Now let us look at other developments that alter our perception of reality. Some of them have to do with science.

There is a convergence of theoretical physics and mysticism, especially Eastern mysticism—a recognition that the whole universe, including ourselves, is "a cosmic dance." In this view, matter, time, and space disappear as meaningful concepts; there exist only oscillations. This change in our conceptual world view is revolutionary.

The holographic theory of the brain's function, developed by Stanford neuroscientist Karl Pribram (described briefly in Ferguson, 1980, pp. 177–187), not only revolutionizes our concept of the operation of the brain, but suggests that the brain may create our "reality."

New epistemologies and philosophies of science see our current linear cause-effect concept of science as just one small example of various ways of knowing. In biological science particularly, reciprocal cause-effect relationships are now seen as the only basis for a rational science. These new ways of science will revolutionize our way of studying and perceiving the world, especially the biological and human world. (Ferguson, 1980, pp. 163–169, gives a brief but clear picture of these new approaches.)

Outside the field of science, we are also perceiving reality in new ways. This is particularly true in the realm of death and dying. We are much more acceptant of death as a reality, and we are learning a great deal about the process of dying as a culmination of living.

Other developments have to do with the ways in which change comes about in the individual. Much of

the material in this book deals with such changes, but I
will list them here:

The women's movement is only one example of various kinds of consciousness-raising activities. The gay
rights and black power movements are other examples.
They are changing people's behavior by calling sharp
attention to the prejudices, assumptions, and stereo-
types that have shaped us.

"Focusing," or being fully aware, in the moment,
of some previously denied experience, brings psychological and physiological change in psychotherapy and
results in changed behavior.

There is a new realization that the person is a *process*, rather than a fixed set of habits. This evokes
altered ways of behaving, increases the options.

There is a strong trend toward the greater use of
individual psychotherapy, and increasing evidence that
this experience brings about change in the self and in
behavior.

There are multitudes of people who have experienced lasting personal and collective change in all
kinds of intensive group experiences. This development has been discussed in previous chapters.

The trend toward more human attitudes in education
produces profound effects in learning and in other
behaviors. This too has been documented.

A final cluster of modern trends has to do with
changes in our belief systems. I will note a few:

There is increased insistence on individual freedom
of choice and a corresponding resistance to conformity
and acceptance of authority.

There is growing opposition to, and dislike for, large
institutions, corporations, bureaucracies, and much

interest and effort going into small, cooperative, group efforts.

There is a growing disbelief in a reductionistic science and an increased interest in the ancient wisdom of earlier cultures, and ancient "sciences" as well.

The Significance of these Trends

What is the meaning, the significance, of all of these current developments in modern life?

Taken together, these trends profoundly transform our concept of the person and the world that he or she perceives. This person has hitherto undreamed-of potential. This person's nonconscious intelligence is vastly capable. It can control many bodily functions, can heal diseases, can create new realities. It can penetrate the future, see things at a distance, communicate thoughts directly. This person has a new awareness of his or her strength, abilities, and power, an awareness of self as a process of change. This person lives in a new universe, where all the familiar concepts have disappeared—time, space, object, matter, cause, effect—nothing remains but vibrating energy.

In my judgment, these developments constitute a "critical mass" that will produce drastic social change. In the development of the atomic bomb, temperature and other conditions were gradually heightened until a certain mass was attained. The attainment of this critical mass brought about an explosively expanding process. These developments are of that sort, except that the process will be in persons and social systems.

Another scientific analogy is the "paradigm shift." Our scientific view of the world, at any one time, fits into a general pattern. To be sure, there are events and phenomena that do not quite fit, but they are disregarded until they begin to pile up and can no longer be ignored. Then, a Copernicus or an Einstein provides us with a whole new pattern, a new world view. It is not something patched onto the old paradigm, although it absorbs the old. It is a totally new conceptualization. One cannot move gradually from the old to the new. One must adopt one or the other: this is the paradigm shift. It has been pointed out that in science, most older scientists go to their graves believing in the previous paradigm, but the new generation grows up with, and lives comfortably with, the new paradigm.

What I am saying is that the many converging trends I have listed constitute a paradigm shift. We will try, of course, to live in our familiar world, just as people lived upon a flat world long after they knew it was round. But as these new ways of conceptualizing the person and the world sink in, becoming increasingly the basis of our thinking and our lives, transformation becomes inevitable. Ilya Prigogine (1980), the Belgian chemist who won the Nobel Prize in 1977 and who has contributed much to the new concepts of science, says, speaking for scientists: "We see a new world around us. We have the impression that we are at the dawn of a new period, with all the excitement, the hopes, and also the risks which are inherent in a new start."

THE PERSON OF TOMORROW

Who will be able to live in this utterly strange world? I believe it will be those who are young in mind and spirit—and that often means those who are young in body as well. As our youth grow up in a world where trends and views such as I have been describing envelop them, many will become new persons—fit to live in the world of tomorrow—and they will be joined by older folk who have absorbed the transforming concepts.

Not all young people, of course. I hear that young people today are only interested in jobs and security, that they are not persons who take risks or make innovations, just conservatives looking out for "number one." Possibly that is so, but it certainly is not true of the young people with whom I come in contact. But I am sure that some will continue to live in our present world; many, however, will dwell in this new world of tomorrow.

Where will they come from? It is my observation that they already exist. Where have I found them? I find them among corporation executives who have given up the gray-flannel rat race, the lure of high salaries and stock options, to live a simpler new life. I find them among young men and women in blue jeans who are defying most of the values of today's culture to live in new ways. I find them among priests and nuns and ministers who have left behind the dogmas of their institutions to live in a way that has more meaning. I find them among women who are vigorously rising above the limitations that society has placed on their personhood. I find them among blacks and Chicanos and other minority members who are pushing out from generations of passivity into an assertive, positive life. I find them among those who have experienced encounter groups, who are finding a place for feelings as well as thoughts in their lives. I find them among creative school dropouts who are thrusting into higher reaches than their sterile schooling permits. I realize, too, that I saw something of this person in my years as a psychotherapist, when clients were choosing a freer, richer, more self-directed kind of life for themselves. These are a few of the places in which I have found persons who may be able to live in this transformed world.

The Qualities of the Person of Tomorrow

As I have experienced these individuals, I find they have certain traits in common. Perhaps no one person possesses all of these qualities, but I believe that ability to live in this utterly revolutionized world of tomorrow is marked by certain characteristics. I will very briefly describe some as I have seen and experienced them.

1. *Openness.* These persons have an openness to the world—both inner and outer. They are open to experience, to new ways of seeing, new ways of being, new ideas and concepts.

2. *Desire for authenticity.* I find that these persons value communication as a means of telling it the way it is. They reject the hypocrisy, deceit, and double talk of our culture. They are open, for example, about their sexual relationships, rather than leading a secretive or double life.

3. *Skepticism regarding science and technology.* They have a deep distrust of our current science and the technology that is used to conquer the world of nature and to control the world's people. On the other hand, when science—such as biofeedback—is used to enhance self-awareness and control of the person by the person, they are eager supporters.

4. *Desire for wholeness.* These persons do not like to live in a compartmentalized world—body and mind, health and illness, intellect and feeling, science and common sense, individual and group, sane and insane, work and play. They strive rather for a wholeness of life, with thought, feeling, physical energy, psychic

energy, healing energy, all being integrated in experience.

5. *The wish for intimacy.* They are seeking new forms of closeness, of intimacy, of shared purpose. They are seeking new forms of communication in such a community—verbal as well as nonverbal, feelingful as well as intellectual.

6. *Process persons.* They are keenly aware that the one certainty of life is change—that they are always in process, always changing. They welcome this risk-taking way of being and are vitally alive in the way they face change.

7. *Caring.* These persons are caring, eager to be of help to others when the need is real. It is a gentle, subtle, nonmoralistic, nonjudgmental caring. They are suspicious of the professional "helpers."

8. *Attitude toward nature.* They feel a closeness to, and a caring for, elemental nature. They are ecologically minded, and they get their pleasure from an alliance with the forces of nature, rather than in the conquest of nature.

9. *Anti-institutional.* These individuals have an antipathy for any highly structured, inflexible, bureaucratic institution. They believe that institutions should exist for people, not the reverse.

10. *The authority within.* These persons have a trust in their own experience and a profound distrust of external authority. They make their own moral judgments, even openly disobeying laws that they consider unjust.

11. *The unimportance of material things.* These individuals are fundamentally indifferent to material comforts and rewards. Money and material status symbols are not their goal. They can live with affluence, but it is in no way necessary to them.

12. *A yearning for the spiritual.* These persons of tomorrow are seekers. They wish to find a meaning and purpose in life that is greater than the individual. Some are led into cults, but more are examining all the ways by which humankind has found values and forces that extend beyond the individual. They wish to live a life of inner peace. Their heroes are spiritual persons— Mahatma Gandhi, Martin Luther King, Teilhard de Chardin. Sometimes, in altered states of consciousness, they experience the unity and harmony of the universe.

These are some of the characteristics I see in the person of tomorrow. I am well aware that few individuals possess all of these characteristics, and I know that I am describing a small minority of the population as a whole.

The striking thing is that persons with these characteristics will be at home in a world that consists only of vibrating energy, a world with no solid base, a world of process and change, a world in which the mind, in its larger sense, is both aware of, and creates, the new reality. They will be able to make the paradigm shift.

CAN THE PERSON OF TOMORROW SURVIVE?

I have described persons who are sharply at variance with our conventional world. Can they—will they be permitted to—survive? What opposition will they meet? How may they influence our future?

Opposition

The emergence of this new person will be opposed. Let me suggest the opposition by a series of sloganistic statements that may communicate something of the sources of antagonism.

1. *"The State above all."* The past decade has given us ample evidence that in the United States, as well as in a majority of other countries, the governing elite and the massive bureaucracy that surrounds them have no place for dissenters or those with different values and goals. The new person has been and will be harassed, denied freedom of expression, accused of conspiracy, imprisoned for unwillingness to conform. It would take a massive—and unlikely—awakening of the American public to reverse this trend. Acceptance of diversity of values and lifestyles and opinions is the heart of the democratic process, but it no longer flourishes well in the United States. So these emerging persons will certainly be repressed, if possible, by their government.

2. *"Tradition above all."* The institutions of our society—educational, corporate, religious, familial—stand in direct opposition to anyone who defies tradition. Universities and local public schools are the institutions likely to be the most hostile to these persons of tomorrow. They do not fit their tradition and they will be ostracized and ejected whenever possible. Corporations, in spite of their conservative image, are somewhat more responsive to social trends. Even so, they will be in opposition to the person who puts self-realization ahead of achievement, personal growth above salary or profit, cooperation with nature ahead of its conquest. The church is a less formidable opponent. And family and marital traditions are already in such a state of confusion that the antagonism, though existent, is not likely to be effectively implemented.

3. *"The intellect above all."* The fact that these emerging individuals are attempting to be whole persons—

with body, mind, feelings, spirit, and psychic powers integrated—will be seen as one of their most presumptuous offenses. Not only science and academia, but government as well, are constructed on the assumption that cognitive reasoning is the *only* important function of humankind. There is the conviction that intelligence and rationality can solve anything. It was this belief that led us into the morass of Vietnam. This same conviction is held by scientists, faculty members, and policy makers at all levels. They will be the first to pour contempt and scorn on anyone who by word or deed challenges that credo.

4. *"Human beings should be shaped."* A vision of humankind may logically be extrapolated from our present technological culture. It would involve the application of social and psychological technology to control nonconforming behavior in the interest of a regulated postindustrial society. Such controls would be exercised not by some one institutional force, but by what some term the "warfare-welfare-industrial-communications-police bureaucracies." It is clear that one of the first aims of this complex web, if this conforming image prevails, would be to control or eliminate the person I have been describing.

5. *"The status quo forever."* Change threatens, and its possibility creates frightened, angry people. They are found in their purest essence on the extreme political right, but in all of us there is some fear of process, of change. So the vocal attacks on this new person will come from the highly conservative right, who are understandably terrified as they see their secure world dissolve; however, these conservative voices will receive much silent support from the whole population. Change is painful and uncertain. Who wants it? The answer is, *few*.

6. *"Our truth is* the *truth."* True believers are also the enemies of change, and they will be found on the left, on the right, and in the middle. They will not be able to tolerate a searching, uncertain, gentle person. Whether young or old, fanatically left wing or rigidly right wing, they must oppose this process individual who *searches* for truth. Such true believers *possess* the truth, and others must agree.

So, as these persons of tomorrow continue to emerge into the light, they will find increasing resistance and hostility from these six important sources. They may very well be overwhelmed by such forces.

A More Optimistic View

Though they will be opposed, I have an increasing confidence that these persons of tomorrow will not only survive, but will constitute a highly important ferment in our culture.

The reason for my optimism lies in the persistent development and flowering of all of the changes in scientific, social, and personal perspectives. Theoretical physics is not going to be put back into some previous box. Biofeedback can only go forward, not regress, and continue to unfold the undreamed-of powers of our inner and nonconscious intelligence. An increasing number of persons will experience altered states of consciousness. And so on, and so on, through the whole list. In other words the pressures will continue building up until they force a paradigm shift.

The persons of tomorrow are the very ones who are capable of understanding and absorbing that paradigm shift. They will be the ones capable of living in this new world, the outlines of which are still only dimly visible. But unless we blow ourselves up, that new world is inevitably coming, transforming our culture.

This new world will be more human and humane. It will explore and develop the richness and capacities of the human mind and spirit. It will produce individuals who are more integrated and whole. It will be a world that prizes the individual person—the greatest of our resources. It will be a more natural world, with a renewed love and respect for nature. It will develop a more human science, based on new and less rigid concepts. Its technology will be aimed at the enhancing, rather than the exploitation, of persons and nature. It will release creativity as individuals sense their power, their capacities, their freedom.

The winds of scientific, social, and cultural change are blowing strongly. They will envelop us in this new world, this world of tomorrow, which I have tried to sketch. Central to this new world will be persons, the persons of tomorrow whom I have described.

This is the person-centered scenario of the future. We may choose it, but whether we choose it or not, it appears that to some degree it is inexorably moving to change our culture. And the changes will be in the direction of more humanness.

REFERENCES

BROWN, B. *Supermind: The ultimate energy.* New York: Harper & Row, 1980.

CORNISH, E. An agenda for the 1980s. *The Futurist,* February 1980, *14,* 5–13.

FERGUSON, M. *The Aquarian conspiracy: Person and social transformation in the 1980s.* Los Angeles: J. P. Tarcher, 1980.

PRIGOGINE, I. Einstein: Triumphs and conflicts. *Newsletter,* February 1980, p. 5.

SCHEER, R. *Los Angeles Times,* January 24, 1980.

Appendix
Chronological Bibliography

The following list includes the publications of Carl R. Rogers from 1930 to 1980:

1930

With C. W. Carson. Intelligence as a factor in camping activities. *Camping Magazine*, 1930, *3*(3), 8–11.

1931

Measuring personality adjustment in children nine to thirteen. New York: Teachers College, Columbia University, Bureau of Publications, 1931, 107 pp.

A test of personality adjustment. New York: Association Press, 1931.

With M. E. Rappaport. We pay for the Smiths. *Survey Graphic*, 1931, *19*, 508 ff.

1933

A good foster home: Its achievements and limitations. *Mental Hygiene*, 1933, *17*, 21–40. Also published in F. Lowry (Ed.), *Readings in social case work*. Columbia University Press, 1939, pp. 417–436.

1936

Social workers and legislation. *Quarterly Bulletin New York State Conference on Social Work*, 1936, 7(3), 3–9.

1937

The clinical psychologist's approach to personality problems. *The Family*, 1937, *18*, 233–243.

Three surveys of treatment measures used with children. *Amer. J. Orthopsychiat.*, 1937, 7, 48–57.

1938

A diagnostic study of Rochester youth. *N.Y. State Conference on Social Work*. Syracuse: 1938, pp. 48–54.

1939

Authority and case work—Are they compatible? *Quarterly Bulletin, N.Y. State Conference on Social Work*. Albany: 1939, pp. 16–24.

The clinical treatment of the problem child. Boston: Houghton Mifflin, 1939, 393 pp.

Needed emphases in the training of clinical psychologists. *J. Consult. Psychol.*, 1939, *3*, 141–143.

1940

The processes of therapy. *J. Consult. Psychol.*, 1940, *4*, 161–164.

1941

Psychology in clinical practice. In J. S. Gray (Ed.), *Psychology in use*. New York: American Book Company, 1941, pp. 114–167.

With C. C. Bennett. The clinical significance of problem syndromes. *Amer. J. Orthopsychiat.*, 1941, *11*, 222–229.

With C. C. Bennett. Predicting the outcomes of treatment. *Amer. J. Orthopsychiat.*, 1941, *11*, 210–221.

1942

Counseling and psychotherapy. Boston: Houghton Mifflin, 1942, 450 pp. Translated into Japanese and published by Sogensha Press, Tokyo, 1951.

Mental health problems in three elementary schools. *Educ. Research Bulletin*, 1942, *21*, 69–79.

The psychologist's contributions to parent, child, and community problems. *J. Consult. Psychol.*, 1942, *6*, 8–18.

A study of the mental health problems in three representative elementary schools. In T. C. Holy et al., *A study of health and physical education in Columbus Public Schools*. Ohio State Univer., Bur. of Educ. Res. Monogr., No. 25, 1942, pp. 130–161.

The use of electrically recorded interviews in improving psychotherapeutic techniques. *Amer. J. Orthopsychiat.*, 1942, *12*, 429–434.

1943

Therapy in guidance clinics. *J. Abnorm. Soc. Psychol.*, 1943, *38*, 284–289. Also published in R. Watson (Ed.), *Readings in clinical psychology*. New York: Harper and Bros., 1949, pp. 519–527.

1944

Adjustment after combat. Army Air Forces Flexible Gunnery School, Fort Myers, Florida. Restricted Publication, 1944, 90 pp.

The development of insight in a counseling relationship. *J. Consult. Psychol.*, 1944, *8*, 331–341. Also published in A. H. Brayfield (Ed.), *Readings on modern methods of counseling*. New York: Appleton-Century-Crofts, 1950, pp. 119–132.

The psychological adjustments of discharged service personnel. *Psych. Bulletin*, 1944, *41*, 689–696.

1945

Counseling. *Review of Educ. Research*, 1945, *15*, 155–163.

A counseling viewpoint for the USO worker. *USO Program Services Bulletin*, 1945.

Dealing with individuals in USO. *USO Program Services Bulletin*, 1945.

The nondirective method as a technique for social research. *Amer. J. Sociology*, 1945, *50*, 279–283.

With V. M. Axline. A teacher-therapist deals with a handicapped child. *J. Abnorm. Soc. Psychol.*, 1945, *40*, 119–142.

With R. Dicks & S. B. Wortis. Current trends in counseling, a symposium. *Marriage and Family Living*, 1945, 7(4).

1946

Psychometric tests and client-centered counseling. *Educ. Psychol. Measmt.*, 1946, *6*, 139–144.

Recent research in nondirective therapy and its implications. *Amer. J. Orthopsychiat.*, 1946, *16*, 581–588.

Significant aspects of client-centered therapy. *Amer. Psychologist*, 1946, *1*, 415–422. Translated into Spanish and published in *Rev. Psicol. Gen. Apl.*, Madrid, 1949, *4*, 215–237.

With G. A. Muench. Counseling of emotional blocking in an aviator. *J. Abnorm. Soc. Psychol.*, 1946, *41*, 207–216.

With J. L. Wallen. *Counseling with returned servicemen.* New York: McGraw-Hill, 1946, 159 pp.

1947

The case of Mary Jane Tilden. In W. U. Snyder (Ed.), *Casebook of nondirective counseling.* Boston: Houghton Mifflin, 1947, pp. 129–203.

Current trends in psychotherapy. In W. Dennis (Ed.), *Current trends in psychology,* University of Pittsburgh Press, 1947, pp. 109–137.

Some observations on the organization of personality. *Amer. Psychologist,* 1947, *2,* 358–368. Also published in A. Kuenzli (Ed.), *The phenomenological problem.* New York: Harper and Bros., 1959, pp. 49–75.

1948

Dealing with social tensions: A presentation of client-centered counseling as a means of handling interpersonal conflict. New York: Hinds, Hayden and Eldredge, Inc., 1948, 30 pp. Also published in *Pastoral Psychology,* 1952, *3*(28), 14–20; *3*(29), 37–44.

Divergent trends in methods of improving adjustment. *Harvard Educational Review,* 1948, *18,* 209–219. Also in *Pastoral Psychology,* 1950, *1*(8), 11–18.

Research in psychotherapy: Round Table, 1947. *Amer. J. Orthopsychiat.,* 1948, *18,* 96–100.

Some implications of client-centered counseling for college personnel work. *Educ. Psychol. Measmt.,* 1948, *8,* 540–549. Also published in *College and University,* 1948, and in *Registrar's Journal,* 1948.

With B. L. Kell & H. McNeil. The role of self-understanding in the prediction of behavior. *J. Consult. Psychol.,* 1948, *12,* 174–186.

1949

The attitude and orientation of the counselor in client-centered therapy. *J. Consult. Psychol.,* 1949, *13,* 82–94.

A coordinated research in psychotherapy: A non-objective introduction. *J. Consult. Psychol.,* 1949, *13,* 149–153.

1950

A current formulation of client-centered therapy. *Social Service Review,* 1950, *24,* 442–450.

Significance of the self-regarding attitudes and perceptions. In M. L. Reymert (Ed.), *Feelings and emotions.* New York: McGraw-Hill, 1950, pp. 374–382. Also published in L. Gorlow & W. Katkovsky (Eds.), *Readings in the psychology of adjustment.* New York: McGraw-Hill, 1959.

What is to be our basic professional relationship? *Annals of Allergy,* 1950, *8,* 234–239. Also published in M. H. Krout (Ed.), *Psychology, psychiatry, and the public interest.* University of Minnesota Press, 1956, pp. 135–145.

With R. Becker. A basic orientation for counseling. *Pastoral Psychology,* 1950, *1*(1), 26–34.

With D. G. Marquis & E. R. Hilgard. ABEPP policies and procedures. *Amer. Psychologist,* 1950, *5,* 407–408.

1951

Client-centered therapy: A helping process. *The University of Chicago Round Table,* 1951, *698,* 12–21.

Client-centered therapy: Its current practice, implications, and theory. Boston: Houghton Mifflin, 1951, 560 pp. Also translated into Japanese and published by Iwasaki Shoten Press, 1955.

Perceptual reorganization in client-centered therapy. In R. R. Blake & G. V. Ramsey (Eds.), *Perception: An approach to personality.* New York: Ronald Press, 1951, pp. 307–327.

Studies in client-centered psychotherapy III: The case of Mrs. Oak—A research analysis. *Psychol. Serv. Center J.,* 1951, *3,* 47–165. Also published in C. R. Rogers & R. F. Dymond (Eds.), *Psychotherapy and personality change.* University of Chicago Press, 1954, pp. 259–348.

Through the eyes of a client. *Pastoral Psychology,* 1951, *2*(16), 32–40; (17) 45–50; (18) 26–32.

Where are we going in clinical psychology? *J. Consult. Psychol.,* 1951, *15,* 171–177.

With T. Gordon, D. L. Grummon, & J. Seeman. Studies in client-centered psychotherapy I: Developing a program of research in psychotherapy. *Psychol. Serv. Center J.,* 1951, *3,* 3–28. Also published in C. R. Rogers & R. F. Dymond (Eds.), *Psychotherapy and personality change.* University of Chicago Press, 1954, pp. 12–34.

1952

Client-centered psychotherapy. *Scientific American*, 1952, *187*, 66–74.

Communication: Its blocking and facilitation. *Northwestern University Information*, 1952, *20*, 9–15. Reprinted in *ETC*, 1952, *9*, 83–88; in *Harvard Bus. Rev.*, 1952, *30*, 46–50; in *Human Relations for Management*, E. C. Bursk (Ed.). New York: Harper and Bros., 1956, pp. 150–158. French translation in *Hommes et Techniques*, 1959.

A personal formulation of client-centered therapy. *Marriage and Family Living*, 1952, *14*, 341–361. Also published in C. E. Vincent (Ed.), *Readings in marriage counseling*. New York: T. Y. Crowell Co., 1957, pp. 392–423.

With R. H. Segel. *Client-centered therapy: Parts I and II*. 16 mm. motion picture with sound. State College, Pa.: Psychological Cinema Register, 1952.

1953

The interest in the practice of psychotherapy. *Amer. Psychologist*, 1953, *8*, 48–50.

A research program in client-centered therapy. *Res. Publ. Ass. Nerv. Ment. Dis.*, 1953, *31*, 106–113.

Some directions and end points in therapy. In O. H. Mowrer (Ed.), *Psychotherapy: Theory and research*. New York: Ronald Press, 1953, pp. 44–68.

With G. W. Brooks, R. S. Driver, W. V. Merrihue, P. Pigors, & A. J. Rinella. Removing the obstacles to good employee communications. *Management Record*, 1953, *15*(1), 9–11, 32–40.

1954

Becoming a person. Oberlin College Nellie Heldt Lecture Series. Oberlin: Oberlin Printing Co., 1954. 46 pp. Reprinted by the Hogg Foundation for Mental Hygiene, University of Texas, 1966; also in *Pastoral Psychology*, 1956, *7*(61), 9–13, and 1956, *7*(63), 16–26. Also published in S. Doniger (Ed.), *Healing, human and divine*. New York: Association Press, 1957, pp. 57–67.

The case of Mr. Bebb: The analysis of a failure case. In C. R. Rogers & R. F. Dymond (Eds.), *Psychotherapy and personality change*. University of Chicago Press, 1954, pp. 349–409.

Changes in the maturity of behavior as related to therapy. In C. R.

Rogers & R. F. Dymond (Eds.), *Psychotherapy and personality change*. University of Chicago Press, 1954, pp. 215–237.

An overview of the research and some questions for the future. In C. R. Rogers & R. F. Dymond (Eds.), *Psychotherapy and personality change*. University of Chicago Press, 1954, pp. 413–434.

Towards a theory of creativity. *ETC: A Review of General Semantics*, 1954, *11*, 249–260. Also published in H. Anderson (Ed.), *Creativity and its cultivation*. New York: Harper and Bros., pp. 69–82.

With R. F. Dymond (Eds.). *Psychotherapy and personality change*. University of Chicago Press, 1954, 447 pp.

1955

A personal view of some issues facing psychologists. *Amer. Psychologist*, 1955, *10*, 247–249.

Personality change in psychotherapy. *The International Journal of Social Psychiatry*, 1955, *1*, 31–41.

Persons or science? A philosophical question. *Amer. Psychologist*, 1955, *10*, 267–278. Also published in *Pastoral Psychology*, 1959, *10*, (Nos. 92, 93).

With R. H. Segel. *Psychotherapy begins: The case of Mr. Lin.* 16 mm. motion picture with sound. State College, Pa.: Psychological Cinema Register, 1955.

With R. H. Segel. *Psychotherapy in process: The case of Miss Mun.* 16 mm. motion picture with sound. State College, Pa.: Psychological Cinema Register, 1955.

1956

Client-centered therapy: A current view. In F. Fromm-Reichmann & J. L. Moreno (Eds.), *Progress in psychotherapy.* New York: Grune & Stratton, 1956, pp. 199–209.

A counseling approach to human problems. *Amer. J. of Nursing*, 1956, *56*, 994–997.

Implications of recent advances in the prediction and control of behavior. *Teachers College Record*, 1956, *57*, 316–322. Also published in E. L. Hartley & R. E. Hartley (Eds.), *Outside readings in psychology.* New York: T. Y. Crowell Co., 1957, pp. 3–10. Also published in R. S. Daniel (Ed.), *Contemporary readings in general psychology.* Boston: Houghton Mifflin, 1960.

Intellectualized psychotherapy. Review of George Kelly's *The Psychology of personal constructs, Contemporary Psychology*, 1956, *1*, 357–358.

Review of Reinhold Niebuhr's *The self and the dramas of history.*
Chicago Theological Seminary Register, 1956, *46*, 13–14. Also
published in *Pastoral Psychology*, 1958, *9*, No. 85, 15–17.

Some issues concerning the control of human behavior. (Symposium with B. F. Skinner) *Science*, November 1956, *124*, No. 3231, 1057–1066. Also published in L. Gorlow & W. Katkovsky (Eds.), *Readings in the psychology of adjustment.* New York: McGraw-Hill, 1959, pp. 500–522.

What it means to become a person. In C. E. Moustakas (Ed.), *The self.* New York: Harper and Bros., 1956, pp. 195–211.

With E. J. Shoben, O. H. Mowrer, G. A. Kimble, & J. G. Miller. Behavior theories and a counseling case. *J. Counseling Psychol.*, 1956, *3*, 107–124.

1957

The necessary and sufficient conditions of therapeutic personality change. *J. Consult. Psychol.*, 1957, *21*, 95–103. French translation in *Hommes et Techniques*, 1959.

A note on the nature of man. *J. Counseling Psychol.*, 1957, *4*, 199–203. Also published in *Pastoral Psychology*, 1960, *11*, No. 104, 23–26.

Personal thoughts on teaching and learning. *Merrill-Palmer Quarterly*, Summer, 1957, *3*, 241–243. Also published in *Improving College and University Teaching*, 1958, *6*, 4–5.

A therapist's view of the good life. *The Humanist*, 1957, *17*, 291–300.

Training individuals to engage in the therapeutic process. In C. R. Strother (Ed.), *Psychology and mental health.* Washington, D.C.: Amer. Psychological Assn., 1957, pp. 76–92.

With R. E. Farson. *Active listening.* University of Chicago, Industrial Relations Center, 1957, 25 pp.

1958

The characteristics of a helping relationship. *Personnel and Guidance Journal*, 1958, *37*, 6–16.

A process conception of psychotherapy. *American Psychologist*, 1958, *13*, 142–149.

1959

Client-centered therapy. In S. Arieti (Ed.), *American Handbook of Psychiatry*, Vol. 3. New York: Basic Books, Inc., 1959, pp. 183–200.

Comments on cases in S. Standal & R. Corsini (Eds.), *Critical incidents in psychotherapy*. New York: Prentice-Hall, 1959.

The essence of psychotherapy: A client-centered view. *Annals of Psychotherapy*, 1959, *1*, 51–57.

Lessons I have learned in counseling with individuals. In W. E. Dugan (Ed.), *Modern school practices, Series 3, Counseling points of view*. University of Minnesota Press, 1959, pp. 14–26.

Significant learning: In therapy and in education. *Educational Leadership*, 1959, *16*, 232–242.

A tentative scale for the measurement of process in psychotherapy. In E. A. Rubinstein & M. B. Parloff (Eds.), *Research in psychotherapy*. Washington, D.C.: Amer. Psychological Assn., 1959, pp. 96–107.

A theory of therapy, personality, and interpersonal relationships, as developed in the client-centered framework. In S. Koch (Ed.), *Psychology: A study of a science*, Vol. III. *Formulations of the person and the social context*. New York: McGraw-Hill, 1959, pp. 184–256.

The way to do is to be. Review of Rollo May, et al., *Existence: A new dimension in psychiatry and psychology*, in *Contemporary Psychology*, 1959, *4*, 196–198.

With G. Marian Kinget. *Psychotherapie en Menselyke Verhoudingen*. Utrecht: Uitgeverij Het Spectrum, 1959, 302 pp.

With M. Lewis & J. Shlien. Time-limited, client-centered psychotherapy: two cases. In A. Burton (Ed.), *Case studies of counseling and psychotherapy*. Prentice-Hall, 1959, pp. 309–352.

1960

Dialogue between Martin Buber and Carl Rogers. *Psychologia*, December 1960, *3*(4), 208–221.

Psychotherapy: The counselor, and *Psychotherapy: The client*. 16 mm. motion pictures with sound. Distributed by Bureau of Audio-Visual Aids, University of Wisconsin, 1960.

Significant trends in the client-centered orientation. In D. Brower & L. E. Abt (Eds.), *Progress in clinical psychology*, Vol. IV. New York: Grune & Stratton, 1960, pp. 85–99.

A therapist's view of personal goals. *Pendle Hill Pamphlet, No. 108*. Wallingford, Pennsylvania, 1960, 30 pp.

With A. Walker & R. Rablen. Development of a scale to measure process changes in psychotherapy. *J. Clinical Psychol.*, 1960, *16*(1), 79–85.

1961

The loneliness of contemporary man, as seen in "The Case of Ellen West," *Review of Existential Psychology & Psychiatry*, May 1961, *1*(2), 94–101. Also published in expanded form, in C. R. Rogers & R. L. Rosenberg, *A Pessoa Como Centro*, São Paulo, Brazil: Editoria Pedagógica e Universitária Ltda., 1977.

On becoming a person. Boston: Houghton Mifflin, 1961, 420 pp. (Also in Sentry Edition, softcover.)

Panel presentation: The client-centered approach to certain questions regarding psychotherapy. *Annals of Psychotherapy*, 1961, *2*, 51–53.

The place of the person in the new world of the behavioral changes. *Personnel and Guidance Journal*, February 1961, *39*(6), 442–451.

The process equation of psychotherapy. *American Journal of Psychotherapy*, January 1961, *15*(1), 27–45.

A theory of psychotherapy with schizophrenics and a proposal for its empirical investigation. In J. G. Dawson, H. K. Stone, & N. P. Dellis (Eds.), *Psychotherapy with schizophrenics.* Baton Rouge: Louisiana State University Press, 1961, pp. 3–19.

Two divergent trends. In R. May (Ed.), *Existential psychology.* New York: Random House, 1961, pp. 85–93.

What we know about psychotherapy. *Pastoral Psychology*, 1961, *12*, 31–38.

1962

Comment (on article by F. L. Vance). *J. Counsel. Psychol.*, 1962, *9*, 16–17.

The interpersonal relationship: The core of guidance. *Harvard Educ. Rev.*, Fall 1962, *32*(4), 416–429.

Niebuhr on the nature of man. In S. Doniger (Ed.), *The nature of man.* New York: Harper and Brothers, 1962, pp. 55–71 (with discussion by B. M. Loomer, W. M. Horton, & H. Hofmann).

Some learnings from a study of psychotherapy with schizophrenics. *Pennsylvania Psychiatric Quarterly*, Summer 1962, pp. 3–15.

A study of psychotherapeutic change in schizophrenics and normals: Design and instrumentation. *Psychiatric Research Reports*, American Psychiatric Association, April 1962, *15*, 51–60.

The therapeutic relationship: Recent theory and research. Lecture given under sponsorship of the Los Angeles Society of Clinical

Psychologists in Beverly Hills, California, January 19, 1962. Privately printed.

Toward becoming a fully functioning person. In A. W. Combs (Ed.), *Perceiving, behaving, becoming, 1962 Yearbook.* Association for Supervision and Curriculum Development. Washington D.C., 1962, pp. 21–33.

With G. M Kinget. Psychotherapie et relations humaines: Theorie et pratique de la therapie non-directive. Louvain, Belgium: Publications Universitaires, 1962, 319 pp.

1963

The actualizing tendency in relation to "motives" and to consciousness. In M. Jones (Ed.), *Nebraska Symposium on Motivation, 1963.* University of Nebraska Press, 1963, pp. 1–24.

The concept of the fully functioning person. *Psychotherapy: Theory, Research, and Practice,* 1963, *1*(1), 17–26.

Learning to be free. In S. M. Farber & R. H. Wilson (Eds.), *Conflict and creativity: Control of the mind, Part 2.* New York: McGraw-Hill, 1963, pp. 268–288.

Learning to be free. (Condensation of above.) *Nat. Educ. Ass. J.,* March 1963.

Psychotherapy today: Or, where do we go from here? *American Journal of Psychotherapy,* 1963, *17*(1), 5–16.

1964

Freedom and commitment. *The Humanist,* 1964, *24*(2), 37–40.

Some elements of effective interpersonal communication. Lecture at California Institute of Technology, November 1964. Unpublished.

Toward a modern approach to values: The valuing process in the mature person. *J. Abnorm. Soc. Psychol.,* 1964, *68*(2), 160–167.

Toward a science of the person. In T. W. Wann (Ed.), *Behaviorism and phenomenology: Contrasting bases for modern psychology.* University of Chicago Press, 1964, pp. 109–140.

1965

An afternoon with Carl Rogers. *Explorations,* 1965, *3,* 104.

Can we meet the need for counseling? A suggested plan. *Marriage and Family,* September 1965, *2*(5), 4–6. Queensland, Australia: National Marriage Guidance Council of Australia.

Dealing with psychological tensions. *J. Appl. Behav. Sci.* 1965, *1*, 6–24.

Foreword. In H. Anderson, *Creativity in childhood and adolescence.* Palo Alto: Science and Behavior Books, 1965, pp. v–vii.

A humanistic conception of man. In R. E. Farson (Ed.), *Science and human affairs.* Palo Alto, California: Science and Behavior Books, 1965, pp. 18–31.

Psychology and teacher training. In D. B. Gowan & C. Richardson (Eds.), *Five fields and teacher education.* Ithaca, New York: Project One Publications, Cornell University, 1965, pp. 56–91.

Some questions and challenges facing a humanistic psychology. *J. Hum. Psychol.,* 1965, *5*, 105.

The therapeutic relationship: Recent theory and research. *Australian Journal of Psychology, 1965, 17,* 95–108.

(A wife's-eye view of Carl Rogers. *Voices,* 1965, *1*(1), 93–98.) By Helen E. Rogers.

1966

Client-centered therapy. In S. Arieti (Ed.), *Supplement to American handbook of psychiatry,* Vol. 3. New York: Basic Books, Inc., 1966, pp. 183–200. (See also 1959.)

Dialogue between Michael Polanyi and Carl Rogers. San Diego: San Diego State College and Western Behavioral Sciences Institute, July 1966, 8-page pamphlet.

Dialogue between Paul Tillich and Carl Rogers, Parts I and II. San Diego: San Diego State College, 1966, 23-page pamphlet.

To facilitate learning. In M. Provus (Ed.), *Innovations for time to teach.* Washington, D.C.: National Education Association, 1966, pp. 4–19.

1967

Autobiography. In E. W. Boring & G. Lindzey, *A history of psychology in autobiography,* Vol. V. New York: Appleton-Century-Crofts, 1967.

Carl Rogers speaks out on groups and the lack of a human science. An interview. *Psychology Today,* December 1967, *1*, 19–21, 62–66.

Client-centered therapy. In A. M. Freedman & H. I. Kaplan (Eds.), *Comprehensive textbook of psychiatry.* Baltimore: Williams & Wilkins, 1967, pp. 1225–1228.

The facilitation of significant learning. In L. Siegel (Ed.), *Contem-*

porary theories of instruction. San Francisco: Chandler Publishing Co., 1967, pp. 37–54.

The interpersonal relationship in the facilitation of learning. In R. Leeper (Ed.), *Humanizing education.* National Education Association, Association for Supervision and Curriculum Development, 1967.

A plan for self-directed change in an educational system. *Educ. Leadership,* May 1967, *24,* 717–731.

The process of the basic encounter group. In J. F. T. Brugental (Ed.), *The challenges of humanistic psychology.* New York: McGraw-Hill, 1967, pp. 261–278.

With E. T. Gendlin, D. J. Kiesler, & C. Truax. *The therapeutic relationship and its impact: A study of psychotherapy with schizophrenics.* University of Wisconsin Press, 1967, 625 pp.

With B. Stevens et al. *Person to person.* Moab, Utah: Real People Press, 1967.

1968

The interpersonal relationship in the facilitation of learning. *The Virgil E. Herrick Memorial Lecture Series.* Columbus, Ohio: Charles E. Merrill Publishing Co., 1968.

Interpersonal relationships: USA 2000. *J. Appl. Behav. Sci.,* 1968, 4(3), 265–280.

A practical plan for educational revolution. In R. R. Goulet (Ed.), *Educational change: The reality and the promise.* (A report on the National Seminars on Innovation, Honolulu, July 1967.) New York: Citation Press, 1968, pp. 120–135.

Review of J. Kavanaugh's book, *A modern priest looks at his outdated church. Psychology Today,* 1968, p. 13.

To the Japanese reader. Introduction to a series of 18 volumes of Rogers' work translated into Japanese. Tokyo: Iwasaki Shoten Press, 1968.

With W. R. Coulson (Eds.), *Man and the science of man.* Columbus, Ohio: Charles E. Merrill Publishing Co., 1968, 207 pp.

1969

Being in relationship. In *Freedom to learn: A view of what education might become.* Columbus, Ohio: Charles E. Merrill Publishing Co., 1969.

Community: The group. *Psychology Today,* Del Mar, California: CRM Books, Inc., December 1969, *3.*

Freedom to learn: A view of what education might become. Columbus, Ohio: Charles E. Merrill Publishing Co., 1969, 358 pp. Available in hardcover or softcover.

Graduate education in psychology: A passionate statement. In *Freedom to learn: A view of what education might become.*

The increasing involvement of the psychologist in social problems: Some comments, positive and negative. *J. Appl. Behav. Sci.,* 1969, 5, 3–7.

The intensive group experience. In *Psychology today: An introduction.* Del Mar, California: CRM Books, Inc., 1969, pp. 539–555.

The person of tomorrow. Sonoma State College Pamphlet, 1969. (Commencement address, June 1969.)

Self-directed change for educators: Experiments and implications. In E. Morphet & D. L. Jesser (Eds.), *Preparing educators to meet emerging needs.* (Papers prepared for the Governors' Conference on Education for the Future, an eight-state project.) New York: Citation Press, Scholastic Magazine, Inc., 50 West 44th Street, 1969.

1970

Carl Rogers on encounter groups. New York: Harper & Row, 1970, 168 pp. Available in hardcover or softcover.

Foreword and Chapters 9, 16, 22, 25, 26, 27. In J. T. Hart & T. M. Tomlinson (Eds.), *New directions in client-centered therapy.* Boston: Houghton Mifflin, 1970. (All have been published elsewhere, except the Foreword and Chapter 27, "Looking back and ahead: A conversation with Carl Rogers," conducted by J. T. Hart.)

1971

Can schools grow persons? Editorial. *Educational Leadership,* December 1971.

Forget you are a teacher. Carl Rogers tells why. *Instructor* (Dansville, New York), August/September 1971, pp. 65–66.

Interview with Dr. Carl Rogers. In W. B. Frick (Ed.), *Humanistic psychology: Interviews with Maslow, Murphy & Rogers.* Columbus, Ohio: Charles E. Merrill Publishing Co., 1971.

Psychological maladjustments vs. continuing growth. In *Developmental Psychology.* Del Mar, California: CRM Books, Inc., 1971.

Some elements of effective interpersonal communication. *Washington State Journal of Nursing,* May/June 1971, pp. 3–11.

1972

Becoming partners: Marriage and its alternatives. New York: Delacorte, 1972, 243 pp.

Bringing together ideas and feelings in learning. *Learning Today,* Spring 1972, *5,* 32–43.

Comment on Brown and Tedeschi article. *J. Hum. Psychol.,* Spring 1972, *12*(1), 16–21.

Introduction to *My experience in encounter group,* by H. Tsuge, Dean of Women at Japan Women's University, Tokyo, Japan. *Voices,* Summer 1972, *8*(2), Issue 28.

The person of tomorrow. *Colorado Journal of Educational Research,* Fall 1972, *12*(1). Greeley, Colorado: University of Northern Colorado. (Commencement address, Sonoma State College, June 1969.)

A research program in client-centered therapy.* In S. R. Brown & D. J. Brenner (Eds.), *Science, psychology, and communication: Essays honoring Willliam Stephenson.* New York: Teachers College Press, Teachers College, Columbia University, 1972, pp. 312–324.
*This paper—exclusive of the new Introduction (1971)—was originally published in *Psychiatric treatment, Vol. 31, Proceedings of the Association for Research in Nervous and Mental Disease.* Baltimore: Williams & Wilkins, 1953, pp. 106–113.

Some social issues which concern me. *J. Hum. Psychol.* Fall 1972, *12*(2), 45–60.

(Wood, J. T. Carl Rogers, gardener. *Human Behavior,* November/December 1972, *1,* 16 ff.)

1973

Comment on Pitts article. *J. Hum. Psychol.* Winter 1973, *13,* 83–84.

An encounter with Carl Rogers. In C. W. Kemper (Ed.), *Res Publica,* Claremont Men's College, Spring 1973, *1*(1), 41–51.

The good life as an ever-changing process. Ninth of newpaper series, *America and the Future of Man,* published by the Regents of the University of California, and distributed by Copley News Service.

The interpersonal relationship that helps schizophrenics. Contribution to panel discussion, "Psychotherapy is Effective with Schizophrenics." APA Convention, Montreal, August 28, 1973.

My philosophy of interpersonal relationships and how it grew. *J. Hum. Psychol.* Spring 1973, *13*(2), 3–15.

Some new challenges. *American Psychologist*, May 1973, *28*(5), 379–387.

To be fully alive. *Penney's Forum*, Spring/Summer 1973, p. 3.

With B. Meador. Client-centered therapy. In R. Corsini (Ed.), *Current psychotherapies*. Itasca, Illinois: F. E. Peacock, 1973, pp. 119–166.

(Mousseau, J. Entretien avec Carl Rogers. *Psychologie*, January 1973, *6*, 57–65.)

1974

Can learning encompass both ideas and feelings? *Education*, Winter 1974, *95*(2), 103–114.

The cavern. (unpublished)

Foreword. In H. Lyon, *It's me and I'm here*. New York: Delacorte Press, 1974, pp. xi–xiii.

Foreword. In A. dePeretti, *Pensee et Verite de Carl Rogers*. Toulouse: Privat, 1974, pp. 20–27.

Foreword. In Japanese translation of *Person to Person*. Tokyo, 1974.

In retrospect: Forty-six years. *American Psychologist*, February 1974, *29*(2), 115–123.

Interview on "growth." In W. Oltmans (Ed.), *On growth: The crisis of exploring population and resource depletion*. New York: G. P. Putnam's Sons, 1974, pp. 197–205.

The project at Immaculate Heart: An experiment in self-directed change. *Education*, Winter 1974, *95*(2), 172–196.

Questions I would ask myself if I were a teacher. *Education*, Winter 1974, *95*(2), 134–139.

Remarks on the future of client-centered therapy. In D. A. Wexler & L. N. Rice (Eds.), *Innovations in client-centered therapy*. New York: John Wiley & Sons, 1974, pp. 7–13.

With J. K. Wood. The changing theory of client-centered therapy. In A. Burton (Ed.), *Operational theories of personality*. New York: Brunner/Mazel, Inc., 1974, pp. 211–258.

1975

Client-centered psychotherapy. In A. M. Freedman, H. I. Kaplan, & B. J. Sadock (Eds.), *Comprehensive textbook of psychiatry, Vol. II*. Baltimore: Williams & Wilkins, 1975, pp. 1831-1843.

The emerging person: A new revolution. In R. I. Evans (Ed.), *Carl Rogers: The man and his ideas.* New York: E. P. Dutton, 1975, pp. 147–176.

Empathic: An unappreciated way of being. *The Counseling Psychologist*, 1975, *5*(2), 2–10.

Foreword. In To Thi Anh, *Eastern and Western cultural values.* Manila, The Philippines: East Asian Pastoral Institute, 1975.

Interview. In R. I. Evans (Ed.), *Carl Rogers: The man and his ideas.* New York: E. P. Dutton, 1975.

An interview with Dr. Carl R. Rogers. *Practical Psychology for Physicians*, August 1975, *2*(8), 16–24.

A person-centered approach to intergroup tensions. Paper at Association of Humanistic Psychology Conference, Cuernavaca, Mexico, December 19, 1975. (unpublished)

With J. K. Wood, A. Nelson, N. R. Fuchs, & B. Meador. An experiment in self-determined fees. (unpublished)

1976

Beyond the watershed in education. *Teaching-Learning Journal*, Winter/Spring 1976, pp. 43–49.

1977

Beyond the watershed: And where now? *Educational Leadership*, May 1977, *34*(8), 623–631.

Carl Rogers on personal power. New York: Delacorte Press, 1977, 299 pp.

Ellen West—And loneliness. In C. R. Rogers and R. L. Rosenberg, *A Pessoa Como Centro*, São Paulo, Brazil: Editoria Pedagógica e Universitária Ltda., 1977. (Written in 1974)

Freedom to be: A person-centered approach. *Studies of the Person* (Japanese), 1977, *3*, 5–18. Japan Women's University, Department of Education, Tokyo.

Growing old—Or older and growing. (unpublished)

Nancy mourns. In D. Nevill (Ed.), *Humanistic psychology: New frontiers.* New York: Gardner Press, 1977, pp. 111–116.

Personal power at work. *Psychology Today*, April 1977, *10*(11), 60 ff. (Condensation of Chapter 8 of *Carl Rogers on personal power.*)

The politics of education. *J. Hum. Educ.* January/February 1977, *1*(1), 6–22.

Therapeut and Klient. Munich, West Germany: Kindler-München, 1977. (Various papers translated from the English.)

Tribute to Professor Haruko Tsuge. *Studies of the Person* (Japanese), 1977, *3*, 35–38. Japan Women's University, Department of Education, Tokyo.

With T. L. Holdstock. Person-centered personality theory. In R. Corsini (Ed.), *Current personality theories.* Itasca, Illinois: F. R. Peacock, 1977, pp. 125–151.

With R. L. Rosenberg. *A Pessoa Como Centro.* São Paulo, Brazil: Editoria Pedagógica e Universitária Ltda., 1977, 228 pp. (Introduction and Chapters 2 and 5 by Rosenberg. Other pages are translations of papers by Rogers.)

(Holden, C. Carl Rogers: Giving people permission to be themselves. *Science,* October 1977, *198*(4312), 32–33.)

1978

Carl R. Rogers' Papers. In *The Quarterly Journal of the Library of Congress,* October 1978, *35*, 258–259. (This describes the collection of personal papers, tapes, films, etc., which, upon invitation, Rogers donated to the Library of Congress.)

Do we need "a" reality? *Dawnpoint,* Winter 1978, *1*(2), 6–9. (Written in 1974.)

Education—A personal activity. (unpublished)

The formative tendency. *J. Hum. Psychol.,* Winter 1978, *18*, 23–26.

From heart to heart: Some elements of effective interpersonal communication. *Marriage Encounter,* February 1978, *7*(2), 8–15. (Talk given to California Institute of Technology, November 9, 1964. Revised version is Chapter 11 in *Freedom to Learn.*)

Meeting my needs as a facilitator. (unpublished)

My political stance. (unpublished)

The necessary and sufficient conditions of therapeutic personality change (1957). Abstract and commentary. *Current Contents,* 1978, *18*(27), 14. (No. 27 of "Citation Classics.")

Some directions in AHP. (unpublished)

Some new directions: A personal view. (unpublished)

With M. V. Bowen, J. Justyn, J. Kass, M. Miller, N. Rogers, & J. K. Wood. Evolving aspects of the person-centered workshop. *Self and Society* (England), February 1978, *6*(2), 43–49.

1979

Foundations of the person-centered approach. *Education,* Winter 1979, *100*(2), 98–107.

Groups in two cultures. *Personnel & Guidance Journal,* September 1979, *38*(1), 11–15.

The security guard: A vignette. (unpublished)

Some new directions: A personal view. In T. Hanna (Ed.), *Explorers of humankind.* San Francisco: Harper & Row, 1979.

With M. V. Bowen, J. Justyn, J. Kass, M. Miller, N. Rogers, & J. K. Wood. Evolving aspects of person-centered workshops. *AHP Newsletter,* January 1979, 11–14.

With M. V. Bowen, M. Miller, & J. K. Wood. Learnings in large groups: The implications for the future. *Education,* Winter 1979, *100*(2), 108–116. (Written in 1977)

(H. Kirschenbaum. *On becoming Carl Rogers.* New York: Delacorte Press, 1979, 444 pp. This biography includes many excerpts from Rogers' writings, from his adolescent days to age 76.)

1980

Building person-centered communities: The implications for the future. In A. Villoldo & K. Dychtwald (Eds.), *Revisioning human potential: Glimpses into the 21st century.* (In press.)

Acknowledgments

Chapter 1, "Experiences in Communication," copyright 1969 by Charles E. Merrill Publishing Co. Published in Carl Rogers, *Freedom to Learn: A View of What Education Might Become,* Columbus, Ohio: Charles E. Merrill Publishing Co., 1969; and in *Marriage Encounter,* February 1978, Vol. 7, No. 2, pp. 8–15, under the title "From Heart to Heart: Some Elements of Effective Communication."

Chapter 2, "My Philosophy of Interpersonal Relationships and How It Grew," copyright 1973 by Association for Humanistic Psychology. Published in *Journal of Humanistic Psychology,* Spring 1973, Vol. 28, No. 5, pp. 3–15.

Chapter 3, "In Retrospect: Forty-Six Years," copyright 1974 by the American Psychological Association. Reprinted by permission. Published in *American Psychologist,* February 1974, Vol. 29, No. 2, pp. 115–123.

Chapter 5, "Do We Need "A" Reality?" copyright 1978 by Association for Humanistic Psychology. Published in *Dawnpoint,* Winter 1978, Vol. 1, No. 2, pp. 6–9.

Chapter 6, "The Foundations of a Person-Centered Approach," copyright 1979 by Project Innovation. Published in *Education,* Winter 1979, Vol. 100, No. 2, pp. 98–107. Pages 124–126, under the heading "A Broader View: The Formative Tendency," copyright 1978 by Association for Humanistic Psychology; from Carl Rogers, "The Formative Tendency," *Journal of Humanistic Psychology,* Winter 1978, Vol. 18, pp. 23–26.

Chapter 7, "Empathic: An Unappreciated Way of Being," copyright 1975 by The Counseling Psychologist. Published in *The Counseling Psychologist,* 1975, Vol. 5, No. 2, pp. 2–10.

Chapter 8, "Ellen West—And Loneliness," copyright 1961 by Association of Existential Psychology and Psychiatry. Published under the title "The Loneliness of Contemporary Man as Seen in the Case of Ellen West," in *Review of Existential Psychology & Psychiatry*, May 1961, Vol. 1, No. 2, pp. 94–101. In its present expanded form, it has been published in C. R. Rogers and R. L. Rosenberg, *A Pessoa Como Centro*, São Paulo, Brazil: Editoria Pedagógica e Universitária Ltda., 1977.

Chapter 9, "Building Person-Centered Communities: The Implications for the Future," will also be published in A. Villoldo & K. Dychtwald (Eds.), *Millenium: Glimpses into the 21st Century*, March 1981, J. P. Tarcher, Los Angeles.

Chapter 10, "Six Vignettes": 'I Began to Lose Me,' copyright 1975 by Williams and Wilkins; published as part of a chapter entitled "Client-Centered Psychotherapy," in A. M. Freedman, H. I. Kaplan, & B. J. Sadock (Eds.), *Comprehensive Textbook of Psychiatry*, Second Ed., pp. 1839–1843 reproduced by permission; further reproduction prohibited. 'Nancy Mourns,' copyright 1977 by Gardner Press, New York; published in D. Nevill (Ed.), *Humanistic Psychology: New Frontiers*, pp. 111–116. Pp. 226–228, "What I Really Am Is Unlovable," from *Carl Rogers on Encounter Groups* (pp. 111–113), by Carl R. Rogers, Ph.D., copyright 1970 by Carl R. Rogers. Reprinted by permission of Harper & Row Publishers, Inc. Barbara Williams, the author of the letter describing 'A Kids' Workshop,' is currently a therapist at the Centennial Center for Psychological Services, 1501 Lemay #3, Ft. Collins, Colorado, 80512.

Chapter 11, "Some New Challenges to the Helping Professions," copyright 1973 by the American Psychological Association. Reprinted by permission. Published under the title "Some New Challenges," in *American Psychologist*, May 1973, Vol. 28, No. 5, pp. 379–387.

Chapter 12, "Can Learning Encompass both Ideas and Feelings?" copyright 1974 by Project Innovation. Published, in slightly different form, in *Education*, Winter 1974, Vol. 95, No. 2, pp. 103–114.

Chapter 13, "Beyond the Watershed: And Where Now?" copyright © 1977 by the Association for Supervision and Curriculum Development. Reprinted with permission of the Association for Supervision and Curriculum Development and Carl R. Rogers. All rights reserved. Published, in abbreviated form, in *Educational Leadership*, May 1977, Vol. 34, No. 8, pp. 623–631.

Chapter 14, "Learnings in Large Groups: Their Implications for the Future," copyright 1979 by Project Innovation. Published in *Education*, Winter 1979, Vol. 100, No. 2, pp. 108–116.

Chapter 15, "The World of Tomorrow, and the Person of Tomorrow": Quotation by Edward Cornish from "An Agenda for the 1980s," *The Futurist*, February 1980, Vol. 14, p. 7. *The Futurist* is published by the World Future Society, 4916 St. Elmo Avenue, Washington, D.C. 20014.

Index